"Barbara Hand Clow has a message that matters tremendously to every single person on this earth. It is about nothing less than achieving relationship with a brilliant and spiritually potent presence that has been offering itself to us for many years, and which has the capacity to transform us, starting with each one of us who is willing to open ourselves to it. This exquisite and powerful book makes that process understandable, joyous and—above all—possible."

—Whitley Strieber

"Weaving science, mysticism, and higher dimensional guidance into a skillful tapestry examining humanity's past, present, (and possible future), Barbara Clow guides us to a needed multidimensional viewpoint of the rapidly changing world in which we find ourselves. Her work can help to lead us up the ladder of evolutionary thinking to access greater understanding and inner balance in a way that may help to transform us on both a personal and planetary level."

—Richard Gerber, M.D.
author of *Vibrational Medicine* and
A Practical Guide to Vibrational Medicine

"Once again Barbara brings her insights of other levels of reality, allowing us to build a wider picture of worlds that lie a breath away from our own physical reality. Such understandings can only improve our sense of seeing, our relationship within the greater scheme of things, and ultimately, a finer understanding of our Self."

—Freddy Silva
author of *Secrets In The Fields: The*
Science and Mysticism Of Crop Circles

"*Alchemy of Nine Dimensions* provides an in-depth, technical discussion of each dimension of consciousness. . . . Working with Clow, Hand Clow once again has provided a powerful book destined to change lives and help move our planet toward greater healing and wholeness. A terrific, extensive glossary will help readers new to Hand Clow's work find their bearings."

—Cathy O'Connell, Ph.D.
in *New Age Retailer*

Also by Barbara Hand Clow

Stained Glass: A Basic Manual (1976)

Eye of the Centaur (1986)

Chiron (1987)

Heart of the Christos (1989)

Liquid Light of Sex (1991)

Signet of Atlantis (1992)

The Pleiadian Agenda (1995)

Catastrophobia (2001)

The Mind Chronicles (2007)

The Mayan Code (2007)

BARBARA HAND CLOW
WITH GERRY CLOW

ALCHEMY
OF NINE
DIMENSIONS

Decoding the Vertical Axis,
Crop Circles, and the Mayan Calendar

HAMPTON ROADS
PUBLISHING COMPANY, INC.

Cover design by Steve Amarillo
Cover photographs © Steve Alexander
Illustrations by Christopher C. Clow

Hampton Roads Publishing Company, Inc.
1125 Stoney Ridge Road
Charlottesville, VA 22902

434-296-2772
fax: 434-296-5096
e-mail: hrpc@hrpub.com
www.hrpub.com

If you are unable to order this book from your local
bookseller, you may order directly from the publisher.
Call 1-800-766-8009, toll-free.

Library of Congress Cataloging-in-Publication Data

Clow, Barbara Hand, 1943-
 Alchemy of nine dimensions : decoding the vertical axis, crop circles,
and the Mayan calendar / Barbara Hand Clow.
     p. cm.
 Includes bibliographical references and index.
 ISBN 1-57174-420-7 (6 x 9 tp : alk. paper)
 1. Pleiades--Miscellanea. 2. Spiritual life. 3. Cosmology--Miscellanea.
4. Dimensions. I. Title.
 BF1999.C586 2004
 133.9'3--dc22

                                2004010432

              ISBN: 978-1-57174-420-3

                  10 9 8 7 6 5 4

Printed on acid-free paper in the United States

Dedication

*To our students, without whom
this book could not have been written.
May your journeys continue to unfold.*

And to Thomas Hand Frazier (1963–2004).

Special Notice to Our Readers

Encountering—and experiencing—the nine dimensions can open up new levels of consciousness. As with all work of this nature, please be respectful of your ability to assimilate new information. When we teach this material to a group, we have healers present, to help each of us make a comfortable passage through the thoughts and feelings that emerge as we contemplate a wider view of reality. Now that we are teaching this material through a book, we realize that you have only *yourself* as your healer. Therefore we recommend that you take in this book at a pace that works for you. Remember to *breathe,* drink good water, make sure you are rested, take a walk, and do comfortable stretching exercises such as yoga as you move through these pages. If you find yourself becoming agitated during any phase of contemplating the nine dimensions, write down what is upsetting you, and then come back to those notes later. Allow yourself to experience all nine dimensions before going back to the ones that particularly excited or challenged you. If you would like continual guidance regarding the acceleration of consciousness as we approach the end of the Mayan calendar, our website, www.handclow2012.com, offers monthly New Moon forecasts and equinox/solstice analyses. Thank you for your attention, and enjoy the book.

Contents

Part One: The Nine Dimensions

List of Illustrations

Five

Six

Seven

Eight

Nine

Ten

Eleven

Acknowledgments

Richard Drachenberg, one of our most advanced and delightful students, thank you for slaving over the manuscript and making the "Pleiadian language"—and the workings of my mind—more accessible.

Freddy Silva, esteemed colleague and prominent crop circle researcher, I am grateful for your significant insights about the Circlemakers. Thank you for your support for this book, and for your helpful comments on the early stages of the crop circle sections.

William Glyn-Jones, mythologist with a beautiful multidimensional mind and eye, I am deeply grateful to you for your insights about Theseus, Ariadne, and Light in the Galactic Center.

George DeSalvo, journalist, your thoughts about the importance of quantum theory for modern humanity challenged me to have greater respect for all the scientists working so hard to advance our world, and thanks for your comments on the manuscript.

John Beaulieu, master of healing, tuning forks, and dimensionality, my studies with you have greatly expanded my understanding of the seventh dimension, and thanks for your comments on the manuscript.

Thea Beaulieu, I see all nine dimensions when I watch you dance.

Tom Cratsley, a great master healer, thank you for healing with us during the Activations at Lily Dale, New York, and for your comments on the manuscript.

Toby and Teri Weiss, leaders and founders of Power Places Tours, if it weren't for your dedication to teaching people about planetary sacred sites and getting Gerry and me to the sacred zones to teach others, and to learn about their dimensional codes ourselves, I never would have been able to think my way through this book; and thank you for your comments on the manuscript.

Aina Allen, long-time student and fellow healer, thank you for your careful proofreading.

Ehud Sperling, president of Inner Traditions/Bear & Company, thank you for your support and encouragement.

John Nelson, writer and editor, thank you for suggesting I bring this book to Hampton Roads Publishing.

John Michell, great writer about geomancy, sacred geometry, and sacred sites, thank you for being my friend and fellow teacher, and for offering me secrets about interacting with the minds of the Circlemakers.

Shawn Randall, wonderful crop circle researcher, thank you for always appearing on Wiltshire Plain whenever I get there myself.

Roslyn Strong, megalithic researcher, thank you for translating Pierre Mereaux's research on Carnac, France.

Barbara Marciniak, the most dedicated, clear, and powerful Pleiadian channel I know, without your friendship, often I might have thought I'd lost my mind.

Brian Swimme, esteemed physicist and cosmologist, thank you for helping me *feel* as well as *understand* science.

David Icke, controversial and brilliant conspiracy writer, thank you for your pyramid model that makes it possible for anybody to see how the Global Elite has captured the human race in chains for at least four thousand years.

Christopher Clow, my third son and the illustrator for this book, thank you for your beautiful work, patience, and joy that we shared during this process. Your finely spiritualized consciousness gives this book deep-feeling qualities, which often characterize your generation.

Judibeth Hunter, artist, thank you for your beautiful renderings of my past lives.

Elizabeth Clow, my only daughter, thanks for coming to England with me in 1997, when your crazy response to the Circlemakers and sacred sites helped me see how we are all players in these mystery plays. You certainly are!

Gerry Clow, my partner of thirty years, thank you for prodding me into writing this most difficult book, and thank you for teaching Activations with me and adding the healing dimension to our work.

Robert Friedman and the staff of Hampton Roads Publishing, thank you for your warmth and professionalism.

And all of our students, this book is dedicated to each one of you, because you have been willing to be *our* teachers from 1987 through 2012.

Barbara's Introduction:
The Story of the Pleiadian Transmissions

In late fall of 1994, a hologram of light appeared in my head, which was familiar to me as a reception of consciousness from unseen dimensions. I call these "thought atoms" or "monads," and they have initiated my previous books. Yet the 1994 monad was significantly more complex than previous ones. It emitted a very high-frequency sound that was higher than my own audible range, and I could also feel it as vibration. This put me on edge, because it felt alien and seemed to be beyond my intellectual abilities.

Before this moment, when thought atoms have come into my mind, I have welcomed them because they integrate my brain and push me to write. This particular hologram seemed to be a twenty-sided sphere with triangular faces. The twelve intersections of the triangles touched the luminous sphere, where rays of blue-white light were emitted out to infinity. I could not imagine what it was. Today I know that this monad was an icosahedron, one of the five Platonic solids, encased in a luminous sphere. Lines of light were shooting out from the twelve intersections of its twenty triangles. The ends of the rays emitted strange high-frequency sounds that seemed to be sourced in spinning geometric forms nested within the sphere. That is what I saw, yet in those days I didn't know anything about Platonic solids. The sphere was entrancing; it shimmered with an otherworldly perfection. Now that I have studied Platonic solids and crop circles, I can see that this vision opened my mind for a new cosmology, a new way to enter the universe. I have also been thrown into a search for its source, a search that still goes on today.

In any case, the monad was extremely annoying. The high-pitched sounds it emitted pierced my head. By November 1994, severe tinnitus or ear-ringing began, and the outside world seemed to be fading away. I wondered if the Pleiadians—the Ps—were contacting me again, since in the past they'd ring my inner head with various harmonic tones. These tones always got louder if I ignored them. (I've been involved in an on-and-off dialogue with beings from the Pleiades since I was four months old, which is described in many of my books.) Since they wouldn't go away, I've learned to "read" their tones, and their counsel has usually been very beneficial.

Because of these past experiences, I concluded that the high-frequency sounds must be from the Ps. The tinnitus was more annoying than in the past, so I gathered together a group of people who wanted to question the Ps. In a deep altered state, I "channeled" answers to their questions, and I hoped this would quiet the tones down.[1] The information in the monad felt scientific and complex, and I sensed I probably could not grasp it in a conscious state. So I simply listened to the sounds vibrating as people questioned the Ps, and I transmitted words out of the tones as if I were a phone translating electrical pulses. The sessions lasted about three hours, and thankfully the tinnitus went away, except when I allowed too much time between each session. Our little group completed eighteen sessions by March 1995; the tapes were typed and transferred into my computer by an editor; and then I organized them into a book, *The Pleiadian Agenda: A New Cosmology for the Age of Light,* which was published in September 1995 and became an instant bestseller.

Before I go on to discuss what happened after the book was published, allow me briefly to describe the book. According to these Ps, they downloaded the story of Earth's role in the Milky Way. This transmission was from the Library of Alcyone, the central star of the Pleiades. The Pleiadians have been deeply involved with Earth over a long period of time, which means they have much knowledge about Earth from a multidimensional perspective. Pleiadian involvement with humans has been detected by archaeologists as far back as 40,000 years ago.[2] The main voice in the book is a saucy Pleiadian goddess, Satya, who describes Earth as a realm that holds nine dimensions of consciousness that all humans can access. This ability, which was natural for humans long ago, is opening up now. This process is accelerating as we approach the end of the Mayan calendar, December 21, 2012.

The nine dimensions are located on a vertical axis that grounds itself in the center of Earth and rises into the Galactic Center. When we incarnate, our locus of perception is on this axis, which was often called the Tree of Life in ancient cultures. We can travel up or down the axis, just like Jack climbing up and down the beanstalk in that famous children's story. By starting with the first dimension—center of Earth—we can travel all the way to the ninth—the Galactic Center. Or, by starting in the ninth, we can return to the first. This really got my attention because I was fascinated by Jack and the beanstalk and the giant as a child. I loved the idea that we could climb beyond Earth—yet also return—even if there was an awful ogre waiting up there. Ironically, when I was a child, no one knew there was a black hole in the center of the Milky Way.

Satya transmitted diagrams that teach how we can live in our dimension—the third dimension (3D)—and access all nine dimensions simultaneously. She said this was once natural to us, but we lost this skill thousands of years ago. As I was writing the book, I noticed that I understood the first four dimensions very well, I had a small grasp of the fifth dimension, and I barely had a clue about the sixth through the ninth. This may reflect the limitations of current science, which usually describes four dimensions. My contact with the fifth resulted from my contact with the Ps from early childhood; I'd stepped beyond the fourth dimension as a child. In recent years, I've learned about all nine by experiencing the Pleiadian models with students and listening to their feedback.

The lower dimensions (1D and 2D) are various levels of Earth (3D)—from core to surface; the fourth dimension (4D) is the realm of collective thought that bridges the physical and unseen worlds; and the fifth through ninth dimensions (5D–9D) are celestial. Most scientists will be unable to imagine the unseen realms except by mathematics that reach beyond the fourth dimension, such as topology and superstring theory. Culturally, the first four dimensions correspond somewhat to Western spirituality, and the higher ones to Eastern mysticism. Satya's diagrams for accessing all nine dimensions simultaneously are actually a wonderful integration of East and West. And having this nine-dimensional model helps me as a Western teacher access Eastern mysticism.

Our students of the Eastern persuasion have found this system enables them to understand the Western mind better. There is no hierarchy in this system, because in it the celestial realms are not superior to the Earth realms. Amusingly, Satya chides the readers of *The Pleiadian Agenda* when she notes that we can only access the higher realms while we are *in* our bodies! Why go out of your body to find God, she asks? Her system glorifies the beauty of Earth vibrating with galactic resonance; everywhere, Gaia is permeated by the divine. Satya calls her work Goddess Alchemy.

Pleiadian Agenda Activations: 1995 to 2012

When I first went out to teach *The Pleiadian Agenda* in public, I barely understood the book, which was most bizarre. Yet I was delighted to find I could easily create classes with it, since the book has a very well designed and simple dimensional structure. As I set up the models and opened the nine-dimensional form for students, some danced or played music to find their body resonance with the various levels. These classes soon became known as "Activations" because so much spontaneous knowledge flowed in through all participants.

In 1996 I asked my husband and partner, Gerry Clow, to join me in adding bodywork and healing during the Activations that fall. In 1998, the brilliant composer Michael Stearns created music to help express the nine dimensions by resonance, since only music can express the higher dimensions in a way we can understand. In 2002, I added a sacred pipe ceremony while we were experiencing the lower dimensions, which enhances and intensifies our resonance with Earth. Today, many of our students teach this material to their own students, and we hope this aspect will grow with the publication of this book.

Speaking of our students, I have been profoundly impressed by how much the Activations help our students with the most basic aspects of their lives. The students seeking spiritual contact are getting it, those who want improvement in their everyday lives are finding it, and many are finding new ways to transform their cultures. We've even activated a few whistle-blowers, since the eighth dimension (8D) teaches how to live impeccably in the material world, and the 8D teaching motivated them. It was initially outrageous to imagine that dimensions influenced by distant star systems—the Pleiades in the fifth dimension (5D); Sirius in the sixth dimension (6D); Andromeda in the seventh dimension (7D); Orion in the eighth dimension (8D); and the Milky Way in the ninth dimension (9D)—can actually inform us here on Earth. Perhaps this is why our ancestors believed the stars had consciousness and were repositories of their stories and myths.

Often we wondered, while the world was going crazier by the day, whether the Activations would continue until the end of the Mayan calendar. Yet our lives, and those of our students, kept improving; students kept coming, and many of them returned three or four more times to go deeper into the material. Meanwhile, I began observing changes in our Galaxy to see if the timetable in the book was corroborated by scientific events, and it has been. Frequently, the latest developments in science have moved into alignment with Satya's versions, which I call Pleiadian science or "dimensional mechanics."

Satya says that our ability to access multidimensional consciousness will be a basic survival skill as we approach the mysterious end-date of the Mayan calendar, December 21, 2012. This possibility seems more compelling since the Twin Towers—Joachim and Boaz—went down September 11, 2001. The world now seems ruled by Chaos Theory, complex mathematics that explores how systems break down amidst order. Being with students while they access heightened and divine states of consciousness has convinced Gerry and me that these demanding Pleiadians must be listened to. They know something very important about us after interacting with us for thousands of years. They seem to be guiding us through the building chaos, while gently teaching us how to find islands of peace within the discord.

Gerry and I have been fortunate to teach in the middle of this wild awakening, mostly because it is fun. We've written this book to transmit as much as we can after living with and trusting the Ps. In the midst of this journey, a marvelous convergence of dimensional science has occurred, which has spurred us on and may inspire or intrigue you. We live during days of miracles, when any one of us can access these levels if we want to—provided we first explore how we lost our multidimensional access long ago.

How We Lost Our Multidimensionality

My most recent book, *Catastrophobia: The Truth Behind Earth Changes in the Coming Age of Light* (2001), considers the indigenous records of Earth changes over the last 20,000 years in light of the latest scientific discoveries.

Throughout my childhood, my grandfather, Gilbert Hand, trained me in the Cherokee records of Earth. He was adamant that science would catch up with the ancient records in my lifetime, and he passed over his five children to give his legacy to his first granddaughter. In 1995, I acquired, as the editor at the publishing house Bear & Company, *Cataclysm! Compelling Evidence of a Cataclysm in 9500 B.C.,* by Oxford anthropologist and geologist J. B. Delair and science historian D. S. Allan. In it, I found the same science as my grandfather's!

I was stunned by the importance of this latest congruence, since the Cherokee, Mayan, and Pleiadian records are so deeply connected. Subsequently, I wrote *Catastrophobia* to explore how the great Earth changes traumatized the collective mind of humanity. Finally, I could see why our consciousness is so limited, and why so few people access the unseen dimensions. The truth is, *we are a multitraumatized species.* We experienced a great cataclysm only 11,500 years ago, which was followed by thousands of years of horrific survivalism. This is a species-level, post-traumatic stress syndrome, which we are only now ready to understand.

While I studied scientific research to write *Catastrophobia,* I considered the scientific theory lurking in the folds of *The Pleiadian Agenda;* I found some current scientific models that in varying degrees supported and described the existence of the nine dimensions. There is a scientific model for each dimension, which is the heart of this current book, and I hope that scientists will find these ideas have merit.

The Emergence of Crop Circles

As the end-date of the Mayan calendar approaches, something has been sending us symbols that are opening multidimensional consciousness for many people. These symbols are called "crop circles," which imprint the crops in the fields each summer, mostly in England. The Circlemakers (capitalized because I think of them as divine beings who are making most of the circles) herald the total awakening of human perceptual tools, which surely will enhance the viability of Earth's species. *The Pleiadian Agenda* offers much wisdom about the dimensions expressed by the crop circles. Satya says that each dimension has a "Keeper," which is an intelligence that holds that level in form. The story of the Keepers was closely held indigenous knowledge until 1994. Now I am free to share it. I am deeply indebted to my teachers, Hunbatz Men, Matthew Fox, J. T.

and Michael Garret, Alberto Ruz Buenfil, Hakim of Giza, and my Cherokee-Celtic grandparents. You will learn much about these mysterious Keepers in the chapters ahead.

We humans, for example, are the chosen Keepers of the third dimension, and we are doing a poor job right now. I believe that humans are destroying Earth because we do not recognize our sacred role in the awakening of the Milky Way, our birthplace. Earth is a rare jewel in the universe, and Satya says Earth is to seed the whole Galaxy with its life-forms in 2012. She reaches us by awakening these deep memories—Goddess Alchemy—which empower us to remember our roles as Keepers of Gaia. In our hearts we know that we are here to bless, not to destroy.

According to *The Pleiadian Agenda*, Earth is penetrated by nine dimensions of intelligence that we all can access, learn from, and consciously utilize in our lives. These levels offer humans extremely enhanced intelligence as well as freedom, yet first we must consider our current condition. After thousands of years of separation from the divine, our collective mind—which functions in the fourth dimension (4D)—is caught in a field of polarized, archetypal thoughtforms that are locked in our bodies and minds as emotional trauma blocks. These days, clever media demons manipulate the 4D collective mind to amuse themselves, make money, capture innocent souls, or merely to avoid looking inside themselves. Yet the 4D zone is *not* their personal territory, since 4D is a bridge out of the physical to the divine. It is not meant to be an insipid frequency zone that crams our heads with stupid images through advertising, pornography, and Internet spam.

We need to own 4D as the zone where our feelings can access alluring high-frequency visions. We are all wired to access higher dimensions through images that are time-released from the Galactic Center, and we can only do this by active intuition and intense feelings. We can locate our personal pathways in the great landscape of cosmic potential by *feeling* our way in the fourth dimension and clearing our heads of junk images. Our brains are more than tangled cassette and video tapes or computer hard drives. Caught in the current media-soaked 4D zone, most people can't see the portal doors to higher worlds. Our objective as an awakening species is to reconstruct and clear the powerful 4D zone, so as to identify the vibrational frequencies of all nine dimensions.

In sharing the essential nine-dimensional structure of Earth's intelligence with students, Gerry and I have seen how varying levels of spatial and temporal dislocation caused by unresolved trauma, originally sourced in the cataclysm and reinforced by traumatic life experiences, afflict our students and people in general. We feel that we have attained a deep understanding of how this trauma locks people up. Having explored Earth changes of the last 20,000 years and how humans are traumatized by them, I can see that humans cease being violent when they release their trauma and recover their story; they get back into the now, or current space and time. This is why we have healers working during Activations.

Gerry is a healer who focuses on keeping students in their bodies, and my work is on expanding their minds, as I work with large mental systems such as the nine-dimensional form. This form was drawn as two models by the Ps: a diagram of a vertical axis of consciousness, and a canopy of dimensions over a person on a healing table. These models help us understand the dimensional structure itself, as well as show how we receive it in our bodies. Here, I introduce these models, and then each chapter of the book is devoted to an in-depth discussion of each dimension.

The Vertical Axis of Consciousness

Through the depiction of a person lying on a healing table, figure I.1 shows how we receive the dimensions. The Ps show human dimensional access this way because many of us have first experienced unseen dimensions during healing sessions, such as massages or past-life regressions. This is because healers can set dimensional fields with which their clients can resonate. The person in this diagram could also be sitting or walking around; however, most people at this time are not able to be in nine dimensions while going shopping. The way it works is simple. While we are alive, we exist in linear space and time—3D—which is a plane; 2D is shown as an isosceles triangle with one side as the 3D plane, and the bottom point is 1D—the iron core crystal in the center of Earth.

Using the image of the person lying on the table in the 3D plane, 4D—the collective mind or archetypal realm—forms a canopy over the person's body, which forms out of the polarizing thoughts and feelings of that person. The higher dimensions—5D through 9D—make portals in

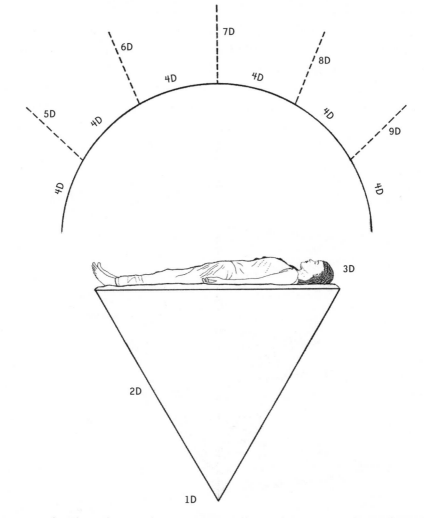

Figure I.1 This shows how we humans receive all nine dimensions. Adapted from *The Pleiadian Agenda*, Barbara Hand Clow, p. 72.

this 4D canopy when the person resolves the polarity and activates subtle consciousness.

This multidimensional model shows how we each perceive the dimensions. The Ps told me to tattoo this drawing on the back of my hand, which was a bit much for me, so I memorized it perfectly. You, too, can avoid tattooing yourself by referring back to this diagram when you can't remember how to contact the nine dimensions. As we move progressively through the dimensions, I ask you constantly to imprint this simple little diagram; this will reinforce the feeling that you can do it all in your own body. Later, you will see that the Circlemakers liked this model so much they made at least three versions of it in the fields in England in 1997!

Figure I.2 shows the dimensional structure of the vertical axis of consciousness from the lowest to the highest dimension. To explain the ener-

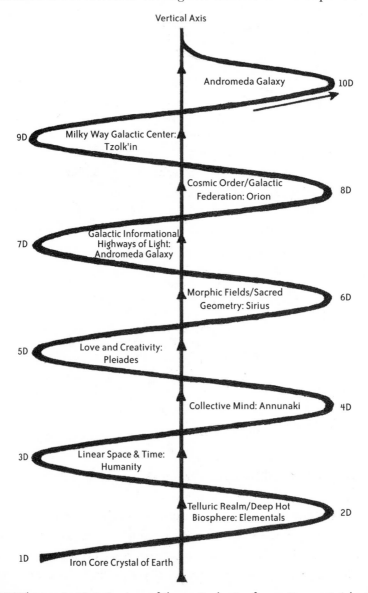

Figure I.2 The progressive structure of the vertical axis of consciousness. Adapted from *The Pleiadian Agenda*, Barbara Hand Clow, p. 163.

getics of the nine dimensions, we must progress from the first dimension to the ninth on the vertical axis. The lowest dimension (1D) is the densest dimension, and the highest (9D) is the least dense; the lower dimensions have less space, the higher ones more. Density is governed by gravity, which coaxes light or photons into forms. Feel how intense and dense the iron core crystal (1D) in the center of Earth must be.

According to science, the center of Earth is a huge iron core crystal, and iron crystals are twice as dense as other mineral crystals. The second dimension (2D) is the area between the iron core crystal and the crust; for example, the mantle. The second dimension is much denser than 3D, Earth's surface. We are solid in 3D, whereas 4D—the collective realm of thoughts and feelings emanating from all living things—is not solid. We all can *feel* 4D and participate in it, such as by sharing beliefs about history and religion.

As we move to higher dimensions—such as being in the heart (5D) or existing in sacred geometry (6D)—we experience each dimension going up the vertical axis as less dense, more spacious, more complex, and more difficult to explain in words. To move into the higher dimensions, we humans must expand ourselves, and to move into the lower dimensions, we must contract ourselves.

We are solid in 3D in linear space and time and have five senses. We stay in our realm by gravity, which I called "grabbity" as a child. Gravity, until we approach it more scientifically, represents the density factor. Gravity also exists in the higher and lower dimensions, and when we go to these levels, our specific gravity changes. Our bodies are located in 3D while we are alive, yet many functions of our energetic systems are stimulated by the lower two dimensions, the 1D iron core crystal and the 2D tectonic or telluric realm. We are also stimulated by the 4D collective thought realm, sometimes perhaps too much. We humans are like an Oreo cookie sandwiched between the denser realms of Earth and the emotionally and mentally charged realm of the group mind that changes constantly according to what it's plugged into.

To be more explicit, 2D is the denser world of minerals and microbes, and 2D is much slower than our pulse, breath, or thoughts. The second dimension regulates all our autonomic body processes, and our health is absolutely contingent upon our resonance with it. Resonance means that our autonomic processes are vibrating in harmony with 2D, which maintains our physicality in 3D. The second dimension itself is a vibrating, pulsing, gushing world of incredibly complex beings that are the source of our vitality.

The Ps use the person on the table as their example because this helps us understand how 2D and 4D resonate in our 3D bodies. Here we see (figure I.3) a healer standing behind the person on the table and using

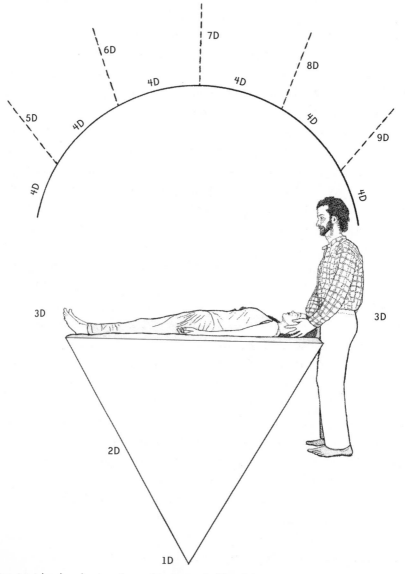

Figure I.3 A healer slowing down the energy fields of the person on the table to encourage healing.

various energetic techniques to slow the vibrational frequency of the person down to the 2D, maybe even to the 1D level. The healer holds frequencies in his or her own body and helps the person shift his or her frequencies to encourage healing. Healing is the modulation of our frequencies in 3D in ways that encourage health. For example, 2D is the realm where inorganic matter becomes organic, and the beings there create all the codes of life. When we bring the 2D frequency into our bodies, our cells heal, DNA repairs, and blood flows like a pure crystalline stream from a high mountain lake. If the healer intuits that the person's block is emotional or mental, the healer will polarize the energy in the client's body, and a canopy of emotional energy stimulated by the collective field—4D—will form over the client's body on the table.

Some people feel the canopy as an emotional field that vibrates or crackles; the healer may also feel this. The healer charges this canopy with even more polarity, and the client will begin to see images or feel pain in various parts of the body. Then the healer can help the client bring forth these images to clear the body block by processing the content of the images and any pain that comes up. The person on the table is presenting previously-blocked energy that he or she is ready to release—that is, clearing trauma. As you will see later, the higher dimensions become available once the 4D blocks are cleared. The higher dimensions cannot be accessed without resolving polarity in our bodies. Also, the person must understand many things about these higher worlds in order to enter them and stay awhile; that material is the essence of this book.

Regarding how to read this book, complex scientific footnotes, as well as sources, have been kept out of the text so as to make it more readable; you can find this information in the endnotes section at the back. You will also find a glossary at the end of the book, in case you've forgotten the definition of a word. Please note that each dimension has been described in such a way as to trigger the actual energy of that dimension. We start with the incredibly dense first dimension, and each successive dimension is less dense and more "spacey." Therefore reading this book is like attending your own mini-Activation; if you find yourself getting agitated, take a moment to relax, have a cup of tea, and let yourself settle. If you find yourself getting sluggish or sleepy, stretch and take a walk. It might be wise to read one chapter a day in a sacred space as you explore these very powerful ancient dimensional teachings. Have a great journey!

Gerry's Introduction: The Healer's Quest

I began teaching with Barbara in Crete in 1996. I was one of nine men in a group of forty women; we men were celebrated by the women for our bravery, and the women were deeply enjoying being feminine in this goddess-rich landscape. I love Crete: the wooded hills, the drone of the locust in the hot, sun-baked mountains, the buzz of the bees collecting honey in the orchards, the crypt-like chapels in the groves of gnarled olive trees, the black cassocks on the Orthodox priests, the sense of fertility and order, simplicity and time. I'm glad I began my journey here.

I tell this story for the benefit of other men out there, and women, who might enjoy knowing how it was for a husband suddenly to be challenged by his wife to WAKE UP! and join her in her quest. No, it was not enough that we were co-publishers and co-owners of Bear & Company, a thriving New Age press in New Mexico. Nor was it enough that I had done my own past-life regressions, received my own profound healings from alternative therapists, and started to feel energy in my hands and sight in my third eye. Nor was it enough that I was a responsible father to our four children and a loving husband to her. She knew—and I knew, deep down inside—that we were on a quest, and the work had just begun.

We remembered our joint lifetime in Minoan times, she as a seer, I as a warrior and protector, and how our lives had been cut short by the cataclysmic eruption of Santorini Thera. Perhaps we did have to complete that work of the sacred temple by bringing it to the people. I thought of how salmon gallantly work their way upstream each year, albeit in diminished numbers, yet doing what their ancestors did before them, what their blood codes told them to do.

I spent a whole night out under the stars that trip. I puffed through a pack of Camels that night, too, to keep me company. I am not a smoker, yet the familiar smell of tobacco and the burning of the match cheered me up, gave me my own momentary bit of starlight. I remember feeling very small on that landscape, as I walked back and forth. What was I to do? Was objecting going to be this hard? What inspired me to take such drastic measures—I am a man who likes his full-night's sleep and a warm bed beside my woman—was the sight of Barbara teaching, and realizing who she really was.

She was in her prime as a shamanic teacher in those times; anyone watching her in *Nine Initiations on the Nile* (our initiation video on Egypt filmed in 1994) or who traveled with us in those days knows what I mean. (You still see this side of Barbara when she leads us through the nine dimensions during our Activations.) She was dressed in a Minoan-style painted silk dress, made for her by an old friend of ours in Santa Fe; she was channeling in public for the first time (having channeled earlier to a private group to create *The Pleiadian Agenda*), and each evening she brought in a new message: The Library of Delos, The Alexandrian Library, The Library of Alcyone, The Grandmother Cave of Crete. With all of my being, I knew she was operating at full potential, and it scared me, because it made me wonder about when and how I would operate at my full potential. Thus the Camels and the puffing out under starlight for a whole long night.

Well, he who protests loudest, resists strongest. I put up a good fight, but I was skewered, toast, done for. I did my own teaching—attempting to discuss "relationships in the Aquarian age," given that I am an Aquarian, like Barbara—and I made the plunge. I had a long way to go, but I had begun. Shortly thereafter, I began my formal training in healing, first at Lily Dale, New York, home of America's oldest spiritualist community, with Rev. Elaine Thomas and healer Tom Cratsley, then in Santa Fe with John Kemper in Polarity Therapy.

I completed my Polarity training with John Beaulieu in Stone Ridge, New York, and then embarked on a two-year training in craniosacral resonance with Paul Vick in Vermont. During this time I began to see clients, first as a hands-on spiritual healer, then as a Polarity Therapy practitioner, and finally as a craniosacral therapist. I am currently using this training to teach others, clients and students alike, what I have learned and what seems most appropriate to share at these times.

I am aided always by a deep memory of when I was a healer and teacher in another time. We call that time Atlantis, but that is not how the people thought of themselves at that time. We were part of a global maritime civilization; our technology was far advanced from today's; and yes, the end came, through a giant cataclysm with which you are all now familiar. The reason I share this memory with you is to say: We can do this, we can make the critical leap happen, we can return and continue on the path we once followed. Yes, we were all once less dense, and yes, we are moving, through personal healing and transmutation, to that lighter place, where there is more room for the Light in our bodies, in our consciousness—and at the same time we are still a part of Earth.

My work is now twinned with Barbara's work; we balance each other well. Thanks to my training and my years as an athlete, I love the body, honor the body, begin with the body—the diamond essence of physicality. Barbara, thanks to her tireless self-education and the training from her grandfather, loves the mind, the diamond essence of mental acuity. Together, we treat students the way we treat our family members: each as a unique being, allowing plenty of room for experimentation and growth. As Aquarian teachers, we like to empower our students, let them stand on their own, and see what happens. We like to combine the power of presence with the discipline of detachment. I like to call it "active neutrality." I am honored and grateful to be in such a role, and I treasure every opportunity I have with students and clients. These moments together allow me to be at my full potential, which is something we all can help each other achieve these days.

Now, I'd like to tell you about the meditations that I have written at the start of each chapter and in my own chapter at the end. They are inspired from my trainings with Paul Vick, the extraordinary craniosacral teacher from London, and the insightful Polarity Therapy practitioner, Andreas Lederman, from Switzerland—and from my experiences co-teaching the workshops. I am giving you an image to work with, in a meditative state, that will facilitate your movement, mentally and energetically, into the chapter that follows. Here is how I'd like you to work with them:

Either read them with your eyes in a soft focus; in essence, turn off your brain's analytical focus and just allow yourself to follow along with the words. You can still read words in such a state, you just don't have to analyze them. Just receive, and respond to them. Or, you could read them into a cassette player, and then play them at the appropriate time. You decide. I hope you enjoy them.

"Every philosophy and every psychological system has been based upon inadequate knowledge of certain aspects of existence, upon a partial insight. We need a greater experience, a multidimensioned metaphysics. Now, as never before, we are capable of it. We can learn from all the traditions, from both their strengths and weaknesses. But to do this we must roam these many worlds, high and low."

—Michael Murphy, *Jacob Atabet* (1977)

PART ONE
THE NINE DIMENSIONS

We all live and express nine dimensions of consciousness throughout our lives, yet most of us seem to be aware of the existence of only the second, third, and fourth dimensions. The second dimension is below Earth's surface, the third is our solid world, and the fourth is the realm of our collective mind. The first dimension located in the center of Earth is the source of grounding ourselves, and the higher five dimensions are where the transcendent parts of our essence exist. These five higher levels have been mostly screened out of the fast-moving, technological world we live in, yet without reaching these levels, we cannot find the Divine and know bliss.

In 1995, with the publication of *The Pleiadian Agenda,* the Pleiadians came into our world with these nine-dimensional teachings, insisting that this model helps integrate human consciousness as we approach the end of the Mayan calendar on December 21, 2012. Now the Pleiadians have returned to show us how the rich language of our times—science—opens us to multidimensional levels of awareness that were once common to all people thousands of years ago. To honor these Pleiadian gifts, each chapter first summarizes their understanding of how each dimension influences Earth. The rest of the chapter is an explanation of the science or sciences that seem to be operating in each dimension. Exploring the sciences of each dimension deepens, even sometimes clarifies and substantiates, the Pleiadians' assertions about the levels of creative expression available to us. They say we are missing a great deal of the frequency ranges in our world. By necessity, discussions about quantum and superstring theory are very complex, yet this book has been written to make modern science more accessible to the average reader. Perhaps scientists will find that this multidimensional approach to science is of interest as well.

The First Dimension: The Iron Core Crystal in the Center of Earth

Opening Meditation

Find your breath. Take your time reading these words. Consider the ink making the letters on the paper you are touching. Consider the paper; how does it feel? Find your breath, and find your feet. Move your head from side to side, and very gently, up and down. Let your head drop gently, softly, toward your chest. Go only as far as it will let you. Breathe into the little stretches you are making. Notice how your breath helps lubricate the stretches.

Raise your head back up and take another breath, a long one this time, five full seconds in, and five full seconds out. Now slowly raise your shoulders up, on both sides, toward your ears. Take a deep breath as you do this and hold it, just as you hold your shoulders up as high as they can go. And then, poof, let out the air and let your shoulders drop. Shake your head a bit to loosen your neck even more, and try another breath, with shoulders up to your ears, and then, again, let those shoulders drop, like lead weights. Don't be afraid to experiment; sometimes we're really tight in the neck and shoulders and this takes a number of times to work.

Notice where your attention is. You are focusing just on one thing right now—using your breath to help you relax your neck and shoulders. Now, feel gravity. Feel the weight of your body in the chair you are sitting on, or the bed or couch you are lying on. Let yourself feel the weight. Let yourself feel very heavy. Go ahead. This is called relaxing with gravity. Feel gravity like a blanket, a blanket with little magnetic weights in it. A blanket that has just the perfect amount of attraction to hold you to Earth. Enjoy your blanket; this is your very own Gravity Blanket.

Now find your feet. Where are they? If they are on the floor, begin to feel the floor through all parts of your feet: the edges, the toes, your heels. Take a grip on the floor with your toes, just to feel more connection. If you are lying down as you read this, put your attention on the air touching your feet, and see if this helps you find them. Now find your breath, and find your feet at the same time. Breath, feet . . . breath, feet.

Can you feel the top of your head as you inhale? Can you feel as if there is a tiny air hole on the top of your head? Go ahead, experiment. Maybe the air comes in through the bones of your head, not just through one hole. Just be aware of what's above you, as you become more aware of your feet and your breath. Crown, breath, feet; feet, breath, crown. . . . Good.

Now picture a column of white light, of laser-beam light, coming from the top of your head to your feet. Go ahead. Take whatever time it takes. Read these words, then close your eyes and picture that column of white light running through your body, from your crown to your feet. Make it bigger, more tangible, with each breath you take. This is your column of white light, so enjoy it. Get to know it. Take your time, all the time in the world.

Now, as you begin to feel and see this column of white light, begin to let this column descend beneath your feet, into the floor and space beneath your feet. Go ahead, keep letting it go deeper and deeper. See it entering Earth beneath you, beneath your feet and where you are sitting or lying down. This is your column of light; focus on it. See where it takes you. Begin to picture a crystal, a large crystal, the size of a city, at the center of Earth. See your light begin to penetrate that crystal. See your column of white light descending beneath you as it begins to shine into this gigantic crystal. Notice what is happening. Take your time.

You are very solid now, and you are in the crystal; you are the crystal. See the white light all around you now, bouncing and reflecting off the sides of this gigantic crystal at the center of Earth. You have come Home. This is your center. See if you find anything special, just for you, in this center. Take your time. Breathe gently as you do this.

Notice the column of light above you, running through your head and back to the surface of Earth. This is your lifeline, your way to the world above. Notice how easily you can move from one place to another: core, surface . . . core, surface. Notice how easily you can move with just your breath: core, surface . . . core, surface. You are anchored, yet you can move back and forth, back and forth.

Now, as you read these words, pay more attention to your breath once again: five seconds in, five seconds out. Find your shoulders. How do they feel? Can you find their outer edges, their outer points, where your arms meet them?

Good. Now continue to breathe, five in, five out, and move your neck and head from side to side, up and down, gently. How are you feeling? Are you a bit heavy?

Good. You've slowed down to Earth pulses, to the pulses of the iron core crystal. Take your time reentering your space; drink a glass of pure water. Remember your journey. Write down what you found. Go take a walk, slowly; feel your feet on the ground. Take your time. You have the whole rest of your life to live.

According to the Pleiadians, who I refer to frequently as the Ps, the first of Earth's nine dimensions of consciousness is the iron core crystal in the center of our planet. Satya, the Pleiadian goddess who is the main voice, says that the first dimension (1D) is the only truly solid dimension in this vertical axis. The second dimension (2D), the realm between Earth's core and the surface, seems solid because of its powerful magnetism and gravity. We have been getting much information from science lately about the mysterious realm under Earth's surface. In 1994, an earthquake of 8+ magnitude rumbled 395 miles beneath Bolivia. This quake was a boon to seismologists who had installed seismic sensors on opposite sides of the planet to measure faint vibrations going all the way through its center.

The chemical structures of rocks, magma, and crystals can be analyzed by studying the seismic waves passing through them; this is called seismic tomography. Since the quake was so deep, these scientists detected and measured the waves generated by the quake that traveled through the center of Earth and out to the opposite side. Excitedly, they analyzed the waves and were amazed by their findings: The center of Earth is a huge iron core crystal that is about 1,500 miles wide and is denser than the surrounding outer core, mantle, lithosphere, and crustal zones.[1] This deep-Earth study is one of many scientific confirmations synchronistically released when *The Pleiadian Agenda* was published.

What the Ps say about the center of Earth is much in agreement with science, and they also say this information is very important for us now. What they say about the structure of the vertical axis is that the iron core crystal is the primal activator of electromagnetic waves vibrating through the 2D telluric realm (see figure 1.3).[2] These waves emerge through the crust, where the material planes of our world (3D) are manifested within electromagnetic fields when these waves emerge through the crust and

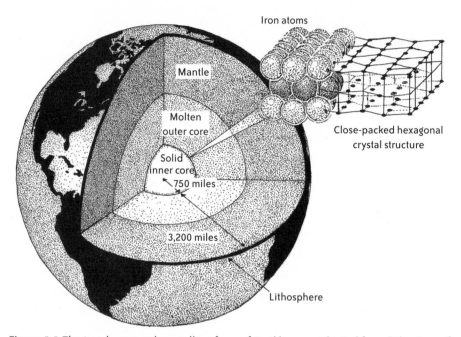

Figure 1.1 The iron hexagonal crystalline form of Earth's core. Adapted from "The Core of the Earth May Be a Gigantic Crystal Made of Iron," William J. Broad, *New York Times*, April 4, 1995, C1.

are triggered by electrical frequency waves in the atmosphere. Much more subtly, the fields of life on the surface vibrate faster and faster, triggered by stellar light frequencies, which are constantly arriving on Earth's surface, even though their radiation is screened by the atmosphere. Earth's crust and atmosphere vibrate with the light of divine intelligence from very high dimensions.

The best way to imagine 1D is as a point—the beginning point of all Earth's manifestation—where materialization happens as a result of the planetary spin. Related to this is the fact that at the 3D molecular level, materialization begins with movement or spin. The 1D core origination point eventually ends in the ninth dimension—9D—in the black hole in the center of the Milky Way. A black hole is formed when a large star dies and collapses under its own weight and it shrinks down to a dense point called a singularity, which distorts space and time. This great spiral draws all kinds of emanations, planes, and spheres into itself on the vertical axis originating in the center of Earth.

The Ps say two more things about the vertical axis of Earth. First, all nine dimensions are totally accessible to humans in 3D, even though there are many other dimensions. For example, the vertical axis, which connects all nine dimensions, is the tenth dimension, and the Ps speak about twenty-six dimensions in all. We humans do not yet have the mental apparatus to apprehend the universe, although we can *feel* it as our container. Second, the Keepers of each dimension are unique to each system, such as Earth. There are different Keepers for the dimensions in other worlds, such as Jupiter, Mars, or Regulus. Other locations generate a dimensional form from their centers, and they have chosen Keepers for their dimensions.

If you've always felt really connected with another place, such as Arcturus or Aldebaran, these stars may be Keepers of other realms that you resonate with. If you feel a great connection with one of the Keepers of Earth, such as Sirius, the Pleiades, Orion, or the Galactic Center, then you may be residing in some form in that other realm while you live here. I freely admit that I feel some part of me exists in the Pleiades while I also live here on Earth. This "other" life enhances my earthly data bank, just as travel to another country educates me and makes me feel free to come and go in my mind.

As we prepare to enter 1D, let us begin with the realization that all of us share something very special: We incarnated here on Earth to experience life activated by the iron core crystal, known by many as Gaia. What gives Gaia life? Spin creates movement, which causes particles to become waves; then matter is created, and eventually we have life within the cells of our bodies. Yet where does spin come from? Actually, this is all simple from a cosmic perspective.

The Ps say that the iron molecules in the core crystal *pulse* because the planet is spinning in orbit while vibrating to all the planets, moons, and asteroids in our solar system, as well as to the Sun itself. All these bodies vibrate by the forward motion of the Galaxy as well as its spin, and the Galaxy vibrates to quasars, supernovas, stars, and galaxies. The Galaxy swishes through space like a plasma wave, or perhaps like a jellyfish or a beating heart. Plasma is slightly less material than gases, liquids, and solids, and plasma holds together by gravity. The orbiting stars vibrate and pulse by orbital spin and forward motion, as the Galaxy churns around with its spiral arms that fan out from its hungry black hole. The

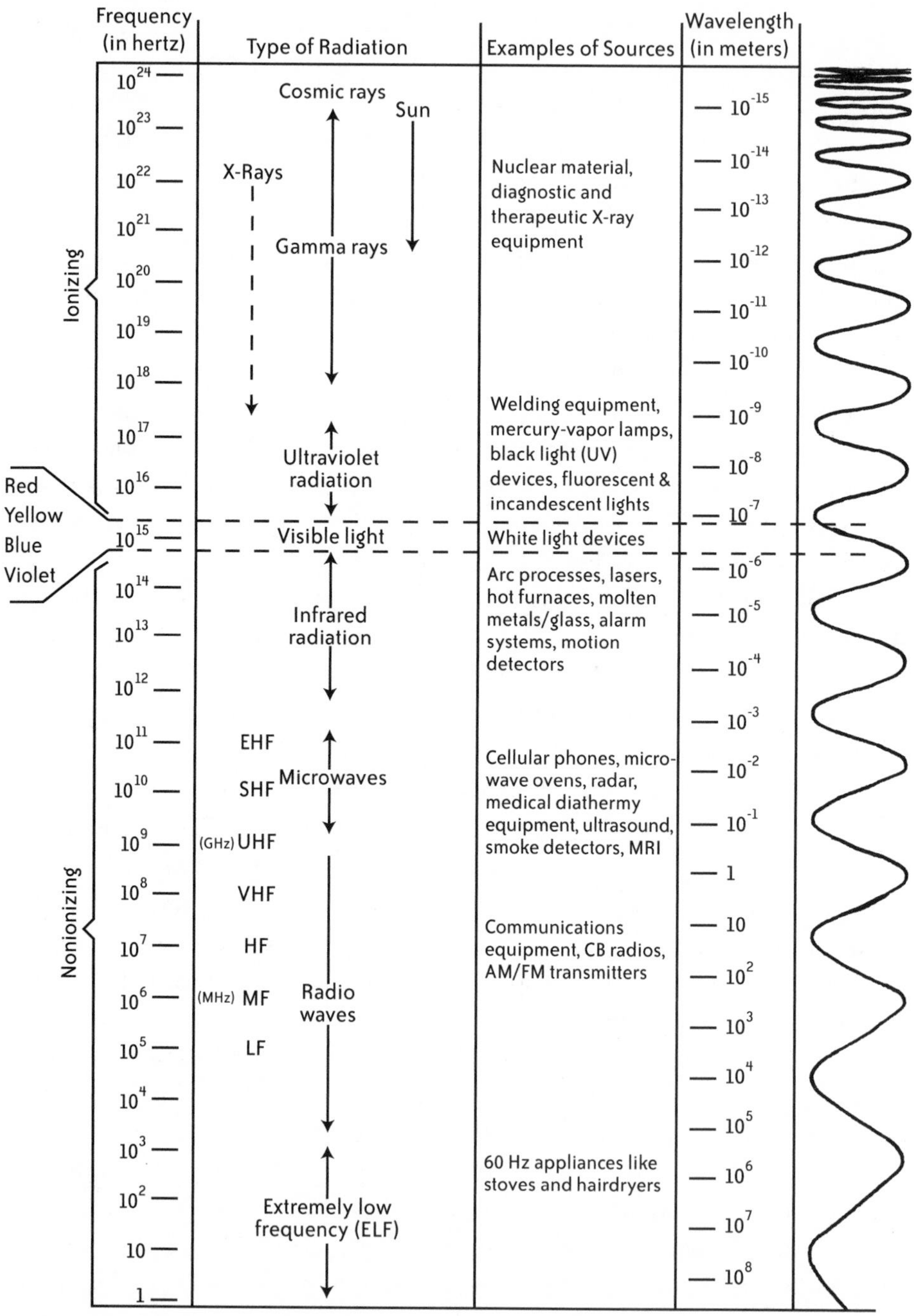

Figure 1.2 The electromagnetic spectrum chart. Adapted from *Electromagnetic Fields,* B. Blake Levitt, p. 43.

Galactic Center is the 1D center of the Milky Way, just as the iron core crystal is the 1D center of Earth. Everything vibrates, which determines the qualities of matter, light, and consciousness. The core is the origination point of Earth's materialization and its transmutation to light in the Galactic Center. We humans are wired in our brains and nervous systems to vibrate with the whole frequency range of the vertical axis.

The Center of Earth According to Science

According to science, Earth's core resonates at 40 hertz (Hz), or forty pulses or vibrations per second, which sends electromagnetic waves into 2D, 3D, and beyond. Earth's crust vibrates at 7.5 Hz.[3] By comparison, if we examine the electromagnetic (EM) spectrum chart (see figure 1.2), you can see that we exist as seemingly solid in the frequency range of the visible light spectrum, where solid things manifest at about 10^{15} Hz in 3D. In fact, relative to the size of atoms, the distance between one atom and another in your body is equivalent to the distance of a few miles; we are empty inside and made of vibrating waves. Frequencies beyond 3D—such as X-rays and gamma rays—vibrate much faster; and the frequency ranges of higher dimensions eventually become invisible. The incredible truth is that we vibrate with the pulse of Earth, which aligns us with all other beings—including light—in the ladder or chain of existence. This is the vertical axis of consciousness.

Also, according to Satya, because we have iron in our blood, we are wired to vibrate with Gaia in our blood. The blood coursing in our veins pulses with the iron core crystal because it has crystalline iron components. This is what makes it possible to be in our bodies and vibrate in other ranges simultaneously. Since the iron core crystal *is* gravity and we organize by much weaker gravity in 3D, then it is possible to imagine why science describes great distances between each molecule in our bodies. We are empty inside, and something holds all that space together.

The higher dimensions, held together by weaker and weaker gravity, are diaphanous. If we ask what started the primal spin, we are asking why we exist in the first place. More important than how it all started, what holds us together? Our glue or physical integrity comes from gravity, the force that emanates from the first dimension. We experience gravity as binding, as allurement, as a formation force, but what adds mystery is the fact that the cells in our bodies are also 1D chains of manifestation. Our cells are intelligent because they vibrate to stars in the universe. As far as how this got started, the Ps yawn. They are much more interested in having humans learn to feel the pulses in their blood, which resonate with the center of Earth.

If you contemplate the spinning orbits of stars emitting light waves that eventually become sound that creates geometry that directs materialization, you will not care how or when it started or ends. You have existence now, and everything else is a distraction. Ask a cellist where the notes come from, and the cellist will simply keep on playing. The core crystal connects you to everything in the universe, its agenda is gravity, and it pulses in your blood.

Many scientists go on and on about how they cannot explain gravity, which is to say they cannot define it as a felt experience. They know that Earth's center is a huge iron crystal, and that iron is more dense than most other metals. They know that things become weightless—gravity lessens—when one rises above the crust of Earth and into space. The Ps say that the way scientists talk about gravity is a great example of how their heads are in the laboratory and not in the world. In September 2002, scientists finally measured the speed of gravity, which does travel at the speed of light, as Einstein theorized. The speed of gravity was the last unmeasured constant in physics.[4] Physicists have developed a new observing instrument, the Laser Interferometry Gravitational Observatory, to detect gravitational waves in space, which means many surprises about gravity are soon to come.

To summarize and clarify the Pleiadian point of view regarding gravity: The 1D core is gravity, and as it moves to the surface and above, it weakens; all 1D centers in the universe are gravity. The 2D outer core is molten, and deep 2D currents flow under Earth's surface. As the gravity waves emerge from 2D, they respond to electricity in the atmosphere and create the surface electromagnetic fields. Gravity holds all the dimensions together on the vertical axis rising into the black hole in the center of the Milky Way. Gravity is less dense as the dimensions ascend because the dimensions move out from the vertical axis in great circular planes, which makes it difficult to measure on the vertical axis. Gravity is the central intelligence or center that gives form to the planar matrices of all nine dimensions (see figure 5.2). The weaker gravity is, the more complex the dimensionality. In the higher dimensions or hyperspace, gravity travels much faster than the speed of light as measured at 186,000 miles per second.[5] The actual measurement of gravity waves in space will probably confirm this model in the near future.

The Science of the First Dimension

All the dimensions of Earth's chain of being are sourced in 1D, Gaia. Of course, Western science does not conceive of this vertical axis structure from the center of Earth to the Galactic Center. However, the qualities of the iron core crystal that were discovered by tomographic analysis after the 1994 Bolivian earthquake suggest exactly this possibility. For example, the texture of the huge crystal probably explains many of the mysteries of the Earth's magnetic field. Seismic waves traveling through the center go faster from north to south than when they travel east to west; that is, they transmit at different speeds in different directions (see figure 1.3). These varying directional velocities are called anisotropies, and measuring them yields fascinating clues about the composition of the great unseen crystal. Since the pressures in the center are *three million times greater* than on the surface, and the iron is solid in spite of the temperature being in excess of *7,000º F,* only the final crystalline form of iron—hexagonal—is possible as the structure of this gigantic crystal (see figure 1.1). One scientist suggested the core is like a huge diamond in the center of Earth.[6] Most important, the hexagonal prism form fits the recent seismic evidence.

The inner core may have its own magnetic field, which probably has a different direction from the outer core. This would explain periodic magnetic reversals, as well as the skewing of magnetic field lines, which show a persistent four-degree tilt. Geometry is the key to dimensionality, as you will see, and to my mind the vertical axis propels out of this huge hexagonal form of the core and emerges through the surface.[7] In that sense, there must be trillions of vertical axes shooting out of the hexagonal crystals in the hot center; each emergence must have a unique pattern on the surface.

The spin power of the four-degree tilt of the whole Earth's magnetic field is the kind of energy that could generate multidimensional planes all the way into the Galactic Center. In light of what I just described, it is easier to see how Earth may truly be unique in the universe or the Milky Way. Furthermore, the Ps say that the Galactic Center pulses in resonance

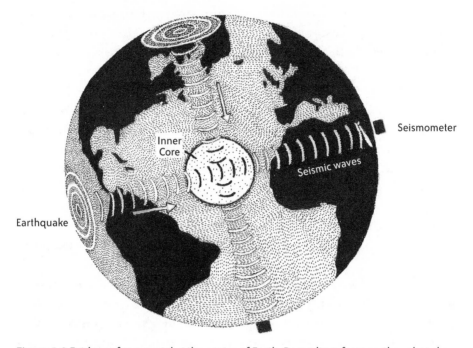

Figure 1.3 Evidence for a crystal at the center of Earth. Recordings from earthquakes show that seismic waves take about four seconds longer to go through Earth from east to west than they do to travel from north to south. The waves must pass through an object that transmits them with different speeds in different directions; a crystal would have this property. Adapted from "The Core of the Earth May Be a Gigantic Crystal Made of Iron," William J. Broad, *New York Times*, April 4, 1995, C1.

with Earth. Recently, scientists have discovered that the black hole in the center of the Milky Way emits X-rays approximately equal to the energy that streams from our Sun.[8] This suggests vibrational connections between our solar system and the Galactic Center. Letting science go for a moment, I'd like to share what we have learned about the core crystal by traveling down into it during hundreds of Activations.

Entering the Iron Core Crystal

From the very first Activation, which I led in "America's Stonehenge" at Salem, New Hampshire, on the Fall Equinox in 1995, the crystal informed us that it has very specific laws: Like any center in the universe, including the DNA in our bodies, the core can only be entered by offering the right prayers. For humans, Earth's center is the ultimate sacred realm, since it is the source of all the lifeforms that have ever existed in 2D or on the surface. Both Earth's surface and the areas deep below are ecosystems that can potentiate lifeforms, and 3D includes the atmosphere, which supports life.

During an Activation, participants are located in 3D by the *medicine laws*—the indigenous way of understanding the natural laws of Earth—which are the only way anyone can enter Gaia. To enter the core, participants are taught to orient themselves to the four directions—East, West, South, and North. The entrance down into Gaia exists in the center of the four-directional altar, which is the place where the vertical axis emerges in a specific location. Once participants are aligned to the directions in this sacred landscape, I offer prayers, and then I go into a meditative state and bring the Ps into our circle. (The Ps actually conduct the Activations.)

We've discovered that the core crystal is always emitting images, symbols, colors, forms, beings, or coded sounds at specific places on Earth.

Figure 1.4 Images emitted from Earth's core.

The Ps translate these keys through me, and then I translate them for the group. Some students can see Earth's frequencies themselves; sometimes they see similar images, colors, and so on, and sometimes different ones. These visions are always unique to the place and time, and I see as many as I can for the group and attempt to translate them. These images somehow help participants shift the frequencies in their own bodies, which admits them to Earth's core. The Ps orchestrate frequencies by color and sound that harmonize everyone, making it possible to enter the core.

Once our energy bodies are prepared, the Ps lead us out of our hearts and heads, down through our spines, and then down below our sacred circle into Earth. As the Ps shift the energy frequencies in our bodies, we travel together as a complex energy dynamic down through 2D into the core. Eventually, we pass easily down into Earth's center to explore our primordial source. In each of the Activations, I receive a unique set of symbols unlike any other. I think the energetic frequencies of a specific place and time, as well as Earth's core, have constantly changing unique vibratory patterns. I find it fascinating that when we are the most alert mentally, our brainwaves are in the beta range—40 Hz—which is the same as the frequency of Earth's core!

Since the inner and outer cores are the source of surface electromagnetism, often the journey through the outer core and into the inner core is intense. For a few students, experiencing the density can be very challenging. For other students, the experience can be so sacred that it is almost overwhelming. This is why we always have healers available. Yet, if we are to experience all nine dimensions, we must first resonate with the qualities of the 1D and 2D frequencies. We have conducted many Activations at sacred sites and power points where clear access to Earth's center was marked by our ancestors. We will continue to do this ceremony until December 21, 2012, as will many of our students with their own groups. It is our hope that this work will help all humans remember that we are the Keepers of Gaia.

Gerry and I have learned much about the iron core crystal by traveling in it with people, and many students discover grounding for the first time in their lives by experiencing the core. When the Ps look at humans, they see seven light centers as our chakra system; *five* are on the body, and one is above and one below. To them, the first chakra of the human chakra system is the Earth chakra, which resonates with the iron

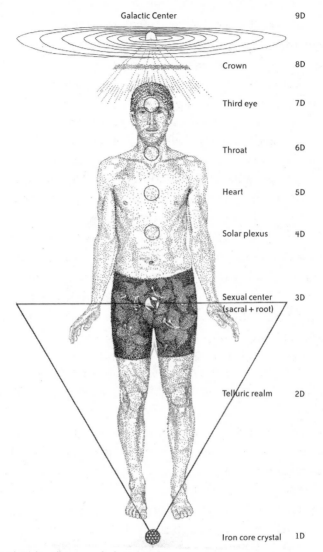

Figure 1.5 The Pleiadian/human chakra system.

core crystal and the telluric realm; this chakra grounds us while we are alive (figure 1.5).

We humans, on the other hand, experience chakras as part of the subtle energetic systems in our body that acupuncturists use for healing, and we experience *six* major chakras located in our body and one above our head at our crown. One difference between the Pleiadian and human systems is over the first and second chakras; to the Ps, the first chakra is off-body (at the iron core crystal), and for humans, we experience that first chakra as our root or coccygeal chakra. That is why we have labeled the first chakra in the body as our *sexual center,* which is a combination of the root (coccygeal) chakra and sexual (sacral) chakra. Interestingly, the Ps say as our root chakra resonates with the 1D iron core crystal, our sexual (sacral) chakra resonates with the 2D telluric realm. Likewise, our crown chakras resonate with the 8D divine realm.[9] The important thing to notice, as you consider this illustration of the Pleiadian/human chakra system, is that our chakras operate *between* Earth and the Galactic Center.

Many students are overwhelmed when they see the molecular matrix of the crystalline facets of the core, and some see in it the species and ecosystems that inhabit the higher dimensions as well as the lower ones. Like films in a gigantic film library, all records and memories vibrate in the dense, organic, iron crystal. Sometimes it feels like one drop of rain on a crystal facet could spawn a pristine new Amazon jungle. We've seen Precambrian flora and fauna—and even dinosaurs—at the center, and many have seen magical creatures such as unicorns or gnomes. As in the higher dimensions, there is no time, background noise, or space limitations, and some actually feel in a visceral way the space between the cells in their bodies.

We've relaxed in great mountain valleys and primeval forests, and we often hear the words "Garden of Eden." Many of us have felt Earth's true pulse so many times that now we can feel it easily in our own bodies. We have experienced sounds that can be heard at sacred sites, such as stalactites being struck in the Mayan caves at Lol Tun in the Yucatan. Michael Stearns recorded these resonating stalactites, which the Maya use to connect people to Earth's heart. The sounds of Earth are audible in the music we play for each Activation.

There is no doubt our distant ancestors were in tune with Earth's core, and attuning with it is probably the key to megalithic science. People living six thousand years ago moved stones around that weighed hundreds of tons, which suggests they may have mastered a science of manipulating frequencies in objects to change their weight. Reducing the weight of stones by sonics is probably possible, since frequency shifts can cause lower density in objects. The megalithic scientists may have discovered powerful natural laws that are ruled by the iron core crystal and are only now being rediscovered. And they probably knew a lot more about how to work with gravity than we do today.

What we have experienced personally in the Activations is that the more we resonate with the heart of Earth, the more we open up vast spaces within ourselves. Once we feel less dense, we resonate more easily with the highest dimensions, which makes it possible to detect them. The more we experience traveling through all the dimensions and going into the Galactic Center, the more we feel how the Galactic Center pulses with Earth.

Students who have experienced many Activations are developing themselves on new intelligence pathways, which begin right in the iron core crystal. Since the core contains the memory records of all species and systems, and since these records are encoded in hexagonal iron crystals, attuning ourselves to the 40-hertz frequency range helps us to access these records. The Ps say that all the species "stored" in the core can rejuvenate on the surface or in the 2D worlds below if viable ecosystems make a home for them. After great catastrophes on Earth, there is always a biological rejuvenation of species that adapt to new habitats. We seem to be destroying the mental, emotional, and physical habitats of the human realm as we come to the end of the Mayan calendar, yet all the data for life on the surface is stored in the iron core crystal. Also, information in other dimensions can generate new creative options; for example, a gamma-ray explosion from a magnestar—a collapsed star—may have done this in 1998 (see chapter 9).

Unique pathways to higher consciousness are now appearing, such as the crop circles during the last twenty years. The most potent pathway for us now seems to be a return to the Paleolithic mind, which was global, ecosensitive, and multidimensional. I believe this because the younger generation represented by my children know this. Specifically, the Paleolithic mind still lives in the core, which holds all possibilities for humans. As the 3D world devolves into chaos during this period, Earth's more gentle, slow, and silent intelligence is regenerating. Using the seven sacred directions to enter Gaia, the key to accessing this is to work from a chosen center of the four directions; to add "above" and "below" so as to activate the vertical axis; and then to move your consciousness into your heart center, the seventh sacred direction. This can be done during Activations, or in your own choice of sacred space and time.

As you will see when we move into 2D and 3D, the core pulses out resonating waves that actually create the dimensions of the vertical axis. These core pulses are the source of energy pathways and systems in the crust and surface. The 2D vital energy pathways—ley lines, vortexes, and water pathways—carry the intelligence of the core and direct 3D ecosystems and habitation patterns. Leaving the core to return up through 2D, we image Earth as a sphere with the core in the center, and we visualize waves of energy moving out from the sphere, through 2D, and emerging as patterns in the crust. These patterns are also responding to light waves from the sky. As we live on the surface, we are constant expressions of these waves. How we materialize as our bodies—how waves become organic—is explored in the next chapter, as this occurs in the second dimension.

The Second Dimension:
The Telluric World

Opening Meditation

Feel your arms on the surface of where you are sitting or lying down. Feel how they make contact with the surface. Feel what is inside your arms, and what is outside your arms. Feel all the tiny things going on inside your arms. Feel all the tiny things going on outside your arms, all around you. Consider all the surfaces you are touching with your body, and with your mind. Your mind observes, notes; it is curious. It just wants to feel, with your body, where you are, inside your body and outside your body.

You are not alone. Notice all the life around you, and inside of you. Little tiny creatures that only microscopes can see: You know they are there, even though you cannot actually see them. You know they are there just by the feel of them. You are full of millions of little creatures, little bodies inside your body. They live with you, inside your cells, inside your molecules, in your blood, your skin, your tissues, your bones.

Feel, get in touch with the creatures outside your body, in the air, in the water, in the ground. See where they come from. See their source. See how many of them there are. See if you can even begin to imagine how many there are.

Now, begin to notice the creatures you like, the ones you feel good about, the ones you feel close to. And, if you can, notice the ones that you cannot see so well, that you don't feel as close to, that seem to be there visiting; the uninvited ones, like hobos sleeping under a bridge at night. See, with your expanded, observing, all-intelligent mind, if you can find a way to speak with all these creatures. See with the power of intention, or with the power of just knowing and observing, if you can contact them. Like sweeping them with a great light from the beacon of your brain. See if they pay attention. Go ahead, give it a try. Be creative; no one else is watching, just you. See what you can do.

Go on doing this, for as long as it takes to get in touch with these creatures. Find out ways to do this best. Try sitting very still, or lying on the ground in a safe sunny place, and let your body find its creatures, those on the inside, and those on the outside. Notice how the creatures on the inside seem connected to the ones on the outside, and those on the outside to those on the inside. Notice the families, clans, alliances. Get to know them by feeling them and seeing them with your incredible sight. . . . When you are ready, bring your attention back to your present moment.

According to the Pleiadians, the second dimension (2D) is the realm between the iron core crystal and the curved crust of Earth. The Keepers of 2D are the elementals—radioactive, chemical, mineral, viral, and bacterial intelligences—who are trillions of workers who maintain this dimension. The same elements all exist in 3D, although with less density. This means that it is easy for us in 3D to comprehend the qualities of 2D and resonate with them intentionally. This zone is often called the telluric realm—the outer core, mantle, lithosphere, and inner crust—because it contains and expresses the great inner Earth forces that vibrate out from the core. By Earth's spin, these forces rise toward the curved surface and then are changed in 3D by powers in the atmosphere.

The 2D realm is incredibly dense and intense, yet it vibrates more slowly than the core. It is held in form by gravity while being pulled to the surface, where Earth's sphere expands out into the solar system by the power of Earth's spin and orbit. Earth's core, although generating gravity and vast in size, functions geometrically as a gigantic, hexagonally structured iron crystal (see figure 1.1). In 2D, lines of materialization are generated that evolve forms in 2D and 3D. The 2D crystals, metals, rocks, magma, bacteria, and viruses are the source of surface life; the Ps insist that surface life first began in 2D.

Due to great compression, the telluric world exudes extraordinary powers, which have powerful influences on the surface. Having evolved out of 2D, we humans still resonate with it by "cords" made of different elemental forms that reach into our four bodies of consciousness—physical, emotional, mental, and spiritual. The crystals, elements, and minerals that comprise our physical bodies are symbiotic with the 2D elementals; it is potent to think of them as your ancestors, or to conceive of your body within your skin as 2D and your outer body as 3D. The Ps say our blood is a 2D crystalline realm, which is physically and energetically alive as a flowing multidimensional connector pulsing with the iron core crystal like a great river system of flowing energy. This flow of 2D forces is exquisitely responsive to all the higher dimensions; when you "know" things, you are feeling this field, and such information is of a high order.

The second dimension is contained by the spherical curvature of Earth's surface, which causes it to be a pressured realm of life. The forms of 2D and 3D are direct reflections of all the higher-dimensional intelligences on Earth's vertical axis; in that sense, we are created in God's image. The dense spherical geometry of 2D draws the higher dimensions down by the magnetic force swishing and churning in the hot, molten outer core. This enriches the planes of the higher worlds, the subtle dimensions. The second dimension is much richer and more brilliant, ancient, balanced, powerful, and conscious than we imagine.

For most people these days, 2D is a dead world to be mined, exploited, and processed for the needs of 3D.[1] Yet the Ps say this world is the source of life, and harmonizing with it heals and enlivens the surface. Thousands of years ago, people believed in the powers of 2D, and they intentionally aligned with them by means of an ancient science—geomancy. The ability to relate to the consciousness of the telluric is an ancient art—alchemy. The Ps also warn that the power group that works to control the world of politics and finances—the Global Elite (the Elite)— is trying to harness 2D so it can control the world (see chapter 4). A crisis looms for Earth's inhabitants because the telluric realm will erupt in response to humans using and abusing its sacred powers; it always does.

The 2D elementals have very specific desires and powers in relation to 3D. The elementals, who are the Keepers of 2D, engage us by resonating with our energy vibrationally through the chemical, radioactive, mineral, crystalline, and biological essences in our bodies. By the laws of the vertical axis, all dimensional intelligences are interdependent and connected by resonance—vibrational frequencies that respond by octaves, such as middle C to higher C on the piano. When the essence of one dimension is diminished, resonance in all the planes of the vertical axis is reduced. When this happens, as it is now by humans bringing too many 2D elements to the surface, the higher dimensions infuse the lower worlds with great powers, which can cause 2D to erupt.

These days, the inhabitants of 3D are having difficulty with this intense energy; for example, microbes are erupting. Yet active microbes and viruses are also a sign that 2D is reformulating. The lifeforms in 3D are incredibly delicate and complex, since they exist on the curved surface of Earth within the atmosphere. The same delicacy and balance exist in 2D, even though this world is intense and chaotic, expressing itself with volcanoes and earthquakes.

The diversity we see on Earth's surface is formed by the complex world within interacting with higher dimensions. All that matters to the 2D elementals is that the biological, chemical, mineral, and crystalline forms of 3D resonate with them; they are our ancestors that hold memory. The surface is impulsed by many higher dimensions which link directly with 2D through force fields on the surface. The Ps say that humans will not protect these inner worlds until they realize they live on a delicate blue sphere that is the skin of a live universe within. Our blue sphere expands geometrically ad infinitum by conscious linkage and total connection with the universe. Earth's surface transforms into a vibrating film of complex intersecting points of spherical geometry that orbit and spin in space when Earth's surface connects with the higher dimensions.

Since the Platonic solids—five geometric forms that are the basis of all matter—direct the surface lifeforms, then certainly these five primordial geometric forms must be the creators of Earth's sphere. Miraculously, we are wired by our five senses to apprehend all of this matrix. Once we remember that we emerged out of 2D, we will naturally seek primal symbiosis with the lower worlds. Then by our consciousness, we will flow frequently in the higher realms again. The Ps insist that this is the natural way for human life. The big question is, how did we lose this vital link to life itself in the first place?

The History of Humanity Being Trained to Fear the Earth

Humanity has been taught to fear and be alienated from 2D by the Roman Catholic Church, a union of politics and religion—Caesar and Church. Around 500 A.D., the Church was run by a cabal of ambitious alchemists and geomancers, who wanted to turn the people into dreaming sheep. The controllers of Judeo-Christian systems have been using alchemy and geomancy for two thousand years, while they've murdered those who dared to use these powers themselves, such as the Cathars and the Templar Knights.[2] However, according to the Mayan calendar, it is time for all people to master these powers in order to harmonize with 2D because 2D will be totally revitalized by 2012. Alchemy is the art of understanding resonance, which makes it possible for humans to materialize things by raising or lowering frequencies. Geomancy is the art of working with the powers of Gaia in order to harmonize with Earth's frequencies. When alchemists and geomancers become adepts, occasionally they have used these arts for greed and personal power. This is sometimes irresistible because we humans really can be healthy, wealthy, and free by aligning with 2D. If you doubt this, check out the Vatican art collection and library, or notice how some humans get rich quickly mostly because they are very creative.

The Ps do not judge this, they simply say that alchemy is not meant to be a tool to get rich—taking Earth's elements for gain. Alchemy is a tool for being multidimensional, or conscious with the elementals and stars. Using alchemy correctly, humans become free, which in turn frees the elementals. Psychics, for example, never need telephones to "know" what they know; that's because they are in touch with the elementals. You can easily see what others are doing with these powers by observing the results.

When too many humans overuse Earth's powers to become rich, 2D will generate a meltdown; it will make people or the atmosphere sick and the land will go fallow. The great plagues during the Middle Ages and the Renaissance were examples of 2D responses to the Inquisitions. The second dimension always wins. And if people try to steal these powers, they often die unnatural deaths, such as modern chemical manufacturers and scientists getting cancer. Notice the number of cellphone users who are getting brain cancer.[3] Another large example is the sexual and financial perversion in the Roman Catholic Church, which is the natural result of its phenomenal geomantic and alchemical sins. When the Church spread itself all over the planetary sphere around 500 A.D., it built its churches on the ancient power places, or sacred sites, which are capstones of 2D telluric forces that draw down the higher dimensions. These churches were designed to be the houses for their alchemical systems so they could harvest the human spirit. A hideous deformation of the human spirit—*blood manipulation*—has been perpetrated for the last fifteen hundred years, which needs to be clarified because the Caesars and the Church have enslaved the elemental forces to control the people.

Here's a brief history from a Pleiadian perspective of how this manipulation took place. It started around the end of the Age of Aries (around 2160 B.C. to 60 A.D.), which was humanity's first age of warfare. Before 2000 B.C., there is little evidence of massive armies and warfare, just mere camp robbing and sacking. When the Age of Aries ended and the Age of Pisces began around the time of Christ, the alchemical powers of human blood, after thousands of years of animal sacrifice and the ritual of the seasonal dying god, were already thoroughly understood by the early Church fathers.[4] Considering the plight of humanity during the previous two thousand years, the Caesars and the theologians identified the ultimate tool for controlling the human spirit: blood.[5] Like any group that wants to command a territory, they made a plan and then created a timeline to further their aims. This plan required teaching the people to fear 2D, since it is the source of their personal power, freedom, and health.[6]

At this time, two thousand years ago, people resonated with 2D at power places by celebrating with the seasons, planetary cycles, and the Moon. Healers and shamans understood the correspondences between minerals, plants, animals, and crystals, and they employed these potent analogs to heal individuals, groups, and the land. They knew that people must be in resonance with the telluric to survive the potent energies on the surface as well as cosmic powers. They practiced alchemical and geomantic arts to maintain health, happiness, harmony, and wealth.[7] They thought of the elementals as the workers and poets of the inner Earth who make everything possible on Earth's surface. The Church had to break the people's connection with these arts and powers by making them fear the inner Earth.[8] So they ranted and railed about Hell and the devil, seductresses in the night, and evil dragons and demons. They ended the seasonal festivals and murdered the healers and shamans, except for the ones who were working inside the Church or for kings. People were taught to trust the priest and fear the witch. They were told to believe that their soul is in heaven and not within Earth. Now the tide has reversed: Many people realize the priest in the confessional or rectory is more dangerous than any witch stirring her cauldron or casting her spell!

When the Caesars and the Church plotted to take control of humanity, they decided the people would never forsake Earth and run into the sheep pen unless they were manipulated through their blood, the ancient practice for controlling people. This work was accomplished in many ways. The blood rites of women fertilizing Earth were condemned, and blood was spilled on Earth during mass warfare for two millennia. This plan culminated in two horrific world wars. The people's connection with the potent dark forces of the inner Earth was broken. When 2D elementals—coded to resonate with us in prayer and ceremony at power places—are abandoned, they dry up and abandon humanity. At this time, almost no one can imagine the exquisite peace and harmony that prevails on Earth when 2D resonates by means of human joy and ceremony. Meanwhile, these forces were secretly culled by the inner circles of the Elite. If you doubt this, see Stanley Kubrick's final film, *Eyes Wide Shut*, which shows how the Elite inner circles use sacrifice and sexual rituals to control the world today.

The consummate power play that used the power of blood at the beginning of the Age of Pisces was the invention of Holy Communion. For thousands of years before the great teacher, Christ, came to Earth, people were often manipulated by priests using various forms of blood sacrifice. Masses of people were taught to obey, since *any form of sacrifice takes away human will*. The Church created Holy Communion based on the ancient sacrificial rituals, with Mount Moriah—the sacrificial hill in the Temple of Jerusalem—as the center.[9] In the new ritual, the nexus point of Christ's life—his Transfiguration—was crafted as a sacrifice. When Christ wanted the apostles to see his essence, he allowed them to watch him raise his frequencies until he transfigured into Light.

This miracle explicitly described in the Bible was a big problem for the Church, since Christ's Transfiguration shows any one of us how to become enlightened. So they melded blood sacrifice—changing the wine into the blood, which they called Transubstantiation—with higher consciousness (i.e., Christ "changing" into his light body), which they called Transfiguration.[10] By this ritual, the blood codes of Christ—and therefore, those of humanity—sucked the higher dimensions into the lower worlds.

This is a classic form of possession, in which a higher energetic is sucked into lower vibrations, and people seeking the higher frequency get possessed by lower energy.

The practice of Holy Communion over the past two thousand years may also have transmuted the lower world with Light. However, mixing blood sacrifice with Transfiguration cut most people off from both the light and the inner Earth.[11] Most of us are profoundly separated from 2D, yet now we must reconnect energetically. Cut off from this link, humans began exploiting the elemental world by mining 2D metallic elementals. These mines were initially small, even though the Roman Empire may have fallen due to pollution from the lead mines. When the amount of mining was small, Earth transmuted the displaced elementals by water, temperature, and seismic movements. But in the eighteenth century, the balance was tipped. Great male-dominant control forces instigated global mining. In the nineteenth century, oil was sucked out of Earth and burned on the surface; chemical and radioactive manipulation was the specialty of the twentieth century; and "mining" frequency waves is the agenda of the twenty-first. Whenever 2D powers are consumed in 3D, great elemental imbalances are incurred. However, such abuses can be corrected by scientific advances in transmutation as well as by people taking back their spiritual powers.

Reconnecting with the Second Dimension

Access to the higher dimensions is being rebuilt by many people. Group thoughtforms are transmuting disturbed elementals by love, which is a regular practice of indigenous people. Anyone can pray and do ceremony with 2D, which is very enlivening. At the time of the New Moon each month, the vertical axis transmits higher dimensions directly into Earth. During this potent transmission time, 2D metallic elementals respond vibrationally to stellar light. This light, as a potent multidimensional connector, vibrates in our blood and makes us very psychic. When we are psychic, we naturally resonate to dense telluric energy; we *know* our path. This is why I have often taught New Moon meditations and continue to analyze the qualities of the New Moon on our website.

The microbial elementals are constantly informing us about everything we need. When I feel uncomfortable or even sick, for example, I slow my frequencies down to the 2D level, and the right healer, substance, or exercise becomes apparent within hours. Scientifically, it is possible to transmute elementals that have been sucked into 3D and are polluting our bodies and the atmosphere. Once people understand the dimensional laws, there will be a massive economic boom based on transmutation technologies. Our New Moon clan in New Mexico often conducted meditations to transmute radiation, another elemental, around Los Alamos National Laboratory during the 1980s.

The reason we must understand our relationship with the lower realm is because 2D vibrates in our bodies whether we know it or not. When we resonate with lower-dimensional forces unconsciously, archetypal forces can take over our minds. We can be overwhelmed and controlled by others, which is why the Judeo-Christian system encourages fear instead of respect for the dark, yet *we need to know the dark.* When you can feel differences by density, you can use these forces as you wish. This ability can be taught, which is one of the main goals of Activations.

When I feel any nausea, dizziness, or unease, I slow my vibrations to see if any viruses or bacteria have made their way from 2D into my body, or if there is an emotion or thought I must clear. If I discover bugs, I think of myself as a hotel, and I'm willing to commune with the visitors. However, I insist they spend a short vacation with me, and they are not allowed to multiply or take over the ballroom. I do not "nuke" 2D life-forms with antibiotics. They can have a short vacation in my field, as long as I don't get an infection. Consequently, antibiotics would work very well if I ever needed them for an extremely serious infection, since I am not antibiotic resistant.

The Elite uses the Internet and the media to inject unrecognized dark forces into people to cull their energy into the latest scenario of fear; this weakens our minds. These technologies are metallic, and since we are not accustomed to these new frequency ranges that bombard us, we are open to forces we don't recognize.[12] If people can feel and identify vibrational frequencies, even these new potent metallic ones, fear is eliminated. We know this is possible because we have seen our students accomplish this. Our hearts need to be strong during the latter days of the Mayan calendar, since we are witnessing unspeakable atrocities. Becoming insensitive is not a solution, and true empathy cleanses collective pain. No one who respects 2D plays around with pornography or the media; both feed slavery and violence in the collective mind. These things

Figure 2.1 A great tree with 2D as the roots, 3D as the trunk, and 4D as the canopy that accesses 5D to 9D.

make human blood resonant with dark forces, which can possess the collective mind. The Elite uses the 4D collective mind to rule us in 3D, yet all you have to do is turn the dial to "Off".

The Ps insist we must now reject war in all ways, since spilled blood feeds these dominant powers. This is a deep pattern that is thousands of years old, is based on blood sacrifice, and now is manifesting in medical practices. We must avoid having our blood drawn and needled into other bodies except in dire emergencies. Notice that great amounts of blood were drawn for weeks *after* 9/11, even though there were no survivors that needed it! These practices are tools of the dominant ones that have little to do with your personal well-being; you do not have to volunteer for any of it. No one has to donate body parts, since transplants are a vile desecration of our physical inner worlds, and animal parts are not to be implanted in human bodies, since humans are not animals. These issues are very unpleasant and painful, yet the Ps say we must stop being so stupid because dimensions are being rent as our bodies are assaulted by medical practices that will someday be deemed barbaric.

A useful Pleiadian image for the structure of 2D through 4D is the tree (see figure 2.1). Regarding the tree, 2D is the roots, 3D the trunk, and 4D the branches into the sky. The tree is the plant realm's closest analog to a human. Trees cannot move around, and each thriving tree has discovered its own sacred site. In that place, the tree draws energy from the core and allows gravity to suck its roots down into 2D; here it seeks water and minerals to grow straight and strong in 3D, while its canopy radiates feelings to the Sun. As the tree is attracted to the light, the canopy of the tree spreads. All the divine forms and dimensions shiver with the tree's ecstasy, as it shoots powerful energy into Earth. This is how we humans should exist on the surface, yet we can move around. We can travel from sacred site to sacred site resonating with the elementals— which is how our ancestors lived in 3D—while resonating with the lower world. We can tap into the vertical axis anywhere we want.

The Science of the Second Dimension

I am comfortable with the idea that elements are alive, yet the Pleiadian description of 2D seemed very bizarre. Orthodox science at the time said that the inner Earth is mostly inorganic and changes by tectonic forces that build and wane. Certainly, science has never said that human blood resonates with the inner Earth, or that our inner bodies are like the inner Earth. Still, I was puzzled and impressed by the power and vitality of the Pleiadian description of the inner Earth—and also very wary. Adolf Hitler tried to take over the world and control human genetics based on his scientists' beliefs about the inner Earth. Many fanatics have gone off the deep end about the inner Earth, a world some call Agartha.[13] Fortunately there is at least one contemporary researcher who understands the uniquely creative powers of the first dimension.

In *The Deep Hot Biosphere* (1999), written by the brilliant twentieth-century scientist Thomas Gold, the entire crust down to several miles is found to be populated with living creatures which have been examined in deep ocean vents and rifts in active volcanoes. This world beneath the surface—Archea—is a fully functioning and robust biosphere that feeds on primordial hydrocarbons. Near the surface, photosynthesis developed offshoots of this subterranean life that progressed to the surface and evolved a way to use photons to supply chemical energy. Once the conditions for surface life—temperature, water, filters of solar radiation, and reduced cosmic bombardments—occurred, the surface life exploded. That is, Gold says that hydrocarbons are not biology awakened by geology, they are geology reworked by biology. That is, *surface life is the descendant of life deep within Earth.*

Where *The Deep Hot Biosphere* gets very "hot" indeed is with Gold's theory on the creation of oil, the "Deep-Earth Gas Theory." We were all taught that the oil fields were created when dinosaurs and vegetation fell into piles and rotted, which created reservoirs in the deep Earth. Either way, since 1860 oil has been considered a nonrenewable resource, which is simply a story that has been disproved by Thomas Gold. He is well known and respected for his Deep-Earth Gas Theory, since subsequent science is verifying it, and it is exactly the same as the Pleiadian description of 2D.

According to Gold, beginning with the creation of the solar system, the planets *accreted,* or formulated as solid bodies from the solids that had condensed from a gaseous planetary disk. During the early stages of Earth, as melting occurred, melts of higher density, such as iron—which is twice as dense as rock—sank toward the center, and materials of lesser density moved upward and formed the crust. The heat that generated this was from radioactivity in the disk, and gravitational compression sorted out the materials by density. This once-liquid Earth contained enzymes, which are catalysts for biochemical reactions. From these enzymes, a huge microbial biosphere, which eats petroleum and gives it the signature of life, exists at least *five miles down.* Down even deeper, there is a transition to zones that cannot harbor life. Oil wells do not drill down this far, hence all oil shows biological enhancement, which is where the rotting-dinosaur theory came from. Chemical analysis shows that expressions of life on the surface and the deep realm almost certainly have a common derivation, since both have the same genetic signature.

Regarding oil, hydrocarbons have existed deep in Earth since it accreted. They well up to the surface through holes and cracks, which allows microbial life to flourish, and they ooze into pools that are captured under domes created by ideal geological formations in the crust. Gold's Deep-Earth Gas Theory has been totally substantiated by testing the oil fields, which are filling up as they are drilled. *Oil is a renewable resource.* It would seem that the Americans intuit this, judging by the cars they drive and the houses they live in. It would also seem that the best domes that pool the oil are the most valuable; possibly the dome under Iraq is an especially good one? The public needs the correct theories on energy resources, since what we're being told is grossly outdated, while the Elite makes plans and money for itself.

The inner Earth is a rich and live realm loaded with energy and consciousness, which offers new horizons in healing and awakening for humanity. Gold's *Deep Hot Biosphere* supports most of the Pleiadian description of 1D and 2D—and contradicts none of it. This affirmation of Pleiadian science by one of the top twentieth-century scientists makes me take the Pleiadian view of the higher dimensions much more seriously. There are many scientific theories about the subtle worlds yet to be discussed in this book; however, nowhere has science better verified channeled material than in Thomas Gold's brilliant and totally scientific description of the second dimension.

THREE

The Third Dimension:
Linear Space and Time

Opening Meditation

You are free and floating on your back on a warm body of water. There is water under you, air above you, and you are relaxed, safe, content, as you float perfectly on this body of water. Your head is relaxed, heavy, supported. Your thoughts are slow, and all you have to do is to notice things, observe things going on inside your head. See what you can see going on in there and in the rest of your body. Take your time.

Did you know that you have four brains inside your head? First, let's find your reptilian brain. It is down low, at the base of your cranium, deep inside, protected, and ancient. Your reptilian brain knows, it is instinctual. It listens to your body, perched right there close to your spine and neck and to the rest of your body. Your blood supply goes right through it. This brain is wise and gives you insights, as long as you listen to it. It knows touch, hot and cold, and wet and dry. It knows what is good for it and what is not good for it.

Next, find your mammalian brain. It sits above, and wraps around the edges of, your reptilian brain. It knows when you need to fear, and when not to, when to run, and when not to. It uses the powers of sight and scent to find food and safety; it uses the powers of discernment to decide what action to take next. It warms when it has companionship with others.

Now, let's find your human brain. It's right there through the middle of your head, front to back, wrapped over your mammalian brain like a sheathing, like an insulation, like a second growth, a second thought, opening a new possibility. It came about through thousands of years of discernment, and wanting to remember those discernments. It wants to store bits of information as food for thought, like a squirrel saving acorns in the ground. Notice thoughts; this brain has many of those. Brilliant bits of energy bursts, shooting through these circuits at close to light speed: thoughts.

Finally, let's find your neocortex brain. It is the extra stuff in front, behind your forehead; you feel it like an energy burst there. It pulses when you have an especially brilliant insight or vision: It loves ideas, and ideals—the things you want to create, to see happen in your life or in the lives of those you know. Sometimes those ideals become real, and our neocortex warms our foreheads, causing our whole face to relax and a smile to form on our lips. See if one is ready to form on yours.

Now come back to floating on the surface of the water. Feel the Sun rise in the sky and warm your head. Feel the four brains inside your head, and enjoy the feeling of new understandings. Return your focus, so you can begin to read once again.

The third dimension (3D) is the dimension of linear space and time that we humans live in with other biological creatures and plants. We humans are the Keepers of 3D, and the Pleiadians say there is much more going on in this world than most people realize. I've noticed that the Pleiadian description of 3D is the same as my childhood understanding of 3D, which comes from my Cherokee and Celtic grandparents, and which was confirmed by my adult study with various indigenous elders.

From this perspective, many worlds operate in 3D. In the dimensional scheme, 3D is the zone where the physical and nonphysical dimensions intersect. The physical realms—1D through 3D—are measurable, and all the nonphysical realms—4D through 9D—operate as subtle frequencies in 3D. These nonphysical realms are experienced; for example, having archetypal thought patterns is a way of being in 4D, or seeing geometric visions in 6D. As the Ps see it, our bodies are held in form by frequencies that vibrate physical matter; we are oscillating, vibrating beings of light. According to quantum physics, our bodies are much more filled with space than matter, and we are slowly comprehending this new definition of ourselves.

When our consciousness vibrates in 4D, such frequency ranges are not solid, yet they feel very real. For many people, experiencing 4D feelings is more intense than feeling their own bodies. The potent emotional energy of a really angry person often seems greater than the energy in this person's physical body. Thus we become very aware of 4D frequencies in 3D, especially in our childhood homes. When we mature, many of us realize that we are living out a complex story, a great drama that is much orchestrated by our feelings. The Ps and most indigenous teachers say in 3D we are mostly asleep, while we use most of our energy trying to avoid feelings. Meanwhile, feelings are our access to enlightenment!

This is why indigenous teachers and the Ps like to awaken us from our sleep and encourage us to get used to intense emotions. They say that if we learn to orient ourselves by feelings in 3D, we will be able to explore 4D with confidence. We are more aware when we know our personal stories; these stories entice us to feel the full range of our emotions, and then the frequencies of the higher-dimensional realms can be detected. Each one of us is a magical being journeying in the field of an immense, cosmic oriental carpet—the third dimension where the physical and non-physical intersect. This is what 3D looks like from the higher dimensions. Our ability to be fully present during our journeys is the key to navigating time.

What is time? Time in 3D, by the frequency-based view, is simply a locater for past, present, and future. Time is not real, yet we accomplish things by it in 3D. When we use time intentionally, instead of just floating along day by day like a piece of driftwood, we realize that the past is a data bank that is useful in the present moment, or the "now." The now is the unique moment in which we can craft our future according to what we already know—the past. Knowing a lot about the past helps, which is why we need our own stories about our journeys in time. The Ps say boredom or fascination are the best guides: We are advised to stop doing anything that bores us and to spend all our time creating things that fascinate us.

Then, since 3D is linear space and time, what is space? Space surrounding us is comprised of energy fields permeated by all the other dimensions. We can detect and interact with these dimensions when we are located correctly in our bodies, or are "grounded." To be grounded, we must open ourselves to the full range of feelings. If you watch people carefully, often they are not clearly located in the present moment, yet you can detect various feeling patterns. For example, in a discussion you may be interacting with a four-year-old child in the body of a forty-five-year-old person; the four-year-old plays out various rages, needs, and demands that were appropriate many years ago. The adult person is immobilized by 4D feelings that rule his or her body; often for this person, 3D feels like a net drawing ever tighter as time passes along. The truth is, he or she is navigating in 4D and not living 3D, and this gets worse with age. If you watch closely, this person is not physically "home" because 4D frequencies outside the current place and time are overamping 3D. Let's explore how this works, since this is the reason most people use so much of their energy to block their feelings.

When you incarnated, you were born in a direct line from the center of Earth, your own multidimensional vertical axis. In the beginning, as you grew your body was like a spiral shell that moved outward, making more curved layers. This maturation of our bodies by morphogenesis—the overall pattern that guides growth—is a miracle that is actually orchestrated by 6D.[1] Why then does so much go awry? If it were not for experiencing feelings, you would end up expressing this 6D perfect form. Since you live in 3D, your feelings hone your body according to how you register your experiences in time. Each one of us is a vibrating, oscillating record of our whole life, including our sense of our ancestors and previous lifetimes, which good psychics can see and read. Feelings connect all beings in 3D, thus by participating in this collective, each one of us is caught in time.

When feelings are unresolved, they lock you in your body in various stages of your life; you stop flowing naturally in the now. For example, people say, "Oh, my achin' back," and if you watch them, they are isolated in their pain. After many years, these emotional blocks disorganize your physical form, and eventually your mind, unless you learn to work on your feelings when your back aches. Eventually, people calcify and end up looking like old crabs or loping wolves. The Ps and healers have evolved many methods to help you move through these blocks and back into the now. Remember, the now is the place where you are informed by the past as you create your future.

The Seven Sacred Directions and Making an Altar

To be in the now, it helps to think of yourself as a point in 3D—a perceptual locater—and become conscious of the seven directions moving out from your body. Even though your emotional connections are the essence of your life and weave you into the fabric of life, to handle the 4D realm, your orientation in 3D should be by the seven directions at all times. Begin with the four directions in a circle: East/West, South/North. Feel yourself as the center in that four-directional matrix. At any moment, your front, backside, and two sides are facing one of the four directions. A traditional way to pray in your altar is to face the East with the West at your back, and North to your left and South to your right. Once you get accustomed to feeling yourself this way, activate the sides of your body to each direction. Your awareness of the rising and setting Sun—the source of your vitality and energy—will increase; and your sensitivity to how the poles and the equator relate you to Earth's journey may awaken. Most important, knowing your orientation anywhere and anytime on Earth enables you to feel the spirits of each direction.

Energies coming to you from the East are spirits who come to offer you creative guidance for the day; energies coming to you from the West are spirits who come to show you what you need to transform and possibly throw away; energies coming to you from the North will inspire you to seek the most challenging outcome of the day; and energies coming to you from the South are spirits who want to support and nurture you. The fifth direction is straight down into Earth, which feeds you with unlimited powers and strength, and the sixth direction is the vertical axis into the sky to all the higher worlds, the gateway to the libraries in higher dimensions. The seventh direction is your heart, your center. When you orient your body in the first six directions as instructed, interact with all the energies coming to you, and locate yourself in your heart, you can feel yourself as a vibrating, oscillating body. An artist who sees and paints the human structure this way is Alex Grey, the author of *Sacred Mirrors*.

Like any intentional practice, this orientation to the seven sacred directions entrains your body and transforms you. Located in the seven directions as a heart-centered person, you are able to attract to your field what you really want. When your heart and mind are informed by the six sacred directions, and your heart resonates with the totality of your energy field, you are fully expanded. Once you experience correct orientation, you will never go back to being contracted, unless you are traumatized emotionally and knocked out of your center. Even then, you can reorient yourself when you are ready. As with any new practice in life, it is best to learn it in a reserved space away from the hustle and bustle of 3D. You should all have an altar space in your house that is oriented to the four directions. There you can sit facing the rising Sun and meditate, receiving knowledge from East/West, South/North. Then you will easily move your consciousness down into Earth and up into the sky and exist in your heart.

This space in your house can be very small, or it can be a room with altars at each of the four directions. The houses of indigenous people were oriented to the seven sacred directions, and people were born into this. Altars are repositories of special objects that help you to feel and commune with the energy of each direction: spiritual guides in the East, chaos forces in the West, nurturing spirits in the South, and great record guides in the North. Special objects on your altar also help you to remember your story and the stories of your ancestors. If you create this space and work with it, at least three things will happen in your life. Very soon, you will notice that your heart melts and opens just by you sitting in your center because the structure of your altar activates you right away; things you struggle with will seem easier when you center in your heart. Next, you will notice that you are orienting yourself by the directions when you are out in the world; you'll become more aware where the Sun rises and sets, for example. And once you've meditated a lot in your center and sense your directionality in the world, you will notice that interference by other people in your energy field is alleviated. When you are in your heart center, you are sovereign.

Various people and forces drawn to manipulate you, to take your power away, or to harm you cannot affect you while you are in your center. For example, Homeland Security cannot reach into your heart, even if it imprisons our culture. If you *are* in prison reading this, create altars in your jail cell to access freedom. Once you are oriented this way in the world, invasive influences bounce off you like water. The Ps say we all will need these skills in the coming days.

Maintaining Physical Integrity in 3D: The Science of the Third Dimension

The science of the third dimension is Newtonian physics, which I will not cover in this chapter since the laws of physical causality are commonly known. Instead, I will focus on the *indigenous* laws of physical integrity, the awareness of which is rarely included in modern life. Being fully expanded in 3D is difficult, since usually our bodies have gotten bent out of shape by physical, emotional, and mental stress. Imbalances and blocks can be healed by working with our feelings and minds, as well as our bodies. Here we are interested in what happens in the solid world: in 3D.

Imbalances in our bodies, such as incorrect posture or physical problems, are the result of the physical, emotional, mental, and spiritual blocks caused by life. You can unlock them at any level; however, our bodies are the most direct access. The great thing about working with our bodies is that pain, reduced flexibility, and illness do not go away until we address what we are feeling. All forms of bodywork can move you directly into a problem, and your body will reveal solutions. Of course, you have to do the work, which is why most people just go to the doctor to get fixed. Our times are bizarre because many people are realizing the doctor doesn't fix them. If you hold with the pain and listen to its message, problems often correct with frequent internal cleansing, good diet, and regular exercise.

Allopathic medicine should only be used for surgery or diagnosis, which are sometimes needed. The Ps are very wary of drugs, since they bypass the messages your body is offering you and lock the problem deep in your body. The bad feeling goes away because the ailment draws back into deeper levels. Eventually, you become sick, since the underlying cause has not been discovered. Physical ailments are signals of energy imbalances, which can be healed with bodywork, emotional processing, mental reorientation, and spiritual contact. If a condition is hereditary, you have chosen to work on something your parent or grandparents didn't learn from. If you are caught in a family emotional conflict that you haven't identified and processed, and it remains locked in your body, eventually you will assume hereditary conditions.

Working with your health is basic maintenance, and it is fun to notice how your physical body reveals your feelings and thoughts; your body is a miraculous temple of spirit. When you expand the field of your body, you will learn how to move better in 3D, to navigate well in space and time. Many people lose this natural flow and synchronicity when the blocks add up. Practices like yoga, dance, tai chi, meditation, mindful walking, and playing music are essential because they enable you to expand your body into your 6D morphogenetic form, which is your ideal incarnational pattern. When you move in 3D, your body is supposed to operate in perfect symmetry with 6D. You incarnated and grew by this special patterning, just like an oak seed grows into a great oak tree. If you maintain this form, you will not often have backaches, arthritis, knee problems, and poor posture. You must have a practice that allows all the parts of your body to resonate with your 6D morphic field!

For example, if your knees or hips are creaky, painful, and not bending well, and you take drugs instead of getting your flexibility back by moving these parts correctly, you are already dying in that part of your body. If you put plastic parts in your body, you are plastic in that zone. Of course, some people need to use such parts for a while, yet this should always be the last resort. Cats are the best teachers about moving in symmetry with 6D geometry. They exhibit ideal form, which is why they were always revered by sacred cultures, such as the Maya and the Egyptians. Notice how your cat lies around all stretched out and then gets up and walks around stretching and pulling its limbs. Just as you need to slow down to feel the resonation of your organs and blood to maintain your body, so must you also stretch and move your whole body to keep it linked up with your 6D incarnational form.

If you live this way in 3D, you will feel fantastic, and then it will be possible for you to identify blocks whether they are emotional, mental, or physical. The release of physical blocks opens emotional blocks, while your mind apprehends how your body is working with your thoughts. This is complex, and it just so happens that the cycles of the Moon can greatly assist your growth.

Living on Lunar Time

The fastest way to deal with blocks in 3D is to handle them right in our bodies. Our ally is the Moon, which is part of 3D because we can watch it wax and wane and observe its effects in the world, such as water level changes caused by the tides. All biological species respond profoundly to the lunar cycles month after month, since living things are mostly water. Once the clock was invented a few hundred years ago, humans began dividing time up into hours, minutes, seconds, and moments. Meanwhile, animals, plants, and spirits live by natural cycles. The more humans divide time, the greater the materialization in 3D and the separation from other living things.

You may have noticed that your reality is getting too filled up with stuff and that there is less and less room for you. This is because when you divide time, space expands, and eventually your reality will be uninhabitable. Meanwhile, the Moon is your best timekeeper. If you will realign with the Moon, you can waltz right out of the dilemmas invented by the holy clock. The Ps say that the division of reality by the clock is moving toward infinity as of December 21, 2012. The only people who will know they live on Earth will be those living by lunar time.[2]

The biological realm waxes and wanes by the Moon, and when you live by the lunar cycles, time is balanced with space. At the New Moon every month, a new story is implanted that is to be played out for the month. For example, take notice of the weather on the day of the New Moon. Whatever the weather is—hot/cold, rainy/sunny—will persist through the Full Moon and beyond.[3] Even if you don't know astrology, anyone can feel the qualities of the current story just by tuning in at the New Moon. Once you feel the elements, play your role consciously in them as the collective field expands and expands up to the Full Moon. Then the Full Moon expresses the energy with a great explosion, like the culminating moment in a Beethoven symphony. Subtly after the Full Moon, the lunar vibes help us to play with the threads of the story as they weave along.

In each year, there are also eclipses, when the Moon blocks the Sun or Earth blocks the Moon. Eclipses attune us to the larger cycle of the Moon, the Metonic Cycle, which is the cycle that relates the Moon to the Sun.[4] This cycle, which is more than eighteen years long, directs a much longer path in life, and informs us when to seek knowledge in the outside world or from deep inside the inner realm. The Moon shows us when to shine and produce, or when to swim in darkness and regenerate. None of these cycles require astrology, although it is most helpful. The lunar light guides us very well if we learn to live by its guidance and drop the clock, except for appointments we need to keep. We are not here to divide reality; we are here to integrate reality by weaving the intersections of the dimensions.

The Six Polarities on the Wheel of Twelve

Our dimension (3D) manifests many worlds in physical forms. Yet, while we live in our world, often we are torn apart by dualities. Because so many worlds manifest here by passing through the emotionally polarized fields of 4D, we perceive issues as either/or, black or white, good or evil. When considering a dilemma, one side or the other is just a range of possibility. Since dimensionality is so subtle and rich, this great polarity system exists to connect and widen our feelings sufficiently. Then the higher dimensions open more, and we can feel ourselves being impulsed by advanced beings. Like the holy clock, we can divide everything by defining our belief as this or that. Yet then we've lost the whole range in our consciousness because we've stuck ourselves in one collective mind-set.

The Ps say this is limited imagination, which didn't matter so much in the past. Now that the end of the Mayan calendar approaches, duality is splitting our world. The Ps offer a tool that I've found helps most people to expand beyond duality—the circle divided into twelve parts that functions as six living polarities in our lives.[5] This wheel enables us to pull ourselves right out of the archetypal 4D field to get a wider view and ground ourselves firmly in 3D. This wheel teaches us to balance our consciousness by observing polarities with wisdom (figure 3.1).

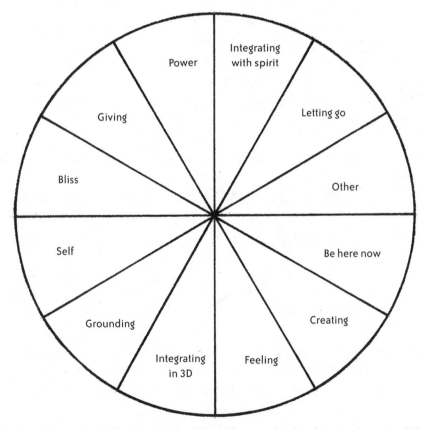

Figure 3.1 The Wheel of Twelve. Adapted from *The Liquid Light of Sex*, Barbara Hand Clow, pp. 41–50.

Intentionally using the six polarities—self/other, grounding/letting go, integrating in 3D/integrating with spirit, feeling/power, creating/giving, be here now/bliss—is the ideal way to manage the 4D feeling range. When we use polarities to navigate 3D, we can handle our connections with archetypal dramas, such as the battle between Christianity and Islam. Rather than be pulled back and forth by dead-end archetypes—the West is Good/Islam is Evil, or the reverse—we can process and balance our personal beliefs and not be sucked into dualities. Individuals who balance polarities and unitize dualities are "grounders" in 3D, since dualities are false and dangerous divisions in the collective that can infect 3D. Here is how any one of us can function as a grounder and balancer of our dimension by means of the six polarities:

1. When we balance self/other, we have a clear sense of self while we are in harmony with others. We cannot destroy the lives of others just because we want something for ourselves.

2. When we balance grounding/letting go, we have what we need for life in 3D, and we let go of anything we don't need. We stop consuming the world because we don't need so many things.

3. When we balance personal integration with spiritual integration, we are effectively in contact with those connected with us, while we are free to tune into spirit realms. We stop disappearing from reality when we get in touch with spirit, and when we are communing with spirit, we are still connected in 3D.

4. When we balance feeling/power, we are very sensitive to others when we use power. We cannot lord power over others because we can feel how they feel about life.

5. When we balance creating/giving, we create what we came to create, and we find ways to circulate our gifts. We cannot avoid expressing ourselves because we are continually impulsed to share this joy.

6. When we balance be here now/bliss, we are in the now while flowing in bliss. We stay in a high state of consciousness by staying in our center.

This simple paradigm offers self-mastery. When we live this way day after day, we are grounded in 3D. We can feel and enjoy the 4D forces as they participate in our minds, and it is fun to observe the great archetypal story. It is a weaving made of all our thoughts and feelings that connects us with everyone else. This is living every day comprehending the collective flow of meaning in the world, flowing in the great story of time.

F O U R

The Fourth Dimension:
The World of Myths and Archetypes

Opening Meditation

Ask yourself: Do you know feelings that come from inside yourself, and feelings that come from outside yourself? Do you know feelings you have created, for yourself, and feelings others created, for themselves? We all have many feelings. All I am asking is: Can you sort them out a bit, instead of feeling them as one big ball of feelings? Can you follow the threads back to their source?

Pick a big feeling. *Any* big feeling. Whatever comes to you at this time. It could be just a feeling, or a feeling with an image attached. Go ahead. See what comes to you. A good way to do this is lying on your bed, or the floor, or out on the ground where no one will bother you. Put your hands behind your head; cradle it. Good.

Now catch that feeling. No matter what it is, catch it. See what it is. Okay, now take that feeling, and any image attached to it, and make it bigger. See it from all sides. See and feel what it does inside your body, especially to your solar plexus. Your solar plexus is like the face of a drum; it sounds when you strike it with a drumstick. Boom, boom . . . boom, boom.

Do you have a big feeling? Are you feeling it at your drum belly, your solar plexus? Are you seeing any images, or feeling any other feelings attached to this feeling? If so, follow them, make them bigger too. It is like a big knot, that you can only untie when you make it bigger, just like a knot in your shoelace. Take your time. Feel space opening in the knot as you untie it. Breathe, remember your body, your own energy, and this is only an exercise, an entertainment, a learning experience.

Are you beginning to *see* this giant feeling? To really *feel* this giant feeling? Can you find where it is coming from, where it started? Can you see how you can change it by knowing where it began? How it will go away once you understand how it got there? Sometimes this is hard, and sometimes this is not too hard. Take whatever time you need. If you think this is more than you can handle right now, stop, and find your breath, find your body. Find your way back to gravity, to your feet.

If you want to continue, continue, and let the learning begin. Once you know where the feeling is coming from, see how you can change the feeling, how you can make it go away by understanding why it got there in the first place. Maybe there is some action you need to take, and it will take away this feeling. Maybe it is someone you need to speak to, to tell them how bad they made you feel. Or maybe it is someone you need to say you're sorry to, to ask their forgiveness. That's okay, too. All that matters is that the feeling go away and stop pounding on the drum at your belly. Write something down, if you like, or take a sip of water.

Once the feeling passes, the pounding stops at your belly, you know you have succeeded. Smile to yourself, and know you can do this again anytime one of those feelings gets going in your body. The more you do this, the quicker, more efficient you'll be at getting to the source of what's bothering you. Notice how nice you feel, how relaxed, how safe you feel. Good work! And once you have read about the fourth dimension, you may want to return to this meditation again.

The fourth dimension (4D) is the realm of the human collective mind, the amalgam of individual thoughts and feelings that meld and weave into archetypal patterns. This dimension holds the memory of the experiences of all people throughout time. According to the Ps, the Keepers of 4D are the Annunaki, inhabitants of a planet called Nibiru. In ancient Sumerian records, Nibiru seems to be a planet with an extremely elliptical orbit; it comes into our solar system every 3,600 years and is outside the solar system for most of its orbital path. The Sumerians believed that whenever Nibiru travels into the solar system, its inhabitants could visit Earth. The Sumerian records describe the Annunaki as gods who came to Earth around 3600 B.C.[1] The activities of the Annunaki are very much like the antics of the Greek gods, since they both intervene in human affairs. Regarding solar system dynamics, if this planet is real, one

Nibiru year is 3,600 Earth years, just as one Jupiter year is twelve Earth years. This is because Nibiru's solar orbit is 3,600 years, Jupiter's is twelve years, and Earth's is one year.

After many years of thought about the cycles in the solar system, I think the reason the Ps say the Annunaki are the Keepers of 4D is because Nibiru has such a long solar cycle. Imagine how easy it would be to remember all the myths and stories over thousands of years if 3,600 years was equivalent to one Earth year; the Nibiruan time sense would be immense. They would know a lot more about Earth's history than most humans do. Omniscient humans—such as certain saints, gurus, and clairvoyants—can read 4D, which holds the records of all human experiences in the collective mind. Respecting the Pleiadian view, I've come to the conclusion the Annunaki are the central controllers of the Global Elite, and they (the Annunaki) invented their 4D program around 5,600 years ago, whether they came from another planet or not. Their New World Order (NWO) and its plots are the main subject matter of this chapter.

From our perspective on Earth, the fourth dimension is the first non-physical (yet detectable) dimension, which makes it very confusing for most of us. This dimension seems to be a world filled with great gods and goddesses involved in grandiose dramas, yet few people are conscious of this except when they are dreaming. In fact, these great beings—such as Zeus and Yahweh—are probably creations of somebody's clever mind; these archetypes easily fool humanity. Certainly, these archetypal gods aren't around here very often. They may have never been here in our dimension, yet once they got invented, people couldn't seem to forget them.

According to the Ps, the 4D gods and goddesses want to be deeply involved in the actions of our bodies, which makes many people feel like they are puppets dancing on heavenly strings. Like lost children hoping to avoid facing life and death, we humans seek answers from immortal parents who may not even be real! It is neediness that keeps these gods alive, which creates some very negative patterns on Earth, such as war. People who have figured out how 4D archetypes influence 3D are not ruled by these gods; therefore, we spend a lot of time with our students decoding the great gods during the Activations. I think the Greeks "unmasked" the gods, since they made such mockery of them, especially during their mystery plays. We humans, not the gods, are the sovereign creators of 3D!

The Astral World and Divine Levels in the Fourth Dimension

The fourth dimension is a live and participatory zone—*the astral world between 3D and the stars*—which is filled with messages from divine beings. This zone receives all the messages coming from the higher dimensions, which is why we *feel* so much in 4D. We can more easily receive these messages directly in our hearts and minds once we have decoded the potent collective force of the Annunaki belief systems that pollute human cultures. Recognizing that 4D can be possessed by fanatics, the ancient Egyptians developed a very imaginative animal totemic theology that shows how the gods interact with humanity. Since 4D strongly activates our feelings in 3D, it splits higher-dimensional information, and in 3D, each issue is seen as positive or negative. It is really easy to see this dynamic when you realize 4D as just a big creative game that connects us all.

The source of human creativity is within messages from higher dimensions. As the messages come in, the 4D intelligence forms split the inspiration to intensify our 3D feeling range, so that we can encompass the magnitude. Most humans ignore these juicy impulses, since acting them out might change their lives. Those individuals who *do* strive to see, hear, and feel these messages often become powerful creators, including becoming members of the Elite. This is *seizing the moment,* and all great artists are adept at bringing these ideas into form. Poets, painters, sculptors, and politicians live and breathe grandiose archetypes; they use them to fertilize 3D like good gardeners.

As for the archetypal beings, we humans are the gods and goddesses of 3D, since we can create solid things. Fourth-dimensional beings can think and plot all they want, but they cannot create anything in 3D. So they seed their hot desires in our minds and incite us to create realities. For example, a hapless and confused teenager plays out the killing tendencies that pollute the adult collective, as with the Columbine massacre. It is no wonder that most people try to ignore these juicy impulses.

If a person's emotions aren't under control, 4D energy takes on a low astral hue, and the person might be visited by angels, succubi, monsters,

ETs, or composite creatures. These visitors seem real on the screens of our magnetic minds, all filled up with ancient archetypal images. Some people are triggered and driven mad by such visions in 3D, and others are fascinated. Spiritual masters and many artists learn to distinguish between low astral impulses and true divine inspiration. I believe *we must all become spiritual masters now,* so we can remember how to create what *we* want in our dimension. Otherwise, the New World Order is going to run it, ruin it—or both!

When contacts from subtle worlds arrive in 3D, overpowering emotions run through our bodies. We can respond by simply following our feelings, yet I am suggesting we also use our minds to observe these feelings. *This is the path beyond insanity.* By their very nature, archetypal forces seek vehicles in 3D for their inspirations, and this process is increasing exponentially during the closing days of the Mayan calendar. If they are thwarted by us, these forces get frustrated, overamped, and violent. Thwarted creativity collects in 4D when it is not circulated between 3D and the higher worlds, and eventually cultures get overloaded by black forces, just like overamped electrical circuits that trip fuses. Astral forces are especially attracted to people who are drugged. The percentage of people who are drugged (legally and illegally) is very high in the United States, making it easy for the Elite to control people. Yet, *we humans are the chosen circulators of divine inspiration.*

If you are bored with your life, you are not tuned in to your fullest potential. Wonderful things result from working intentionally with divine forces that birth art, visions, and sacred cultures. The New World Order conspires to dull and stupify humanity to keep it shut down. Modern culture (especially American) is boring, uncreative, and hideously violent because it is polluted with discharging dark energy. We can choose what we want to create in 3D, since we have free will. By not blocking the flow of the rich archetypal stream, sacred cultures are imbued with art, theater, and music.

Some cultures, such as the Australian aborigines, channel the stream by dreaming; others, such as the Minoans with their bull dances and labyrinths, expressed it in mystery plays. These potent forces flow easily through indigenous children who are raised to be very creative. Their elders know that blocking these forces makes the forces bigger, or *inflated.* They become an independent force that weakens the group. Eventually, the force overwhelms people, and waves of collective insanities and sicknesses arise, such as making war. Medicine practices can be used for curing; however, true indigenous people create most of the time because *creating is more fun than curing.*

Ecstatic sacred cultures, such as the ancient Egyptians, the Maya, Minoans, and Celts, spring forth when masses of people just respond to the need for change in the collective mind. Conversely, when enough people suppress the 4D forces within themselves, then very dark, violent, and destructive cultures manifest. At this time, Earth's people are screaming for an end to global domination and violence. Yet screaming for peace doesn't work; it is time to circulate the archetypal stream. The Ps say the big problem is "god poison." Too many people on Earth are waiting for the gods to return. *We are not caring for our own dimension.*

The Fourth-Dimensional Canopy of Light

The fourth dimension looks like a murky canopy over individuals, cities, cultures, and countries. This is astral energy that resembles gooey frogs' eggs; healers can often see it with their clients, and America looks like it is floating in a polluted lake of it these days. These canopies are constantly bombarded by waves of energy and light from the higher five dimensions (see figure 4.1). When higher-dimensional energy rushes into the curved 4D canopy, it acts as a lens that splits thought into two possibilities—positive or negative, good or evil, black or white, right or wrong, and so on, in the consciousness of the person on the table. When people express only one side or the other of an issue, their minds split, making them *unconscious.* The 4D-splitting dynamic exists so that electromagnetic (EM) fields can form in 3D, where 2D magnetism arrives in the curved crust and responds to 4D electricity in the atmosphere. Without this dynamic, things would not solidify into vibrating EM fields in 3D, and this EM dynamic affects our consciousness, since most people can feel this astral force.

Our embodiment comes out of pure energy. When we have learned to allow archetypal forces to flow through us, our bodies easily resolve wide polarity states, and our EM fields, as well as our minds, expand. This is the law of expansion and contraction. We can all differentiate between astral influences and higher-dimensional inspiration, and therefore we are able to see both sides of issues, which enables us to perceive the full range of

Figure 4.1 The 4D murky canopy bombarded by waves of energy from higher dimensions.

information. Astral influences are nothing more than the desires of other humans to invade our minds, which cannot happen to people who have figured out the game.

The issues that present themselves in our minds are collective. We may or may not realize that millions of other people are processing the same thoughts. For example, these days millions are exploring a polarity I call "Judeo-Christianity versus Islam." Some split this archetype into good or evil, safe or dangerous, while others seek to understand both sides to become *conscious*. As the drama unfolds, more and more people tend to become conscious. Yet sometimes the dualistic forces are so strong that a collective insanity—a maelstrom—develops. This is happening with Judeo-Christianity versus Islam, especially now that we are at the end of the Age of Pisces and the Mayan calendar. The ending of long cycles always dredges up unresolved layers of time, which each one of us can process when we are in a polarized (not dualized) state.

The Global Elite uses powerful 4D forces, such as Yahweh, to further its agenda—the New World Order. The Romans and the Vatican materialized these forces through the Age of Pisces during the last two thousand years, building a 4D collective belief in one god—Yahweh.[2] Now the Elite is working to take over 3D for the next two thousand years during the Age of Aquarius. The Ps say it is easier to allow potent 4D forces to flow through ourselves and avoid being dualized during the changing of the ages, while we also open ourselves to higher-dimensional inspiration.

If we humans block the archetypal stream, 3D shreds into manifold dualities, as if a dragon were thrashing the canopy of light. Our EM fields contract, and we lose our ability to trust the divine. By being lazy, stupid, and intoxicated, we are harlots for the Elite. If we give our power away, a great rending of reality can occur—the third dimension devolves into a maelstrom or the whirlwind, which was a geological disaster 11,500 years ago. This time, a religious whirlwind is building, like a tornado made of flaming angels. Great opportunities that were not taken up two thousand years ago, such as Christ's and Muhammad's real teachings, could be resurrected now. Judeo-Christianity versus Islam is the big epic movie that premiered at the end of the Mayan calendar and the Age of Pisces, and it is boring.

Meanwhile, hidden within the secret caves of the world religions are the seed elements of the sacred cultures that created them in the first place. When the people first detected these sacred cultures, the higher dimensions flowed through the Canopy of Light and the divine illuminated Earth.[3] When the God Program began to take over Earth, the Elite began enticing people to kill one another. As long as the people are split into opposing camps, the New World Order can froth up global conflict between the world religions. For those readers who are on one side or the other, remember the Elite does not care who gets killed, only that it wins. To comprehend how humanity might have gotten into such a mess, let's see what science has to say about 4D. Science mirrors and directs cultures, as we especially saw during the twentieth century.

The Science of the Fourth Dimension

Quantum mechanics (QM, or the New Physics) is the science of 4D on the vertical axis.[4] QM studies the properties of light, the microscopic world of atoms and molecules. The discrete energy units—quanta—function as either particles or waves, and mechanics is the study of their movement. QM discovered that light functions as either particles (photons) or waves (frequencies), which fundamentally dualize matter. Since our thoughts are received through 4D, the reception of frequencies in our 3D brains is split by the very nature of the subquantum reality. I am suggesting that particle/wave duality is the inherent cause of dualistic thought patterns in our minds; it is an electromagnetic phenomenon.

A total revolution in physics has occurred since 1900 that is reflected by what's in our minds and what's going on in the world. Yet most people have no idea about this. Our 3D world is adrift in all the things the New Physics has invented—televisions, computers, microwave ovens—yet most people don't understand how these things work. Our consciousness is somewhat hijacked by QM technology, since most people don't think about what it's doing. Meanwhile, these nascent technological aspects of reality will be the main evolutionary theme for the coming *two thousand years*. Astrologically, the Age of Aquarius, which we have just entered, is ruled by the planet Uranus, which rules EM frequencies.[5]

Being able to imagine that material things are actually visible light can rip open your mind. The Global Elite wants to retard public understanding of such vibrational frequencies as long as possible. We are supposed to be obedient consumers who buy cellphones without thinking about what they're doing to our brains, or watch TV so the Elite can run its political programs. Many of us find it hard to comprehend how the other forms of EM radiation, such as radio waves, microwaves, and infrared radiation, are the same as light in the visible light spectrum (VLS); and physics is often poorly described in our schools (see figure 1.2). Once we realize that all matter is made of particles and frequency waves, we will realize that our brains are wired to detect many frequencies. Since a chair is solid in the VLS, and you will bruise your knee if you run into it, then what do the radiation waves of cellphones do to your head? What do microwaves do to food? Comprehending frequencies could be the ultimate freedom, or these new technologies could capture us in the darkest prison—a world in which nature is totally manipulated. The facts are, physicists live in strange universes, creating ever-stranger things, while we don't understand how the things they are inventing actually work.

The QM revolution is the cause of the mind-boggling speed of change in the world and in our minds during the last hundred years. The Elite is going to stay in charge unless we figure out what we want to create in its place. The world according to Newton—3D science—was predictable and understandable. We were able to visualize its laws and be confident where things are, whether they will go this way or that way, and how long it will take. In the Newtonian period, the individual could seemingly master reality without much effort. With QM, light can be either particles or waves (which you can't see), and the individual can only predict what light will do by probabilities. Probabilities are simply tendencies for things to happen, which is easier to understand since life is actually like that; 4D is a big probability range, the collective mind.

The impact of the QM revolution is awesome because QM has been used for making the most successful numerical predictions in the history of science. The world according to Newton causes us to think of nature as a machine, when in fact nature functions by probabilities. On a given day, this or that might happen, and we can see this by watching events. QM explains much about the enigmas in nature and ourselves. It is an incredibly exciting field of study that opens our minds way beyond the mechanical universe. We need a quick refresher of modern physics, just to be sure we know what we're talking about here.[6]

QM is based on the four key forces in the universe as now defined by physics: electromagnetism, the strong and weak nuclear forces, and gravity. The EM force binds electrons and nuclei; the strong nuclear force binds quarks, which make protons and neutrons; the weak nuclear force causes nuclear decay; and gravity is the weakest force, yet its influence is effective at greater distances than the other three. The quanta (or particles) of electromagnetism are photons—particles of light—that have infinite range and no mass. Light as frequency waves functions over the entire EM spectrum of radio waves, microwaves, infrared light, light, ultraviolet light, X-ray, and gamma rays (see figure 1.2).

Gluons—quanta of the strong nuclear force—keep quarks "glued" together inside protons and neutrons. Leptons and hadrons are the quanta of the weak nuclear force, which causes radioactive decay and nuclear reactions in stars, such as supernovas. The quanta of gravity are thought to be gravitons, which have not been found, and gravity has had little effect on experimental verification (gauge theory), which attempts to unify all the forces except gravity. Gauge theory is dependent on *gauge symmetry*, a mathematics that determines the effects of sequences of transformations of objects in time and space. Regarding the particles, they all have antiparticles, particles of the same mass but opposite in some other way, such as electrical charge. When a particle meets its antiparticle, they annihilate each other to produce more energy. Electrons, neutrinos, and quarks make up the ordinary matter of the universe, so I will focus on them. The other two groups—muons and taus—are very unstable or short-lived.

Electrons are the basis of the flow of electricity. Neutrinos are very interesting because they can travel through other matter, even all the way through Earth, which means they probably carry 1D and 2D information. Quarks are fascinating because they have electrical charge and can be three different colors—the primary colors red, yellow, and blue. Quarks have neither structure nor spatial dimension. They have not yet been observed in particle accelerators, but there is much evidence for their existence. Some people can see auras as color envelopes in the three color ranges, so maybe they are seeing the "quirk" of the quarks.

When I think about these particles, great space opens in my body, since this 4D subquantum field is less solid than my 3D electromagnetic field. Contemplating this dancing world tends to open my heart, since the subquantum field is very creative and chaotic. In fact, various aspects of QM seem fifth dimensional. Of course, each dimension morphs up to the next one, and each has lower and higher qualities. Certainly, QM beautifully describes how 4D dualities widen to polarities out of our consciousness in 3D. Regarding the unity of 5D above the duality of 4D, our reality flows in 5D waves—the dimension of absolute unity and synchronicity—where all particles are relational.

For example, J. S. Bell proved in 1964 that two particles that have been split apart communicate by telepathy; they are connected in an immediate and intimate way showing that *the universe has consciousness.* David Bohm's theory of the implicate order or unbroken wholeness (1970) demonstrates that the dynamic relations of particles depend on the whole system. That is, it is impossible to analyze the world by separating its parts. Scientists can mimic parts in nature, but this does not explain our world and the cosmos. In fact, the solidification of reality probably happens only in our minds. The New Physics shows that we live in a holistic and telepathic world instead of being stuck in a Newtonian machine. From that perspective, it is possible to imagine how the universe might work. Nonscientists can understand the universe and realize how they move in the flow by studying QM experiments. A fantastic and clear explanation of this dynamic is in Itzhak Bentov's classic book, *Stalking the Wild Pendulum.*

This has been a very brief summary of the fundamental particles and forces in the universe. The New Physics has resulted in incredible technological advances; for example, decoding the properties of light (especially lasers) and discovering the microscopic world of particles and waves. The bifurcation of particles and the existence of antiparticles mirror the human tendency to live in duality instead of polarity, which causes people to be violence prone. *People annihilate the people who most closely mirror their own behavior,* just as particles and antiparticles annihilate each other when they meet.

With QM as the bedrock of modern technology, materialistic science has been largely reduced to inventing formulas that create destructive technologies, such as the atom bomb. This is a dangerous situation. We must all comprehend these basic forces now that scientists have created the bomb, a hideous materialization of the Yahweh archetype. The question is, are scientists responsible for the results of their own theories and experiments? Often these inventors act like they are gods who may use nature any way they please. QM is not higher-dimensional physics, nor is it cosmological, because for an authentic cosmology, we must contemplate the nature of the universe in higher dimensions. The universe will never be found in particle accelerators; our brains can perceive and integrate much more than accelerators and computers can. Our thoughts can travel faster and easier without cellphones.

Newtonian physics describes how things obey the laws of gravity, motion, and events in a way we can visualize; QM does not. This is because Newton's laws are the real laws of 1D to 3D where we live; QM is the law of 4D; and cosmology operates in 5D through 9D. The New Physics revelation of the subatomic world shows that our EM brains translate frequency waves. The collective 4D mind is a huge screen of frequency waves that we detect and read in our heads, if we learn where to turn the dial and how to adjust the volume. We humans are like radios.

Measurements in QM can only be done by probability distributions, which is exactly how the collective functions. In fact, the more you understand probability, the more you can think clearly and use intentions to direct your actions. You can tune in good stations, instead of bad ones. This is a big deal, because as the Ps noted earlier, 4D beings (as well as other higher-dimensional beings) want to be involved in the actions of our bodies to experience the frequency waves.

Newtonian laws are easier for us to understand because we see them operating in 3D and we can picture them in our minds. Yet four hundred years ago Newton put our consciousness in a mechanized box. As we now begin to comprehend QM fully, our consciousness expands just like the universe. It is time for everyone to study QM to take our power back from the Elite and end the abuse of nuclear forces. Our split consciousness is partly trapped in a mechanistic mentality, while another part is reacting to a new vista ripped wide open only one hundred years ago. Without the larger whole being rediscovered in the New Physics and in the teachings of higher mathematics, we would just sit in the box with the clock ticking along. Let's return to studying 4D directly through our human experience to see how it works.

Life as an Oreo Cookie

In my introduction, I noted that each of us is like an Oreo cookie sandwiched between the denser realms of Earth and the emotionally and mentally charged realms of the collective mind. The fourth dimension changes constantly according to what is plugged into it. For most of us, 3D is an intensely charged arena, because our bodies in 3D are sandwiched between 2D magnetism below and 4D electrical forces above. We already know quite a bit about how 2D affects us, and now we need to understand how 4D actually affects us in 3D.

We can *feel* what is manifesting in our world and *know* ourselves in our lives amidst 3D relationships. The Wheel of Twelve bisected into six polarities (see figure 3.1) is the best tool I've found for detecting how 4D feelings influence our activities; it teaches us how to read our own fields, or become *self-reflective*. Using the Wheel identifies whether we are balanced or not regarding any pattern in life. When you are balanced, you are in 3D or *grounded*. The fourth dimension churns energy because it vibrates much faster than 3D and continually splits energy. Therefore you must maintain constant vigilance to be grounded, especially during a maelstrom, such as was caused by 9/11.

These times are just like being caught in a tornado, and it is difficult to know where to run. George W. Bush and his followers are creating such fast changes on manifold fronts that Americans are profoundly ungrounded most of the time. Living in the U.S.A. is like living in a particle accelerator! People are fearful in their minds while they are churned by fast-moving events to which they aren't even connected. The Wheel of Twelve corrects imbalances and helps us be islands of peace amidst the gathering storm; it teaches us how to ignore the spin-control plots of the Elite masters.

You may be dealing with intense personal issues, such as keeping a comfortable sense of self while involved in a new primary relationship, and politics may seem very far away. However, most people cannot avoid the collective issues that will shape the whole twenty-first century. The maelstrom sucks everybody in, and they are enticed to be on one side or the other. If you are an American, you are caught in duality if you think George W. Bush is good and Osama Bin Laden and Saddam Hussein are bad, or vice versa. Feeling this way makes you angry, judgmental, and fearful, which blocks subtle consciousness. If you are on one side or the other, you will miss seeing your role in the awesome and gripping drama that is unfolding.

The final sorting out of the real story of how world religions have conspired with the Global Elite during the Age of Pisces to control the world is utterly fascinating. If enough of us figure it out, *we can take our dimension back from the Elite.* Each one of us has a choice now. Either be unconscious and get sucked into the 4D maelstrom, or be conscious and create a new world in 3D. If you choose to be aware in 3D, you can follow multidimensional cues and avoid being 4D pawns.

This is not about the roles people play; *it is about where your consciousness is.* You might play a role as an antiwar activist or as a bomber pilot, and it might seem you are on one side or the other. If you are balanced and processing your own actions, however, you create new possibilities in the field just by the frequencies you radiate. This can keep 3D from being swallowed up by the Elite, whose favorite scorecards are battlefields and morgues. As we approach the Age of Aquarius, the Elite has a great plan—the New World Order—to control the whole world. You are sovereign in 3D when you are conscious and creating new possibilities, or new timelines. Then multidimensional forces flow through your body, such as knowing how Christ really lived at the beginning of the Age of Pisces, Muhammad six hundred years later, and certain gurus now living in the world.

What exactly is the difference between a *dualized reality* and a *polarized reality?* When polarized, the two sides of the issue are in resonance; they are interconnected, they link different dimensions, and they expand possibilities. For example, as the battle between the world religions progresses, millions of Jews and Christians could immerse themselves in sacred Islamic art and study the Koran. Muslims could study the life of Christ and offer more of their knowledge about this revered teacher, which could offer new information to Christians. After all, Christ and Muhammad were born and lived in the Middle East, not in Los Angeles. If the three religions studied the ethical teachings of their own teachers, they might notice that war is condemned.

Dualized realities split the issues at hand so that one side cannot recognize the humanity of the other—for example, the Jews and the Palestinians in Israel, where each side is manipulated into attacking the other daily. Because these religions are separated, the Elite froths up the differences between their beliefs while making money on weapons. None of this is worth the life of one person. The Elite has positioned itself to make lots of money, and you also can by investing in arms. Yet, if you give them your money, you will be supporting the Elite. Dualized environments destroy intelligence and kindness, and investing in violence is suicidal.

Let us go through the six polarities through the lens of the New World Order (NWO) versus Islam drama that is being choreographed by the Elite, since this conflict is exceedingly confusing and has only just begun. This perspective is written for American readers, yet it can be viewed from any side of the issue.

Dualities and Polarities

1. The first polarity is *self/other.* When dualized, saving your own skin is the point. You support anything the NWO does or wants; Islam is the enemy, and anything they do is evil. If you choose to hold the polarity of self/other, by observing both players in the drama, it is easy to see

who gains what, and how they browbeat the opposite side to further themselves. Either side will do anything to push its agenda and beat the other side.

2. The second polarity is *grounding/letting go*. When dualized, making as much money on the conflict as possible is the goal. You are looking for every opportunity to profit or to eat, drink, and be merry. If you hold the polarity of grounding/letting go, seeking ways to widen understanding of the needs and desires of the so-called enemy is the goal, and you encourage people to see that everyone is losing, except the Elite.

3. The third polarity is *integrating in 3D/integrating with spirit*. When dualized, watching CNN and Fox News is an obsession, while having real beliefs and feelings of your own or feeling the spiritual aspirations of the "enemy" is impossible. The media is always dualized during a maelstrom. If you hold the polarity of integrating in 3D/integrating with spirit, observing the drama is valuable, since it is being created at such great cost to humanity. This is the Big Movie, and holding the drama and all the players deep in your heart gives them the space and energy to wake up in the middle of it—to become conscious. Magnificent hidden truths become visible when hidden hatred is being exposed, yet what if nobody witnesses it?

4. The fourth polarity is *feeling/power*. When dualized, feeling all the anger, judgment, and pain is obsessive; you need it like a drug. Glued to the TV, you relish the victories or disasters as the high point of the day—Bombs Away! If you are holding the polarity of feeling/power, as a daily practice look deep within yourself for the parts of yourself that are causing the drama. Seeing your own "dictator within" helps defuse the power mongrels as they growl and snarl on the world stage.

5. The fifth polarity is *creating/giving*. When you are dualized, getting involved in the drama is your desire; you want to fight the evil ones. If you were doing much flag-waving after 9/11 (as well as now), you need to examine your stance now. If you hold the polarity of creating/giving,

you see the fantastic creativity that is expressed during great conflict, and compassion becomes a way of life. Your heart is swept into the great drama that unfolds when people's lives and the lives of others are at stake. There was a better way a long time ago, and it can be found again. Blocked creativity always makes people violent; instead of works of art, we have dead bodies.

6. The sixth polarity is *be here now/bliss.* When dualized, the drama is all that is going on for you, and the maelstrom makes you feel ecstatic. If you hold the polarity of be here now/bliss, feeling your individuality play within the mass events is an eye-opener. You can see timelines from similar events weaving in and out of the players, as if they have returned from past lives to get another chance. They have! With clarity in your heart, seeing how this process works in time could make mass trauma events and religious duality impossible in our future.

Back to being an Oreo cookie: You can keep on being trapped in the gooey white sugar layer between the two chocolate cookies, or you can expand and expand in 3D by intentionally maintaining yourself in a polarized state and flowing with the larger field, as if you are one blade in a field of grass in the sunshine and wind. This way of being is very dynamic because the polarized state expands your EM field like a fan. This fan corresponds to the 4D canopy above, which becomes a diaphanous web. This "web" pulls you right out of the current archetypal drama because your mind is sovereign.

You may say, "Oh, I have nothing to do with *that!*" such as the conflict between the NWO and Islam. If this is so, then you are never angry at your partner, you never take something you don't need, you never ignore somebody who is reaching out to you, you never overpower anybody else, you never drop the chance to create, and you never just disappear on people. However, on the other hand, if you examine your life and see that your actions are part of the maelstrom, your situation will collapse like a card game being sucked up in a tornado. Why?

The Ps say they will know when we have changed when we stop killing each other. The interconnectivity of individuals opens the portals to the higher dimensions. This reformulates 4D into a diaphanous canopy that dissolves control agendas. Each one of us can be a key player in the 4D drama—or else our dimension will be reduced to a card game, and then the only interesting thing left will be who wins.

The Nephilim and the Burning Bush

According to the Ps, the New World Order (NWO) and the fundamentalist religions are directed on Earth by the Annunaki—the Nephilim, which in the Bible means "the Gods Who Came Down." These gods are the directors of the current cycle, which began 5,600 years ago, when they began dividing up territory to conquer the world. They turned Earth into real estate. Today the world is being torn apart by the conflicts and divisions of Earth that began long ago and still continue. Because of so much bloodletting, 4D has become a control "net" that ensnares humanity.

As I go into this in more detail, let us remember that Christianity came out of Judaism, and Islam came out of Judeo-Christianity. If everybody knew that, the conflict would end in a day. The same saints, gods, sacred sites, and scriptures are the basis of all three religions, yet the believers have been cleverly split by having their territory divided up. This keeps them fighting. The conflict has grown huge during the last three hundred years, since the Elite believes the end of the world is coming—or it thinks the Annunaki are returning to Earth, or it just wants more money. This is hysterical. The Mayan calendar indicates that the Milky Way is awakening humanity, and Nibiru is not scheduled to return until 3600 A.D. if at all. Maybe the Sumerians "invented" Nibiru to control people, and it worked so well that other cultures have used the same device.

Since today many people personify and invent God—the great white father who will send his son back again—maybe the Annunaki were just made up in the first place. True belief in a transcendent god involves trusting the unfoldment of divinity in time and not manipulating reality. The story of the Caesars and the Church—how the human race got into this dilemma during the last two thousand years—has already been told. Now we need to examine the contemporary version of how the net ensnares individuals and traps them in dualistic states. This net, woven out of the black-and-white threads spun by all the individual dualities, constricts almost every part of the world now. The NWO is sucking people into it to rule the new world during the emerging Age of Aquarius. This is simply good planning for the future, yet we do not have to get sucked in. If we don't figure this out person by person, the future will be run by the Elite.

The NWO uses the same old religio-magico system that was created two thousand years ago by Caesar and Church. Based on the Hebrew calendar, this system is slated to culminate soon, which is why the fundamentalists of all the religions think the world is ending. Systems that harvest Earth's energy at sacred sites are still in use, and the main fundamentalist objective is to take the powerful sites back, especially Jerusalem (see chapter 2).

The NWO is currently in residence in Washington, D.C., a city/state constructed by Masons over two hundred years ago.[7] Washington was to be the center for all the states, as well as a place that would birth a whole new world. It is a classic temple complex with obelisks, pyramids, avenues, and zodiacs, which was originally created to foster life, liberty, and the pursuit of happiness. Things have changed! The Bushites—the Bush father/son regimes—have arranged a reconstruction of this geomantic form by building a World War II memorial right in the middle of the reflecting pool between the Washington and Lincoln monuments, the main energy line of the capital. This disrupts the original geomantic form to pervert the original intentions of America. Now America is to be the leader of the New World Order, the agency of total world domination, which is probably not what the original founding fathers intended.

The Bushites are sincere in what they believe. They do believe that the end of the world is nigh, since a majority of them are Judeo-Christian fundamentalists. They have taken the power to make sure certain things happen on schedule. This is an exciting time for the Elite: The Jews think the Messiah is still coming, the Christians believe Jesus is coming back soon, and both believe they must rebuild the Temple of Solomon in Jerusalem. If they build the Temple, the Messiah will come, like "Shoeless Joe" Jackson in the film *Field of Dreams*. Once this happens, the fundamentalist Christians believe that 144,000 Chosen People will be saved and everybody else will fry in a holocaust. The only thing that matters is to be one of the Chosen People in Jerusalem at the right time, and everybody else be damned. Meanwhile, the Muslims believe their savior, Allah, has already come. Muslims love to visit Allah's sacred sites, as well as the sacred sites in the Hebrew Bible and the Temple Mount.

Since the Americans have the power and are the true believers, they are the good guys. Anybody joining up for the NWO agenda is an American ally, and anybody who refuses is the enemy. Such a big program calls for a total and systemic reorganization of the United States—such as through the creation of omnipotent state-run agencies like the Office of Homeland Security. Mass-trauma events, such as the destruction of the twin towers of the World Trade Center, can easily be created to get the people to fall quickly in line. This is the current situation in a totally dual-ized field that is splitting the people of the world. A book could be writ-ten just about the NWO agenda—and it would need to be revised annually. If we are to retain our sovereignty to the end of the Mayan cal-endar, we must be grounded in our bodies and become adept at locating where our own minds are.

The best way to understand any dimension is to *locate it in our own bod-ies.* We are sovereign in 3D when we meditate in our altars and call in the seven directions. These extremely dualized times are not going to be easy to live through. It is so easy to get ungrounded. This is a time when unre-solved dramas are being replayed, and the old players are back again to get a chance to do things differently in 3D, the only dimension in which timelines can be altered. I find it fascinating, for example, that so many of our leaders today are reminding us of power players of the past. These are amazing days when we can work with 2D elementals and play with 4D archetypes, as we construct new fields and timelines with our minds. By meditating at your altar, you can practice Goddess Alchemy, which is changing the world by changing yourself. If millions did this, the world would change.

The Power Lens of the Fourth Dimension

Imagine yourself at your altar, or go there now. Choose a current dilemma that is bothering you, such as American troops stuck in Iraq. Hold this in your mind, and once you have a feeling for it, tune in to the 2D elementals and the 4D archetypal beings. Ask them to come into your circle, and ask them to have a conference with you; you want to feel and hear what they say. They may want to channel through you, sing through you, or maybe you will feel like playing music with them. When you can actually feel them in your space, you might feel dense and feel, see, or hear a great being. Make some smoke or light some incense, which encourages them to become more solid and present. You will feel the pain of Earth. Just allow yourself to cry, rage, or run any feelings through your body, and remember to breathe.

Pray with the teachers who have come and thank them. You may be impulsed to smoke a pipe, bless the directions with corn, close your eyes and see a vision, or examine a favorite altar piece; just follow your impulses as they show you things. My altar has all kinds of creative things on it, such as important letters, photos of my elders, my children's toys, stones, effigies, and feathers. These things offer my teachers ways to instruct me, since they are not present. Messages come when we receive spirit impulses, and the opportunity leaves when we do not respond, especially while at our altars. They are so happy to be welcomed that you may feel like a happy puppy as you sense them in your own body. Do not worry about this, since you are sovereign in your circle—but do feel their cues. They are the true inner story of yourself right now.

Tune in to your body and notice any place where there is a twinge, a cramp, a heaviness, or a tingling. Then journey into these places in your body and receive teachings. Then reemerge and play a musical instrument (bells or a drum will do) or study something in your space. Knowings will come into your mind and heart when you go in and out of the spirit fields.

Your power in the fourth dimension is your *feelings*. After you've worked for a while with the teachers who have been present, you may feel some very deep emotions. These are impulses from higher-dimensional guides, who play our fields like a piano when we are open. Guides will not come to you until you have processed your own 4D dualities, which are simply parts of yourself that you need to clear. When you process a current dilemma, wounded parts come up to show you where you are involved in the dilemma; these are the shadows on your soul. When you see them, higher-dimensional spirits sweep in to help you clear the energy, and the larger field is transformed by your clearance. You can create these miracles as often as you like; these clearances can cause soldiers to lay down their arms.

The more you meditate in your altar, the more you will know the beings who work with you and the more quickly they will come. This is how I have gotten to know the Pleiadians, who specialize in opening our hearts. Feel what it is like when 5D precipitates into 4D and your heart opens, like soft rain in a secluded garden on a summer night. If your body gets excited and you feel fascinated with whatever is around, it is the Ps. They show you your world through their eyes by exciting you and vibrating in your cells. You might really feel someone is with you, or a shiver might run up your spine. Sit up very straight, feel the energy in your spine, and move your consciousness into the iron core crystal to ground yourself. Feel your body in your center, feel the fire surging through your spine and into your cranium. See the canopy of energy above your body. Feel your heart expand with pink light, see the millions of waves of light shimmering into your space, and then breathe and close your eyes. You are ready to be illuminated and travel into the fifth dimension of your heart.

The Fifth Dimension:
Samadhi and the Pleiadians

Opening Meditation

Take a few minutes to catch up with yourself. Find your breath. . . . Find your feet. Remember how you felt after you tracked your feelings to their source. Remember what it felt like to have the weight off your shoulders, off your abdomen, how freely you could breathe. Remember that feeling, and take another breath, this time a cleansing one, drawing air all the way from your feet to your chest.

Try it again, until, gently, you can create that feeling, from feet to chest. Feel the movement, the air traveling through your body. Remind yourself that you are the one creating this feeling—*you*. See if you can raise the corners of your lips, just a little bit. See what it feels like to have a smile on your lips. Hold that feeling, hold that smile, with your next breath.

Take another breath, and feel this one right at your heart. Let the air come in right through the middle of your chest. This is *you* breathing, no one else. This is *your* movement of air, *your* life force in action. Identify that. Now begin to feel your chest expand, each time you take another breath. Take your time. There's no need to breathe too fast; just slow and easy, enjoying each cycle of inhale and exhale. Breathe—five seconds in, five seconds out . . . see if that makes a difference.

Each time you breathe, expand your chest a bit more. Feel what it feels like to make it bigger, more open. Visualize your heart and seeing it expanding. Tune in to movement—

all things moving in your body—and the color *green*. Open the space around your heart, at the center of your chest, wider, and wider, see how wide you can get it open. Take a few minutes to get fully open. That's okay. Just let it open the way it wants to.

Stay right here, steady, centered. See how your head feels . . . see how your abdomen feels. Take note of those feelings, and stay with your breath. Easy, in and out, rising and falling, opening your heart as much as it wants to open. Now, let yourself become aware of any other energy in the room: Is it sunlight? the sounds from the street outside? the song of a bird? a voice somewhere else in the house? Greet those energies with your heart. See what that feels like. See if you can let a little of this energy into your body, through your heart. See if you can send a little energy from your heart to meet this energy. Be creative: Do this any way you like.

Now, close your eyes, and imagine someone you would like to be with. It can be anyone from your present life, or from your past. Let that person come to your attention. See that person's face, and feel that person from the center of your chest. Feel your heart gently making contact with that person's heart. If you need to ask for—or receive—forgiveness from that person, do so from your heart. Speak to that person from your heart. Let it take time if necessary. Know that there are no time constraints on this feeling.

If you want to just send love to that person with your heart, do so, and enjoy the sensation of sending love from your heart. Experiment with how you send the love energy: Aim it, or let it just glow all around that person. Paint this person with the paintbrush from your heart. This person could be a pet, an animal, a tree, a plant, a friend, a relative, a lover—any living thing, past or present. Whoever it is, stay with that one person, and let the process continue until there is no more energy to send, or to receive.

Now, take another breath, and bring your attention to your chest area. How is it? Does it seem more open than when you started? Does it hurt a bit around the edges? Then breathe, and let your breath be a paintbrush for your heart. Bring cool, moist, healing energy to your opened heart. Thank your body for being able to open up so much, and know that each time you do this, you'll be able to open more and more. The little hurts are just a part of the process of opening. Visualize putting a healing salve on these hurts; thank your heart for being so willing to open and receive.

Now bring your attention to your breath, and to your feet, to the column of energy running from your chest to your feet. Remember the feeling of your open heart, and know that you can return there any time you want. Open your eyes, and take a final cleansing breath. See if you can find another smile on the corners of your lips. Good. Now we are ready to learn more about the Keepers of the heart, of the fifth dimension.

The fifth dimension (5D) is a realm of light that centers in the human heart and is resonant with Earth's biological creatures and plants.

For humans, the light's vibrational frequency is called samadhi, the realizable human experience of communion with the divine.

According to the Ps, the Keepers of 5D are beings from the Pleiades, a star system that is located in the Taurus constellation, the great bull in the sky. The Pleiadians have been the ancestors of many indigenous clans on Earth for at least 40,000 years, as pointed out by several prehistorians.[1] The description of this dimension by the Ps, as well as its connection with Earth, is mind-boggling. They say a great spiral of stellar light from the Pleiades reaches our Sun, and our Sun is the eighth of the large stars of the Pleiades. The generator of the spiral is Alcyone, the central star of the Pleiades from Earth's view. Astronomically, this seems bizarre, yet a few astronomers and early Greeks described this same spiralic geometry of light between the Pleiades and the Sun. My Mayan medicine brother, Hunbatz Men, has written about this system, since it is the basis of the Long Count in the Mayan calendar.[2] Somehow the Ps have a great impact on Earth via this system, as if they slide into our world through a nautilus spiral when significant "nows" arrive, such as the end of the calendar (figure 5.1).

Figure 5.1 Nautilus shell spiral.

According to Satya in *The Pleiadian Agenda,* as well as to Hunbatz Men, our solar system is being awakened by a band of light—the "Photon Band"—which is transmuting Earth's atmosphere. At this time, as the Mayan calendar orchestrates Earth's awakening, the Ps are tuning in to our solar system and updating us with the latest news from Alcyone. It is as if the mysterious stellar spiral is a communications system. As one of the receivers of the "P News," I have since discovered that the Photon Band makes sense in light of some of the discoveries of quantum mechanics (QM). Here we will consider the New Physics from a 5D perspective, having just examined its 4D aspects in the previous chapter.

Photons are particles of light that vibrate with frequency waves, which carry the full spectrum of electromagnetic (EM) radiation from extremely low frequency waves to gamma rays. High-frequency photons have more energy than low-frequency ones, and an unusually large amount of high-frequency photons are coming to our solar system. Very potent gamma-ray bursts have been reaching our solar system since the 1990s (especially in 1998), which are probably much more intense than most previous ones.[3] Of course, we've only had the technology to detect them for a few years, yet it is possible there is an increase that has something to do with the mysterious Photon Band.

As of early 2003, astronomers have determined that high-intensity gamma rays come from *hypernovas*—extremely huge supernovas.[4] According to QM, photons split into pairs and travel independently in the universe, yet they are still able to communicate no matter how far apart they move. *Photons are conscious in some way.* This awakening by high-energy gamma rays must be intensifying the frequency ranges in our minds. Gamma rays are an energy of the highest order we know, which means we're really talking about consciousness itself.[5] Since the publication of *The Pleiadian Agenda,* I have pondered whether there really *is* a Photon Band and what it might cause, and I sense that the matching twins of Earth's photons that are located in high-frequency zones—such as in black holes—are communicating strongly with their Earth counterparts.

The Ps say gamma-ray bursts cause humans to become seers who are conscious in nine dimensions simultaneously. They also say they are 5D intelligences who require EM fields in 3D to see themselves. I have seen the Ps "seeing themselves" three times. They were small, radiant, luminescent beings that quickened my heart. One afternoon in 1985, a group of them spent hours shimmering in my study in Santa Fe. They say they've come into our dimension to inspire us to become masters of love.

Love fosters biological life—the intelligence of the heart—a force greater than our minds, which are merely screens that read frequencies. We are encouraged to empty our minds when we meditate in order to bypass this distracting screen. When we clear it, we flow into a dark inner labyrinth made of pathways into our heart. Unlike 4D, there is no polarization in 5D. Thought travels faster than light, yet love travels even faster than thought. This enables us to recognize our soul mates and great beings who arrive on Earth to radiate high-frequency light, such as Christ, Buddha, and Muhammad. This light vibrates divine immanence, and our response to it is called grace.

According to the Ps, Earth is Alcyone's laboratory, and Alcyone is Earth's library. *The Pleiadian Agenda* and this book are records from the Alcyone Library. A new sacred culture—harmonic biology—is seeding in the Milky Way, now that our solar system has returned to a key location in its orbit around the Galaxy.[6] When the solar system was in this same location 225 to 250 million years ago, Earth was selected (because it holds nine dimensions in its field) to be the laboratory where biological life would be developed for the Milky Way. The Ps say Earth's new biology will be disseminated in the Galaxy on December 21, 2012, like a dandelion releasing silica filaments in the wind. Only life that vibrates in all nine dimensions will be carried out into the stars.

The seeding of the Galaxy will be an ecstatic release of Earth, like Shiva dancing with Earth in the Galaxy. Many Earth experiments are preparing humans to honor the galactic biological laws. For example, what each geneticist does to DNA shows whether he or she honors life or not. In the Milky Way, the Divine first entered our dimension via sound, which is why the Bible says, "In the Beginning was the Word." The laws of harmony are *spiritual science*, which is greater than materialistic science. These laws are the basis of the rest of this book, since materialistic science will never explain or comprehend the five higher dimensions. Materialistic science explains the solid world very well, and it also brilliantly investigates many factors in nature that are actually higher dimensional.

This is why I seek to identify a science for each dimension; these times are a cornucopia of exciting discoveries. Spiritual science thinks of galaxies as conscious living beings who inhabit and structure the universe, just as we do Earth.

Star Lore and Orgasms

The fifth dimension is light. That is to say it is the field of the whole EM radiation spectrum, and we are mysteriously embodied in this field. As we move into the subtle realms—5D through 9D—the Ps say that each higher dimension has a home in the stars, and they maintain aspects of Earth's field. For thousands of years, humanity understood reality by mythology, the stories of the stars or star lore. The modern world has lost this imaginal connection, which is the source of rich ancient traditions. Star lore is the primordial bridge to the higher dimensions.

Gerry and I—two freedom-loving Aquarians—have been reweaving this tapestry of light by exploring higher worlds with groups. Stars are the cells of the galaxies, just like the cells in our bodies. Star lore reawakens "cellular memory," memory that is light-encoded in our cells. We can actually feel ourselves living in other places and times, such as the Pleiades or ancient Egypt. Cellular memory can be accessed through storytelling, which is why some great storytellers sing, chant, and play their own bodies like instruments. If we do not stimulate our EM nervous systems, our memories atrophy. The ancient ones gazed at stars and listened to them singing.[7] It would seem we have lost this thread to the divine mind, yet this is not so. Only a hundred years ago, Van Gogh painted the stars in the night sky as spinning galactic spirals of light. Star lore's eternal records awaken according to the cycles of light, which is happening now. Earth's photons have pairs in the stars that communicate periodically. These lost twins are returning in the gamma rays; we are hearing the music of the spheres in the heavens. We are not lost or abandoned, we are simply waking up.

As Alcyone's laboratory, Earth is where love can be experienced in the physical. The energy in our personal healing fields is directly proportional to the love in our hearts, and we attract Pleiadian partnership by expanding our hearts. As the Ps have said, our EM fields make it possible for them to actualize themselves in our world. The most potent force we humans create is our orgasmic frequencies while making love. The Maya say human orgasms move the Galactic Center![8] This may sound crazy, yet as we ponder the vertical axis through the dimensions, the energetics we are reaching for are quintessential. Seeking orgasmic frequencies is the goal of this book, especially since the great Wilhelm Reich discovered they are the source of the life force, the orgone.[9] The Galactic Center emanates sacred time, then the dimensions spin out of the center, and we are biological on the vertical axis; maybe we *do* spin the Galaxy with our orgasms!

Most sacred teachers point out we can attain enlightenment just by being loving. The only reason to explore the dimensions beyond 5D is to expand our love into even higher dimensions, which is fun. The sixth dimension (6D) holds the forms of 3D; 7D awakens cellular memory by sound; 8D is God; and 9D spins out the cycles of time. The higher dimensions link 5D to the divine source, and then 5D radiates this love down into the lower dimensions. The fifth dimension is the center of the vertical axis, as our hearts are the center of our bodies. You can experience each one of these fields by traveling up the vertical axis, or you can simply sink into love in our magnificent solid world. After all, love is the total frequency range of the universe.

If you choose that path—the way of the heart—Earth is a labyrinth with paths moving into the center and back out again. You can walk the paths, encounter other beings, and shower them with love, just by expanding your field. If you are unitized in the heart, life is a time to seek other beings to love. The only way to know love is to experience it, which draws in the Pleiadians. Many seekers want to understand the universe itself, and you can do so through love.

The Science of the Fifth Dimension

Fifth-dimensional science is outrageous and delicious. I begin with topology, the mathematics of correspondences and continuity. As we move into the higher realms, things are explored by means of Goddess Alchemy. The rules of Goddess Alchemy are: Things must be fun and clear, not cloaked; and exciting, not the cause of snores.

My standard for attempting to identify the sciences of each dimension is that each system must have direct results in its corresponding dimension and make little sense in other dimensions. A science of one dimension never eliminates a lower (or higher) one. For example, 4D quantum mechanics does not supercede 3D Newtonian physics. When the physicist Max Planck introduced QM in 1900 by presenting his theory of the laws of energy radiation (the discontinuous universe), he was afraid it would undermine the foundations of Newtonian physics. It didn't, since the quantum world is simply the microcosmic view. We've needed the 4D/QM view to be able even to locate 5D, the dimension where *matter unifies*. This unification makes more sense when you understand how 4D splits matter.

As we grasp for the higher five dimensions, we must stretch our minds. To assist our students, we asked Michael Stearns to create music that resonates with nine frequency levels; otherwise, it can be so hard to detect really high and low frequencies. Some students have the hardest time resonating with the iron core crystal as it resonates at 40 Hz. One thing is sure, to get to the higher levels, we must fully comprehend the levels we're leaving. It helps to conceive of each dimension as *planar*—nine flat realms that extend out into circular infinity (figure 5.2). Cosmologists believe the universe is flat while space is curved.[10] Some readers may find they cannot grasp the dimensional concept as a whole until they've considered all nine and then go back through to fit things together.

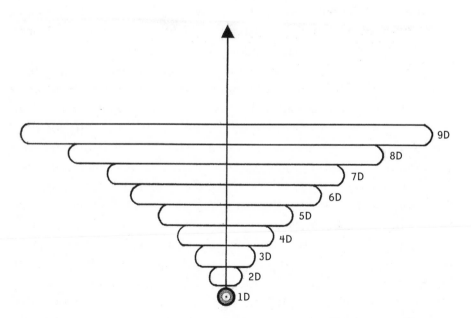

Figure 5.2 The nine dimensions as planar fields that expand infinitely outward from the vertical axis.

Topology or "knot theory," the mathematics of correspondence and continuity, is fifth dimensional in all ways. Mathematics is a highly structured language that relates higher orders to things. Generally speaking, all forms of mathematics are 5D because math seeks to find relationships between complex things. Topology's specialty is finding formulas to describe knots that eventually create things in 3D; it studies the places (knots) where higher orders enter our dimension. Knots are places where cords cross an axis, and the strings that make the knots come from some other place. It's as if the universe were a flat weaving made of knots, like an oriental carpet. Topology is a science that investigates forms from other places that interweave in detectable ways.

Topologists are onto something for sure, since their formulas have achieved major experimental verifications. Topology is behind all kinds of biological experiments such as manipulating DNA and cloning—what I call "Frankensteinian biology." It is also a weird field of study—topologists understand the algebra behind their discoveries but not the geometry. Most people tend to think either geometrically or algebraically. I think geometrically, and I like topology in 5D because it leads us into labyrinths, as you will see in a moment.

Knots form by the weaving of cords, which can be loosened or tightened, just like knots we've all tied and untied, such as in our shoelaces. Can you remember the magical moment you first tied your shoes? It was a mystical moment for me. Well, topologists spend their time inventing formulas that describe the lengths, holes, loops, and curves of knots. If the strings are followed out to their source, the geometry behind the knots—6D—is visually obvious to me, yet linking geometry and topology with formulas would take books of calculations. Using topology as a visual/structural tool, I'm able to imagine the knots vibrating with EM frequencies. String physicists believe that the elementary particles are not points or dots but "tiny, one-dimensional filaments somewhat like infinitely thin rubber bands, vibrating to and fro."[11]

Imagine the world as a vibrating field of looping, intersecting knots that end up being matter. In case you're feeling spacey, welcome to the higher dimensions! As a useful bridge, it helps to pull four dimensions—3D through 6D—together into a working concept. This offers a sense of the relationship between 6D geometric forms and things that replicate in 3D. I first understood the relationship between 6D ideas and 3D things when I studied Plato as a child, and it is very similar to Rupert Sheldrake's "morphogenetic fields" that replicate lifeforms in 3D.[12] As a working idea, use knot theory to bridge 3D through 6D. Knots are intersections of lines in 5D (the lines coming from 6D), and the knots untie (or tie) in the 4D duality field (particles and waves) and form things in 3D within EM fields. Tightening a knot intensifies duality and the consequent dilemmas in 3D, yet loosening a knot fans out polarities and opens perspective.

Labyrinths as the Way to Walk in Higher Dimensions

The French philosopher and painter Patrick Conty bridges topology and geometry. Of course, he is not a mathematician, yet his beautiful exposition *The Genesis and Geometry of the Labyrinth* (2002) shows how geometry is always playing in our bodies. It's as if the solution can be right in our backyard. Labyrinths existed all over the ancient world, and Conty notes they are the primordial archetype that bridges this world to the higher dimensions.

Labyrinths are an advanced topological knot, and they are paths we can walk—*experiential geometry.* Thinking of our births for a moment, 3D is a maze in which we wander around with little sense of direction, without knowing if we'll ever get out, and we don't even get an owner's manual when we're born. Yet the *labyrinth is the ideal pathway through life's maze,* as well as being very much like a vulva. Moving in and out of its center, it is the ideal guide for discovering our inner self while rebirthing consciousness.

Figure 5.3 A labyrinth.

When people walk in labyrinths, they often have profound spiritual experiences. The path guides the walker into its center, which is the vertical axis that links all nine dimensions. If you've ever walked in one, remember how you meandered and circled, and then reversed, the tightest reversal being in the center. Our minds and bodies move beyond duality while weaving and turning in this complex knot. Often symbols precipitate in the mind's eye that awaken cellular memory of the geometry that holds our bodies in form. These symbols vibrate with very complex geometry, and as your body moves along the paths, the geometry also vibrates with sound waves. You can feel the land sing, which melts you into an ethereal knowing.

Ancient labyrinths are often located at sacred sites—places where telluric energy flows strongly—such as near Tintagel in Cornwall, where some ancient stories say King Arthur ruled Camelot. Labyrinths can be found as mosaics on the floors of churches, such as Chartres, where they mark the pathways of strong Earth energy configurations. In the Middle Ages, pilgrims walked the Chartres labyrinth while choirs chanted sacred music above. Labyrinths suck higher dimensions directly down into 2D pathways.

Figure 5.4 The *sma*, which shows how the heart unites Upper and Lower Egypt.

Conty talks about a classic Egyptian knot, the *sma,* that is found on the side of the pharaoh's throne. (I always wondered about this when I was in Egypt.) The axis of this knot is the human heart emerging out of the tracheal column in the center (see figure 5.4). The knot tied on the tracheum unites Upper and Lower Egypt, which resolves duality and opens the flow of the wisdom of the heart. This flow fertilizes the land and supports and enhances living things, which you can see symbolized by the cords that show plants joining. The cords are strings emerging out of 6D that show how plants are replicated from higher-idea forms, an ideal image of morphogenetic fields. The sma unites the heart with the breath of life, which teaches each person to breathe the sacred breath with the pharaoh who leads them. Two strings make up the knot instead of one, which means the union of Upper and Lower Egypt has been achieved; the sma is a potent duality resolution.

For Conty, *the labyrinth is the knot that represents the whole, the essential nature of experience.* The axis of the labyrinth is the will or capacity to materialize, while the cord creates the form. For me, the labyrinth circulates us in multidimensional space as we walk in it on sacred land, change directions, and go in and out of the vertical axis. We can trace its pattern—the geometry of primordial unity—with our bodies in 3D, a great way to find our path through the maze of life. Walking our paths intentionally in 3D, we can discover the way of the heart.

Next we will examine a scientific theory that actually bridges 5D into 6D, which helps us imagine how our bodies are cradled by 6D morphogenetic fields, the ideal forms that replicate lifeforms in 3D, and consider where all these fields come from.

The End of Time and Platonia

Seeking a wide view of the universe, Oxford physicist Julian Barbour begins by asking what time is.[13] Starting with the subject of time moves him beyond Einstein's limited world of only four dimensions. Einstein's relativity theory put time into a spatial framework: space-time as a fourth dimension. According to special relativity, time and space seem to be aspects of a four-dimensional reality where events happen that appear to be relative. Barbour argues that *time is not like space,* and events are not in a fourth dimension since they are not related by time. He says his main aim is to show that *instants of time are real things.*[14] They are static and timeless configurations in the universe that are experienced by us as dynamic and temporal, which is why time seems to be so real. The configurations are the ultimate things; there are infinitely many of them; they are all different instances of a common principle of construction; and they are different instants of time.

Barbour starts with time because the theory used for cosmology—general relativity—and the theory used for the microcosm—quantum mechanics—are incompatible. He notes that the unification of relativity and QM may well spell the *end of time.* This may sound arcane, yet his new theory of how the universe operates makes sense and can be easily understood with visualization, something which hardly works with relativity.[15]

In Barbour's universe—which he calls *Platonia* because his idea is so similar to Plato's ideas and forms—spatial things are primary reality. He begins with *shapes* to discover how things exist and happen. Think about it: What you see are shapes, which we know are composed of frequency waves. Yet the question remaining is: How do these frequencies take on shape?[16] Platonia is configured of triangles, cubes, and other geometric shapes, which are compared qualitatively. The world as we know it is made of these shapes and all their relationships, and we experience them as instants of time.[17] In my system, time is generated from much higher dimensions, and it works to think of time as something that is experienced as instants in a world of shapes.

Considering configurations—*Triangle Land*—Barbour says triangles are formed by three dots connected by lines that create *nows*—events or things in 3D. (These dots can also be strings.) If there are four dots, tetrahedrons form; if there are six dots, cubes form. For each configuration, there is a corresponding thing in 3D, and the possibilities are infinite. In Platonia, the land of nows, there are Platonic forms (as well as other forms)—tetrahedron, cube, octahedron, icosahedron, or dodecahedron—and all the dots in Platonia are potentialities in different quantities.[18]

Since 6D is the realm of sacred geometry, why do I have Barbour's theory in 5D? Platonia *is* also 6D, which comes next, yet we need Barbour's theory here because it brilliantly explains how *5D precipitates out of 6D,* or where the knots come from. His theory also provides a context for the potent imprint of the Platonic solids in nature, where geometry is so visible in shells and plants. Platonia links the forms of nature found on

Earth with cosmology. Reversing directions and going up the vertical axis, Platonia shows how sacred geometry pops out of the 5D fields, where configurations are vibrating with EM frequencies that eventually are seen as "things." Imagine the 6D geometry of a labyrinth holding it in form as it vibrates in 5D!

Certainly, time and space are not in the same dimension (although we humans experience them this way in 3D), which is the reason special relativity and gravity are not resolved. From my point of view, *space* exists in *all* the dimensions, *time* is some sort of function that operates differently in each dimension, and *gravity* is the force behind everything and generates the whole vertical axis.

Returning to the more 5D aspects of Barbour's theory: Platonia—the 6D land of geometric configurations—is permeated with *mist,* which *varies in intensity by the potency of the nows.*[19] That is, our ideas in our nows form into mist in the configurations. Intense and repeated nows create *paths,* which are continuous events played out by systems and cultures, such as technologies, cultural agreements, and beliefs.[20] Barbour comments, "Time is Nature's way of preventing everything from happening at once."[21] History is not something that happens in time; it is a path through a landscape in the mist. We believe in time because we experience the universe in *time capsules,* yet there is no time. Time capsules are fixed patterns that encode change or history.[22]

Platonia is eternal, and I would add that 6D is timeless and eternal; however, things exist in 5D via EM frequencies that split in 4D and become visible in 3D. Time certainly is not what it appears to be in 3D and 4D, although time is linear in 3D and feelings have time qualities in 4D. Think how time seems endless when one waits for one's lover to arrive. All our conscious experiences (in 3D) have their origins in real structures within the nows, and the *intensity of the mist determines the probability of things being experienced.*

Barbour's mist, paths, and time capsules brilliantly explain the connections that create the laws of archetypes, the collective mind, and how probabilities function. For example, history tends to repeat itself unless people learn from it, change the path, and fumigate the mist. His theory also explains how meditation can change outcomes in 3D; groups could thicken the mist for "peace" with their minds. A sacred culture could precipitate instantaneously in 3D, since such original paths are very potent in the mist; many people have experienced ecstasy and initiation in the past, which thickened that mist. The thickness of the mist is critical to identifying sacred cultures, such as the ancient Egyptians and the Minoans. Yet I never mention the Sumerians and the Babylonians this way. This is because the Babylonian/Sumerian culture and its derivatives were, and are not, sacred cultures. They were dualistic and mired in 4D and became obsessed with time; they divided 3D up with calendars that are programs for their agendas. They developed the principle of controlling history by means of artificial timelines. These programs cut off access to unwanted paths in the mist. Seeing this differential is critical, since *Western cultures are based on the Sumerian/Babylonian time divisions* (dividing the day into sixty-minute hours), which cause them to be apocalyptic—always waiting for the end of time. The Western political agenda runs the world by this false time system, yet alternatives to believing "the world is coming to an end soon" do exist in the mists of Platonia, such as living by the four seasons and lunar cycles and understanding the Mayan calendar.

Instantaneous states of the universe do happen, which shows that time is not fused in space, much less is real in 3D or 4D. This is a "many worlds" interpretation of QM that functions in dimensions way beyond 4D, and it beautifully explains how 5D is structured. Most important, all we know about the past exists in current records, such as in our long-term memory, which is chronological. *Our brains are a time capsule,* and exploration of past lives has proven that most people can go back to times before they were born. Barbour thinks of the whole Earth as a time capsule with fossil records and chemical evidence for its creation from a supernova.[23] That is to say, the configurations are part of our cranial structure and our planet. Thus the paths entice us to follow our fascinations to create many nows. The mist explains the continuance of cellular memory and how sacred cultures precipitate from paths into nows when enough people activate a mist to reopen a path.

Barbour's theory actually explains how *geometry precipitates love and creativity.* Platonia describes 5D as a dimension where polarities unitize and where forms exist that resonate with the higher and more subtle realms. This view solidifies the links between 6D and 5D, which opens new potential for penetrating 4D and comprehending how things are solid in 3D. Now that we have a few more links, we are ready to explore sacred geometry to see how 6D is formulated out of 5D on the vertical axis.

The Sixth Dimension:
Sacred Geometry and Platonia

Opening Meditation

Find your breath. Notice where it enters your body. Does it come in from all around you, or just in through your nose or mouth? Take another breath, and see if you can get the breath to come right in through your throat. From the front of your throat, and through the back of your neck. Try a few breaths this way, gently and slowly.

Become aware of your shoulders. Notice how the air comes into your body right in the middle of your shoulders, right where they meet. Close your eyes, and visualize your shoulders like feathers that meet in the middle at your throat. See how light you can make your shoulders. See if you make them rise and fall, gently and gracefully, with each breath. See how your throat is where they meet.

Become aware of all of the outer layer of your body. See if you can see yourself like an envelope, with energy inside and a surface holding it all together. See what that shape looks like, and feel what it looks like. Get a good sense of that shape.

Now, put your attention on the left side of your body. Just see what it feels like, and see what it looks like. Occupy that side of your body with your senses. See what comes to you. See how far off your body this feeling goes. When you have seen and felt enough, for now, put your attention on the right side of your body. See and feel what that looks like. Let your senses go there, to the right side of your body. Take note of what you find. Is it different from the left side of your body? If so, how is it different?

Now, put your attention onto the space in front of your body. Occupy this space with your senses. See what happens when you place your attention on this space. What happens each time you take a new breath in this space? Just notice what you find there. Then, when you have seen and felt enough, go find the back side of your body, the space behind you. What is that like? Can you see it with your inner eye, can you sense it with your senses? See what you find there. Take your time. This can be a little slow at first. Notice what you find there, using any one or more of your senses.

Now, put your attention on the space beneath your feet, whether you have your feet on the ground or are resting on a horizontal surface. What can you feel at the base of your feet, and in the space around the base of your feet? How big is this space? Is there any space at all? Can you feel or see anything in this space? What is it like for you?

Finally, put your attention on the space above your head, above your crown. Visualize what is up there. Is it big and expansive, or is it just a place? Can you feel or see anything at all? See if you can make it bigger, more clear, by taking a new breath. Take note of what you find.

Now, take a new breath, and visualize your whole body once again. See if your body looks any different from before. This meditation allows you to identify and work with your six-dimensional energy body, your wireless anatomy that holds your form in place. This is a good meditation for helping you "take your space" on the planet, by helping you see how you occupy your space on the planet.

The sixth dimension is the realm of geometric forms that replicate as plants, animals, humans, and material objects in 3D, which is called morphogenesis. For example, in 6D exists the idea of "Cow," and then many cows replicate in 3D (see figure 6.1). It is also the home of the *Ka*—the human spirit body—which makes it possible for us to read the vibratory ranges that define our bodies, emotions, thoughts, and souls. Our Ka knows when to take energy in, when to block it, and when to mirror it back to its source; yet, most people are unconscious of its activities. This remarkable subtle-energy body contains the memory of our initiations and therefore holds the records of the greatest potential for any person. Being in 3D (linear space and time) makes us dense and solid, which tends to make our Ka dormant. Most people are asleep throughout their whole lives. You can realize that your 6D form is real just by understanding the relationship between 6D and 3D.

Figure 6.1 The idea of "cow" in 6D replicating as cows in 3D.

According to the Ps, the Keepers of 6D are the Sirians—beings in the Sirius trinary star system, which is only about 8.7 light years from our solar system. Our relationship with the Sirius system is extremely intriguing:

Even though other stars move in different pathways in the spiral arms of the Galaxy, Sirius, the Pleiades, and our solar system all revolve around the Galactic Center every 225 to 250 million years *in the same locational relationship* in the Orion arm of the Galaxy.[1] Astronomically this means there must be some kind of magnetic, gravitational, or geometric system that makes this possible. The Ps also say that Nibiru, home of the Annunaki (the Keepers of 4D), orbits out into space and swings around the Sirius system like a boomerang, and then returns to our solar system. From Nibiru's perspective, our Sun and Sirius are twin stars that are always conscious of each other.

This relationship between Earth and Sirius was known to many archaic medicine keepers, such as the Australian aborigines who staged initiations with boomerangs to teach students about this relationship. Many cultures, such as the Dogon of Africa and the ancient Egyptians, say their ancestors originally came from Sirius.[2] According to the Ps, the library on Sirius A transmits the laws of sacred architecture: the science of building structures that model 6D geometric forms. They say that great feline gods from Sirius periodically come to Earth to build their temples and found new cultures that can discover the vertical axis. The Egyptians, for instance, built very advanced examples of sacred architecture, such as the sphinx and the Great Pyramid; and the classical Greeks built the Acropolis.[3] Just as 4D beings like to incite us into acting out their agendas, so do the Sirians enjoy inspiring us to construct sacred architecture. We humans are the builders, which teaches us to experience 6D while holding form in 3D over long spans of time. The Greeks noticed that *whatever remains in form through time is reflective of the higher dimensions.* The paths and the mist of sacred architecture are very developed.

My grandfather, Gilbert Hand, taught me the same thing. He showed me ancient objects that still exist because people venerate them, and he helped me feel and read their codes—records from the past. Because of this, I have a very complex and ancient sense of time. I did not really understand how 6D holds things in form in 3D until I was able to see it one day while looking at the Acropolis from a hotel balcony in Athens. I had a perfect view as the stars rose behind it in the early evening. Staring at the Acropolis with my third eye open, I saw the sky suddenly explode with lines of blue-white geometric forms. I was witnessing the geometric light that holds the Acropolis in form!

How Our Bodies Exist in the Sixth Dimension

The relationship between our solid world and the 6D world of eternal forms that replicate things in 3D is most easily understood by considering the frequency waves that create our bodies. Just like the expanded 6D field that holds the Acropolis in form, our bodies are aligned with our 6D morphogenetic or morphic field (M-field), which is huge. These M-fields vibrate with many frequencies, and when our hearts are open, we naturally align with this 6D structure. Heart expansion does not work correctly without alignment with this field, just like the Acropolis would crumble into a pile of old stones without its light geometry. Without our M-fields, we'd never look the same in the mirror in the morning. Since you are made of vibrating EM particles with oceans of space between them, what invents you every day?

Egyptian sacred science counsels that we must learn to feel our Ka reading frequencies, which means keeping our Ka "in" to maintain the correct energy boundaries of our four bodies. By feeling the different vibratory patterns of our physical, emotional, mental, and soul bodies, we can be healthy without doctors, have love in our lives, understand our world, and be in contact with spirit *all the time*. With our Ka in, we automatically differentiate the vibratory frequencies of our four bodies, which are radically different (figure 6.2). The physical body has the lowest vibration, the soul body the highest.

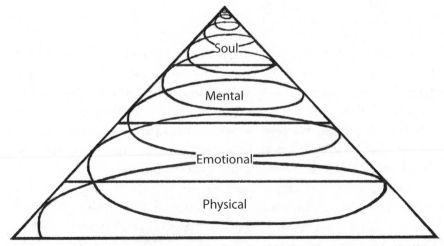

Figure 6.2 The vibratory frequencies of the Four Bodies of Consciousness: physical, emotional, mental, and soul.

When your Ka is in, unseen frequencies are *palpable,* or felt strongly at the physical level. This state enables you to identify whether a problem is physical, emotional, mental, or spiritual. Speaking of boundaries, when your Ka is in, you can feel what other people are doing to you energetically. For example, when encountering a person who emits great energy, it is useful to know whether this is physical (sexual), emotional (love-or-hate), mental (ideas), or soul (spiritual). Knowing the level at which a person is approaching you might save your life, your job, or your marriage.

When you are adept at reading frequencies, your Ka stays in because you are resonating with it; a good model is observing how your autonomic nervous system regulates your body. Many people have learned to observe their autonomic processes, such as breathing, to sense whether they are tense or not. Once you learn how to observe your Ka monitoring the fields you live in, you will not be able to imagine living without it. If you feel ungrounded or lost, you know your Ka is "out." If you embody your Ka well, you can be very psychic. Your body is like a good radio with finely tuned dials, and you are able to be omniscient, or all-seeing, which means your Ka reads frequencies at a distance. This is what Gerry and I mean when we talk about "getting activated."

Yoga

Egyptian sacred science is most relevant in the modern era, and these teachings have come down to us.[4] This suggests they have thick mist in Platonia. Both the ancient Egyptians and the great sages of India taught that *yoga is a necessary practice for activating ourselves,* because yogic practice moves our bodies in and out of postures that align us with our 6D M-fields.[5] When you were conceived, your EM field contained a program to guide you through your growth, the pattern of your unfoldment. An oak seed will grow into a great oak tree. Trees hold their M-fields most faithfully because they stay in one place. We humans lose this alignment more easily because we move around so much, thus we need special practices. *Yoga realigns our physical forms within 6D M-fields.* Instead of slouching around in 3D, yoga lifts you out of being a puppet strung up by 4D-emotional dramas, or being reamed out by the collective mind-set.

If you watch cats, they hold yoga postures all day. When they sleep, they seem to be meditating. Cats are very Sirian, which is why the Egyptians revered them. Doing yoga correctly patterns you with your light geometry, which regenerates your body. You are designed to live with your

Ka embodied, regardless of what is going on around you. You can vibrate at such a high frequency that most people can't even see you. Many "street smart" people have figured out how to do this for survival, and it works if you get stuck in a boring meeting or party.

The Ps say the 6D Sirians like to infuse their intelligence into our 6D M-fields to encourage us to create things that resonate with the primordial forms. Just like the Ps say they require our EM fields to see themselves, the Sirians find themselves in our bodies and auric fields when we do yoga, play tennis, dance, or perform any correct alignment. I also think golf is a very Sirian sport, which is why it is mystical for some people; it certainly is interesting that golf was originally designed with nine holes. Gerry feels the same way about baseball, with its geometric field and nine innings.

Initiations—ceremonies that connect us with our formative nature—synchronize our current growth with the pattern of unfoldment that was imprinted during conception. Our Ka holds *all* the memories of previous initiations, when we were realigned during these key phases. These states can be accessed in past-life regressions, since they exist in our bodies as time capsules. Julian Barbour says: "By a time capsule, I mean any fixed pattern that creates or encodes the appearance of motion, change, or history."[6] The asanas or yogic postures are individual initiations, and since yoga stirs up a lot of fire energy in our bodies, holding them aligns us with the power of our M-fields; the kundalini flows and our bodies change. This activates the natural frequencies of the four bodies of consciousness, making it easier to distinguish them. The rewards of correct alignment—health, joy, fascination, bliss, and regeneration—are so great that many people persevere and discover the great personal radio dial within that reads vibrations.

Personal Altars and Your Ka

Altars are tremendous accelerators. When you pray to the seven sacred directions—East, West, North, South, Sky, Earth, and Heart—of your altar, your Ka embodies, since altars are 6D fields grounded in 3D that have direct access to the mist of Platonia. Memory of important paths, such as ancient cultures, can be stored in the objects of these cultures, which are classic time capsules. All this information opens when you pray to the seven directions in sacred space. You can build an amazing 6D field filled with your own reflections about the world, and there you can be in touch with any place or time.

Altars are doorways into other worlds, places where we can ascend through nine dimensions, which is freedom. This is why the Church got them out of people's homes and took control over sacred space. The Church methodically destroyed the sacred power objects of the originating cultures, or put them on display in the Vatican Museum or in bishops' houses, since the ancient ones had made many effigies and imbued them with potent records.[7] Recently, indigenous cultures all over the planet have been creating them again and selling them to make these records available to the people. When you are meditating in the middle of your altar and tuning in to various objects, as you become more psychic and can discern frequencies better, you may see or feel the lines of light from 6D holding them in form. After all, the frequencies making them solid are vibrating inside. You may find you can feel and read energies in stones and sacred objects, which is really fun. You are more likely to do this when you understand the symbolism and myths of the culture that created them.

You might ask what this accomplishes? We are living in a time when 3D is not sufficiently infused with 6D forms because there is almost no sacred science left in the world. This lack of meaning in life causes our world to be split by the 4D zone, and the higher dimensions have almost no access to us in 3D. The most potent link to higher dimensions is *personal*—such as the special stone or feather you find while on a quest. Photos are another example; they give instant access to people we've lost and miss who are still part of our personal story. The ancient Egyptians were very loving, since they were taught as children to live with their Ka in; their statues of the ancient ones in the Egyptian Museum in Cairo are so imbued with timeless force that you can still feel their love of the Nile when you look into their quartz and lapis eyes.[8] When we reweave our own threads to the eternal forms, the nine-dimensional vertical axis pushes from Earth to sky like a great ancient oak tree. To better understand how this geometric permanence actually exists, let us now consider the science of the sixth dimension.

The Science of the Sixth Dimension

According to astronomers and biologists, the universe is very ordered. Light streams away from stars, while on Earth we find complex molecules and complicated lifeforms that exist in sunlight. Only an exceptional initial condition and a great ordering intelligence could be behind this.[9] Sacred science studies order in the universe and seeks correspondences and relationships in the world that reflect divine forces. A realm of geometric forms directs nature.

For thousands of years people thought the world of forms was real and that it directs the world. This ended only one hundred years ago when Einstein announced his relativity theory.[10] In his way of thinking, concepts such as space and time—which were thought of as separate and absolute—became intertwined and relative. Until the late 1990s, most scientists believed that relativity theory proves that the speed of light is constant and the realm of geometric forms exists only in our minds. Einstein's general theory, however, does not apply to the way I explore dimensionality; and the difference between a relative and ordered universe must be clear. There is a chasm between general relativity and an ordered universe, a dilemma which tortured Einstein in his dotage. A number of physicists are finding fundamental flaws in relativity (see chapter 7); they are realizing that there was no real reason to drop the directing world of forms, since there have to be geometric structures that hold EM frequencies. *Whether thought of as tiny little strings or great big triangles, fundamental forms exist that order the universe.* Otherwise, all would be chaos.

Tetrahedron   Hexahedron   Octahedron   Dodecahedron   Icosahedron

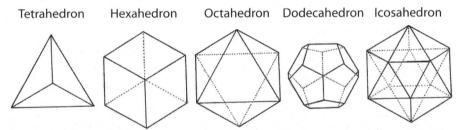

Figure 6.3 The five Platonic solids: tetrahedron, hexahedron (cube), octahedron, dodecahedron, icosahedron.

It is difficult to describe the 6D morphic realm without showing how it is derived from sound (the property of 7D), since *sound generates the geometry in 6D.* Let us begin with imagining Julian Barbour's configurations as Triangle Land: a limitless, timeless, eternal world of triangles. Triangle Land is easier to visualize than *Tetrahedron Land,* a world of tetrahedrons, which already has six dimensions.[11] Another way to visualize 6D is by playing with five quartz carvings of the Platonic solids (figure 6.3), as I have done throughout the writing of this book. Attempting to see these forms in your inner mind will help you visualize 6D. After all, these five forms are the geometric basis of all living things. Imagine the entire 3D universe constructed of these configurations and all their relationships in space. Next, imagine them vibrating with frequencies while replicating things in 3D.

For example, see the 6D form of Cow replicating as cows in our world (see figure 6.1). Platonia is mathematical perfection, which Barbour is able to model, since mathematics relates higher to lower orders. Yet he could not visualize much beyond Triangle Land. Imagine Icosahedron Land and what it might be replicating! Since *The Pleiadian Agenda* was inspired by my vision of a luminous icosahedral sphere (see introduction), the nine dimensions may well be generated from Icosahedron Land. You will need to study Barbour's *The End of Time: The Next Revolution in Physics* to take this further on your own, which I heartily recommend.

In the nine-dimensional model, the vibrating forms from 6D replicate as lifeforms of every possible variety in 3D, and also as nonliving things. The nautilus shell always grows by the Fibonacci spiral,[12] as does the sunflower, as well as many other proportions in plants and animal skeletons.[13] The Golden Mean (*phi*) math ratio of 1:1.618 determines the Fibonacci spiral, and the spiral is the basis of materialization. At the subatomic level, spin generates primal movement, which begins any materialization, which in turn becomes spiralic in matter. These two factors of spirals regulate how 6D geometric forms replicate in the material realm.

The Golden Mean spiral spins energy from one state to another by shifts in frequency ranges, which are measured in hertz. Simple geometric forms, such as a circle or square, vibrate at lower frequencies; more complex forms, such as an icosahedron (made of 20 triangular faces), vibrate faster. The idea is that 6D is filled up with all these configurations—simple and complex—and they replicate in 3D via frequencies in EM fields that can be measured in hertz. To my way of thinking, the less complex geometry manifests less complex things, while the advanced geometric forms generate complex worlds.

From the ancient Egyptians to the classical Greeks, geometry was part of the search for truth, a way to order the universe. Geometry was an integral part of the physical world, and temples were built to access the laws of perfection in higher worlds and to imprint these laws in the minds of the people. Since I have actually seen this higher order (my vision at the Acropolis), I never doubt that we emanate from geometric configurations, and we can embody these configurations with yoga and meditation. I stress relativity theory here because it has caused modern science to make geometry into a separate science, while algebraic theory spins further out into many worlds. This split is making it difficult to recognize the power of the 6D influence right in our reality and in our bodies. Yet this is the way to discover order in nature and be healthy!

Modern science is making us sick by often using only a portion of its own data. We can see sacred geometry—the substratum of all things—in nature, which ought to be taken more seriously than successful experiments in particle accelerators. After all, we can see geometry in ancient fossils; the Platonic solids are the basis of organic life. Julian Barbour has brought back the world of forms and offered a new theory that takes us beyond relativity. By practicing yoga, we can mold our bodies into our 6D M-fields.

Now let's visit some folks on the planet who can actually *see* the eternal forms that replicate, make art that shows these forms, and relate these forms to the organic basis of life.

Shamans, DNA, and Biophotons

In the early 1980s, Amazonian shamans told anthropologist Jeremy Narby that they identify the medicinal properties of plants while drinking ayahuasca, a hallucinogenic brew. He thought they were joking, but he decided to study them because international agencies were planning to "develop" the Amazon. Narby could see that the people were handling themselves perfectly well, and they were deeply comfortable with nature. He wanted to find a way to support the Ashininca tribal people and their deep knowledge of plants. The shamans said the reason for their knowledge was ayahuasca, so he began by figuring out what they were *seeing* in their visions. They see visions of brightly colored images that look like DNA, chromosomes, and triple helixes such as collagen—images similar to those discovered and photographed by molecular biologists.[14]

Certainly, the people knew how to use the plants for medicinal purposes. Narby suspected they might be seeing the actual language of the plants—DNA—through symbols, and they could somehow interpret them. Scientists do not know how vision functions; that is, how the brain gets information and makes coherent images of things, much less how people see visions. Of course, my view is that the brain reads and transmits EM frequencies, which are detected by all of our senses including vision. The people were clearly finding something that actually exists in plants. There was a connection between their plant knowledge and the content of their visions.

Figure 6.4 The Australian aboriginal cosmic serpent compared with chromosomes and DNA helixes. Adapted from *The Cosmic Serpent,* Jeremy Narby, pp. 78, 80. (A) "A painting on hardboard of the Snake of the Marinbata people of Arnhem Land." Adapted by Narby from Huxley (1974, p. 127). (B) Adapted by Narby from *Biology: An Appreciation of Life,* CRM Books, Del Mar, California, 1972. (C) Early prophase: "Each chromosome is visible as two sister chromatids." (D) Anaphase II: "... the migration of homologous chromatids to opposite poles." Images C and D adapted by Narby from *Molecular Biology of the Gene, Vol. 1,* 4th ed., by Watson et al. Copyright © 1987 by James D. Watson, published by The Benjamin/ Cummings Publishing Company.

Shamans often see serpentine images, especially double ones, which resemble the DNA double helix. The DNA molecule is a single long chain made of two interwoven ribbons connected by four bases; DNA is both single and double, just like mythical serpents. While having visions, shamans must find a way to interpret what they are seeing; in this case, serpents are their best representation. In contrast, the biologist who takes ayahuasca might see strands of actual DNA, with which he or she is more familiar.

The DNA replication mechanism is the same for all living things on Earth and always has been. Earth's surface has changed many times, yet DNA and its replication process is always the same. That is, DNA is the mechanism for 6D replication in 3D. Narby concludes that *DNA is the origin of the shamanic knowledge.* Incredibly, these shamans can read DNA language while in an altered state. But how? Is there a neurological basis to this skill?

DNA emits photons, which are electromagnetic waves in the narrow band of visible light; these emissions are called *biophotons.* These emissions have a high degree of coherence. Researchers say DNA is an ultra-weak laser (a split beam that can produce holograms), and "a coherent source of light, like a laser, gives the sensation of bright colors, a luminescence, and an impression of holographic depth."[15] Molecular biologists who study biophotons describe these emissions as "cellular language," a form of subtle biocommunication between cells. These waves direct internal systems, and they communicate among themselves, and even between other organisms. As Narby realizes, this could explain how plankton cooperate in swarms as if they were "super-organisms."[16]

Quartz devices are used for the experiments on biophotons, such as the device used to detect the ultra-weak laser emissions from DNA. Quartz crystals have been used forever as tools by indigenous people to detect frequencies. In fact, they are excellent receptors of EM waves or frequencies, since they are piezoelectric, or flash with light when you rub them together. Quartz crystals always grow by hexagonal or six-sided geometry, and remember, the iron core's crystalline structure is hexagonal (see chapter 1). I use quartz crystals as devices for divining M-fields in things around myself. I also use quartz to hold data banks, so that I need not remember too much all the time. When I am working on a big data bank, I receive data in holograms. When my head gets too packed, I send the monad of thoughts into a crystal, which I keep in my work area, such as one of the quartz Platonic solids. The crystal emanates it back to me when I need a recall or a quick start. That is, I encode the crystal with time capsules, and then I can recall the path that accesses the mist when I want to.

Narby is suggesting that shamans have learned how to defocus their consciousness to see DNA. This is true because any working shaman already knows how to do this; it is just very hard to explain to people who don't think it possible. It is how people just "know" something; for example, how a medical intuitive like Carolyn Myss can read organic imbalances. Next we will explore an incredible ancient system that connects the 6D world of forms with cultures in 3D by means of sacred geography.

Sacred Geography and the Wheel of Twelve

The French scholar and writer Jean Richer studied the orientation and siting of many ancient temples in Greece.[17] The axis of each temple is usually aligned to the rising of heavenly bodies, and the god of the temple is symbolized by various planetary deities. By identifying which planets are which gods, he established the existence of complex astrological systems. He has concluded that the Greek landscape is a huge zodiacal pattern made of wheels of the twelve astrological signs. The landscape mirrors the zodiac, a classic "as above, so below." All the main sacred sites are marked by famous temples and mountain peaks. Jean Richer simply proved his theory, and he left it to other researchers, especially mythologists, to apply it to their own fields, and for others to ask, why these patterns? Why would any culture go to this much trouble?

Luckily, John Michell and Christine Rhone pursued this question in *Twelve-Tribe Nations and the Science of Enchanting the Landscape.* They discovered that astrological systems made of giant zodiac wheels exist *all over the whole world.* Some of these remnants are thousands of years old, and the most famous one is the twelve tribes system of Israel.[18] This complex ancient landscape system that relates the sky to the land is a proven fact about our planet. It is truly remarkable and mind-boggling, yet most archaeologists and anthropologists just ignore this finding.[19]

Michell and Rhone conclude that older civilizations used this system to maintain stability by what they call the *principle of enchantment.*[20] They constructed complex systems of temples utilizing features in the landscape to ground higher-dimensional forces. Within these systems, art and ceremony occurred based on seasonal time cycles that wove together the mundane and spiritual realms. They believe that this form of life is the most conducive to human happiness and freedom, as well as assuring that communities are settled and peaceful, which contrasts sharply with the lack of stability in modern life. These systems were a global method for drawing down the 6D world of ideal forms (in this case cultural) into 3D.

According to Michell and Rhone, in the land arranged and marked according to the zodiac, the activities in each region were scheduled by the seasons. This system regulated every aspect of life from the ceremonial systems to the arrangements of clans, villages, and families. Where you were born was the archetype you expressed during your life, and everyone created art, drama, and music that expressed his or her own archetype. People would travel to enjoy the mystery plays, myth, and music of the other clans, and this maintained the people in harmony with nature. Michell and Rhone think this system is the Celtic version of the Grail. It is said that one who drinks from the Grail will return to the state of being in the primordial vision. This can only be achieved via sharper and more intuitive perceptions. The zodiac wheels made it possible for people to find enchantment by making the landscape into a cosmology, a model of the universe.

Plato says that by musical control the ancient Egyptians preserved their civilization from corruption for more than ten thousand years.[21] In his *Laws,* Plato calls this *a canon of sacred music.*[22] Plato was an initiate of the Heliopolitan Mystery School, which invented the nine-dimensional model.[23] If Plato says the Egyptians did this for 10,000 years, I think we should believe him.

I think of the return of the enchanted landscape—the Grail—as a potent mist, since so many people seek it today. The mystery plays and ceremonies were carried out yearly to express the potent 4D archetypes that were flowing through the people. The patterning of the land by geomancy enhanced the 2D powers, while the temples calibrated heavenly frequencies so that the larger cycles of time could guide evolutionary unfoldment. Michell and Rhone use the term "enchantment" because in medieval times, monks and nuns used chanting to bring higher dimensions to Earth. This is a classic example of 7D sound making forms in 6D that are perceived by us in 3D. These experiences connected all the people to each other, making 4D into a circulating river of time that pulled in higher dimensions. To better understand this idea, we need to consider astrology, a potent mist in Platonia.

Astrology and the Sixth Dimension

Another form of 6D access is through the practice of astrology, which involves knowing the archetypal patterns in your natal chart and observing how the movement of the planets, Moon, and Sun—transits—influence your birth chart. Unlike sacred geography, this practice is still used by many modern people. Astrology was the basis of the principle of enchantment described by Michell and Rhone, as well as the basis of Richer's Greek temple system. Modern astrology is psychodynamic and helps us to pull ourselves out of linear time by showing us how the drama of life is artificially pressed into past, present, and future. Besides offering a wide time perspective, astrology teaches people that various planets have different effects on events and emotions, and links people to higher fields. Once you start thinking this way, often you are able to access very high dimensions available right inside the feelings and events going on around you. Feelings are awesome because they intensify 4D, which makes it easier to detect frequencies from 5D through 9D. Cultures ruled by enchantment taught people how to recognize these influences and express them as a group in geography, art, astrology, and seasonality. What a rich life that was for thousands of years.

Until writing this book, I thought of astrology as a 4D practice, since the planets carry the 4D archetypal forces, such as Mars ruling war or Venus ruling love. However, astrology is a 6D art because it teaches us how to manage the 4D archetypal forces and to align our emotions with our originating form. I discovered the Wheel of Twelve (see chapter 3) when I was called to teach large groups after doing natal readings for many years. I developed it to help students free themselves from 4D duality so they could move up into higher dimensions. There is great similarity between the sacred geography wheels of twelve and my system, which is an instant balancing tool that is suited for modern life. Using the Wheel of Twelve is often magical for people, just as the enchanted landscape must have been. Maybe the ancient people used astrology in ways similar to the Wheel of Twelve, or maybe it is getting charged in the mist by all the people using it these days.

Long ago, the ancient ones lived when it was still possible to hear the sounds of the heavens. They knew about the potent effects of sound on consciousness, and they seemed to know about the science of sound—sonics. They used 7D sound to create 6D geometry to open their 5D hearts, while they spent their days playing with the 4D archetypes to maintain peace and harmony in 3D. As you will see next, sonics was highly advanced for thousands of years, which is perhaps the best explanation for how prehistoric people constructed megalithic complexes from stones weighing many tons apiece. Much evidence for ancient sonics is being discovered at the present time, which is very exciting.

SEVEN

The Seventh Dimension:
The Galactic Highways of Light

Opening Meditation

Sit back and let your body find itself. Find your breath, find your feet. Let go of your brain for a while; it's like a muscle, and it has been working hard for you. Let your eyes relax; they have been working hard, too. Let your eyes just notice the light and colors around you, and the spaces around you, as a big, soft, comfortable blur. The only focus you need is when you read these words, and you can do that slowly, as you breathe, letting your body settle a bit more with each breath.

Become aware of each breath as it comes into your head. See if you can feel how each breath seems to fill your head, right out to the edges. Play with this feeling inside your head. Breathe slowly and mindfully. This is like giving your brain a massage. Experiment. Continue to relax your eyes, to make your focus soft, and continue to relax and settle down in your body.

Now become aware of the middle of your forehead as you breathe. Let each new breath come into your body through this area. How does that feel? Can you feel an opening there? Can you visualize this happening inside your head? Notice any sensations you may be feeling there, and just stay with your breath, and with these sensations.

Now, find your mind. Your mind is where your thoughts come from. Your mind is your brain being conscious of itself. It should feel relaxed and soft. It is resting. Now, see if you are curious about anything, some place or thing you'd like to travel to. See with your inner sight where you go. See if you can hear any tones, high or low, beckoning from a distance. Travel with your mind to anywhere you want to go. Breathe, and see how each breath takes you further, how each breath makes each vision clearer.

Stay with this vision as long as you want to. Let the vision teach you, show you. Enjoy your visit, your ability to see at a distance. When you return, travel into your mind through the middle of your forehead. . . . Dial up another vision: Go to another place, any place. Experiment. You are traveling the lines of light in the Galaxy.

When you are ready, take a deep breath, and find your body. Find your feet. Feel the center of your forehead. Become aware of your breath filling your whole body. Remember the visions you have received, and know that it is there for you to return to at any time.

The seventh dimension is a realm of cosmic sound that generates the 6D geometric forms by vibrational resonance. Sound originates in the vibrational frequencies of the spinning, orbiting bodies in the universe, but what moves the bodies? According to the Ps, the Divine Mind or God influences all the bodies in the universe by movement and measure. In the Milky Way, cosmic sound travels within the great 7D photon bands that structure the Galaxy itself (figure 7.1). Within the photon bands, 8D

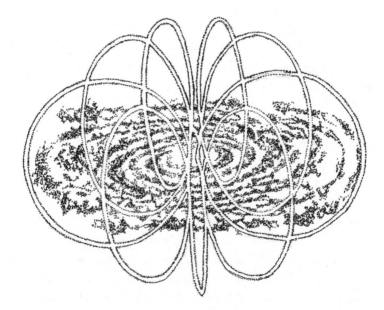

Figure 7.1 Cosmic sound traveling in the great photon bands that structure the Milky Way.

"thought waves of light" step down by octaves into lower frequency 7D sound waves. These waves circulate galactic energy into the spheric field of the Milky Way. Since sound waves are lower frequency than light waves, these waves sing the Divine Mind. The great photon bands spin out of the Galactic Center, circle within the galactic sphere, and then return through the center torqued by the galactic plane's powerful axial spin. This classic torus (doughnut) dynamic is generated by the great vertical axis that rises out of the Galactic Center at right angles to the galactic plane. Fountains of light rush through it and circulate, and these galactic highways of light carry 8D thought waves as high frequency light.

The Divine Mind permeates the whole galactic sphere, while the 7D zone is within the torus that holds the form of the galactic plane. These singing bands generate parallel possibilities in 3D, or *synchronicities*, in which we humans can sense the intentions of the 8D Divine Mind. If we follow these leads, life becomes a dance in the higher dimensions. The Photon Band that is now activating Earth (see chapter 5) is a key part of the great Milky Way structure. The Photon Band has joined Alcyone, our Sun, and the Sirius star system in a synchronistic flow that started 225 million years ago, when Earth was selected to seed the Galaxy with its biology. Now that our solar system is being activated by the Galactic Center, Earth is experiencing the nine-dimensional activation, which is transmuting its biology. Sacred cultures that mastered multidimensional consciousness in the past are needed for guidance, such as the Maya, since scientists are only now beginning to consider multidimensionality by means of superstring theory.

The Keeper of 7D is Andromeda, which is now converging with the Milky Way while all other galaxies are moving away.[1] Andromeda is visible as an exquisite spiral in the night sky spinning just outside our galactic plane. The Ps say Andromeda has a huge influence on the Milky Way, especially within our solar system, since Andromeda has a similar solar system. Within it, there is a planet called *Aion*, which is like Earth in every way, with a similar location to its Sun, good climate and atmosphere, and a fecund biology that replicates. The only difference between these two solar systems is that Aion did not experience a great cataclysm, as Earth did 11,500 years ago. Aion's inhabitants are devoid of collective trauma, and all the higher dimensions freely enhance its biology. Aion directs its cultures with cosmic sound and light codes by using sacred science. In Andromeda there is no splitting or separation from God, while in the Milky Way, as we near the end of the Mayan calendar, we cannot remember Gaia's biological codes. Because Andromeda has retained this biological knowledge, it is the Keeper of 7D for Earth. Andromeda transmits harmonic records by sound from the Aion Library to the center of the Milky Way, and the vibrational intensity of the records is rising exponentially. This is indeed a powerful mist in Platonia. Earth's inhabitants suffer from severe collective post-traumatic stress syndrome, and minds are locked in the lower dimensions, especially in 4D. The Elite manipulates the people, and its members crown themselves Keepers of 3D.

According to the Pleiadians, in light of this gross distortion in 3D, Andromeda created a new program two thousand years ago called the "Cosmic Restart Button." They sent Christ, a 9D Messiah (singer of God's frequencies), to Earth. He came to reawaken love in the human heart so that each person could heal from trauma, and the Ps say our DNA reformulates by love. In those days, the people got the message because Christ was human in all ways and infused his blood into Earth. The truth is, Christ fathered children, a seminal act that awakened Earth's biology.[2] This story—the *hidden* teaching of the Holy Grail—has been carefully guarded; the Messiah threatened the Elite plan to control Earth. Regardless of the Elite agenda, Andromeda is the Keeper of 7D for Earth—their "Cosmic Restart Button" is working—and now our Galaxy is being informed about harmonic biology and undamaged DNA.

The Ps also tell us that the new energy coming to Earth from Andromeda is being received in our hearts. Christ seeded humanity with *grace,* which draws each one of us to a new level. We are withdrawing from the Elite organized religions and reclaiming the sacred. Satya, saucy as usual, says we are remembering the "erotic" Christ, the cosmic progenitor of humankind. Organized religions deny the very nature of the alchemical male, which is why this juicy force has been perverted into sexual abuse. The building wave of grace is freeing the minds of the people, who feel the potency of the Grail. Many people now know that Christ was married to Mary Magdalene, and that he seeded a 9D bloodline into Earth's people.[3]

To elucidate how dimensional shifts work, we will move down from 7D into 6D. Notice in figure 7.1 that the photon bands are all interconnected in the Galactic Center. This central weave distills pure thought into the 6D geometric light forms, the configurations of Platonia. When the Divine Mind (in the Galactic Center) sends out new patterns, the mist in Platonia shifts. Moldy old ideas about big institutions, such as the New World Order and the Vatican, collapse like punctured balloons. New domes of mist vibrate with inspiring ideas, such as Christ being a lover and a father. The erotic responses of the people thicken the nascent, glowing mist. By following whims and creating new realities in 3D, the corresponding mist thickens and new things manifest instantly in the solid world. Have you ever followed up on an intriguing course of action, and it manifested so quickly that you could hardly handle the results? This is a sign you are really in tune. Creation works best when you move quickly to grasp the potential or *seize the moment*. When we ignore hot and juicy ideas, the pregnant mist dissipates; then the old mist grows right back, and Platonia fills up with fog.

The New World Order knows all about Platonia and the mist, which is why the science of geometric forms was eliminated from Elite-controlled education. The Elite reserves real knowledge for its own use while it mind-controls the public; it thickens the desired mist by working with Hollywood (Holyrood) to create ideas to be implanted in the public mind. Remember, *each individual mind has the same power in Platonia;* everyone has one vote and can instantaneously draw down his or her own ideas. Since "we the people" greatly outnumber the Elite, we are the most potent force, which is why the Elite programs are so huge right now. The Elite farms the mist by culling minds, such as through television—"tell-a-vision." The exquisite Andromeda galaxy is beaming out a potent twinning force as it spins and weaves near the Milky Way. The message from Andromeda is *take control of your own mind now.*

The Ps say that 7D sound is the communications system of the Galaxy. In 3D we get threads of this system through birdsong and the migratory patterns of birds. Have you ever wondered how birds migrate? They orient by galactic energy lines, which they follow in Earth's magnetic fields. (An incredible film on birds in flight—*Winged Migration*—came to the theaters while I was writing this book, and it will help you to understand 7D.) The Divine Mind moves energy within gravitational fields, while birds hear this movement and mimic it by their flight and song. Because we are filled with grace, birds enhance our creativity. As bluebirds sing and fly, they attune 3D to the blue band that surrounds Earth, the place where cosmic sound meets the outer boundary of Earth's gravity.

We can radiate our love out into the whole biosphere by attuning our minds to this gravitational "sound" boundary. You can soar beyond terra firma in your heart and see Earth as the blue planet in space and remember your role as Keeper. When you attain this consciousness, birdsong informs you in ways that no language can. Gerry recalls that whenever he felt lonely or lost, he would lie down at the edge of the forest and listen to birds calling in the trees overhead.

Language has divided humanity, simply because it is so mired in 3D. Birdsong and sacred music pull us beyond duality and attune us to high celestial frequencies, which draw our consciousness to the outer edges of Earth's gravitational field. When you are in mystical bliss while living in ordinary reality, you've gone there. There have been times when Earth cultures maintained themselves in bliss by sacred sound. Language and writing were of little interest to them, except in the mundane. Sacred sound thickens and quickens the healthy biological mist. At this time, celestial sounds quicken Earth as Andromeda beams our Galactic Center. Cosmic consciousness is becoming audible on Earth by sacred sound from the Galactic Center. We are being reattuned with nature.

The Science of the Seventh Dimension

I will begin by summarizing what is known about sound and frequency waves. Sound functions in both the audible and inaudible frequency zones, which are of lesser magnitude than light. All sound vibrations are grouped in octaves, or sequences of eight notes. The easiest way to grasp this is to consider the piano (see figure 7.2). The white keys play seven or eight octaves, or groupings of eight notes. Each octave is C-D-E-F-G-A-B-C, with C repeating as the beginning of the next higher octave. Each key vibrates at a certain number of pulses per second—hertz (Hz)—and each octave is a doubling of frequencies. For example, lower A is 220 Hz, middle A is 440 Hz, and higher A is 880 Hz, and when one A is struck, all the other As in the piano vibrate with it. This is the principle of resonance, the vibratory responses of frequencies, such as the As on the piano. What is going on?

Figure 7.2 Octaves on the piano.

Sound is the vibration of air molecules, which we measure by pulses per second, or hertz. The vibrations of molecules create solidity, sound, color, light, and all living beings. Light vibrates at a very high frequency many octaves above sound waves. White light is a frequency range (like sound) called the visible light spectrum (VLS), which breaks down into color. Red is the lowest frequency, violet the highest, and it goes red-orange-yellow-green-blue-indigo-violet. This means you resonate with higher frequencies by wearing violet and lower frequencies by wearing red, which is why gurus wear violet robes and barflies wear red dresses. These simple octaves underlie all matter; *everything is made of vibrations.* Once this is fully comprehended, it makes sense that the many dimensions could form in planes where certain frequencies vibrate. We cannot see or hear extremely high dimensions, just as we cannot hear sound much above the range of the piano keyboard. But literally anything could be vibrating in these higher zones, but such things would not be physical, as we are in 3D.

The easiest way to grasp dimensionality is to think about frequency waves in octaves and to visualize objects as frequency-wave patterns. The human audible range is of a much lower frequency than the visible light spectrum. Pianos and tuning forks demonstrate the audible vibratory ranges. Crystals set in sunlight project the VLS as color spectrums on walls; similarly, raindrops make light frequencies visible in rainbows. These simple things in nature help us know that higher frequencies (that we cannot see or hear) are there.

The principle of resonance and octaves shows that frequencies get higher and higher; every time the notes of the scale—C through C—are doubled, we have a new octave. Imagine doubling them over and over, and moving off the piano and out of the audible hearing range. If you could do this, eventually you'd be up to the frequency of light, and if you kept on doubling, you'd discover gamma rays. *We resonate with all these frequencies.*

Like C resonating with C on the piano, we resonate with very high octaves of sound and light whether we are conscious of it or not. How light *functions* is the subject of 8D, yet for now it helps to know that *we are resonating with light when we hear sound.*

Cymatics

Moving back down dimensionally, we will consider how sound creates 6D geometric forms. There is an actual science that studies this action: cymatics, the study of the geometric patterns that are made by sound, which makes "sound-creating-form" visible. As we discussed above, frequencies are just molecules moving in air, many of which we cannot see, yet devices have been constructed that register and measure them. To "see" sound frequencies, all we need is a *medium*—something that makes visible the geometric forms of the molecules. Actually, this is quite elementary, but I sure got knocked over the first time I saw a cymatics machine!

Gerry and I took a course in sound healing with John Beaulieu, who demonstrated how sound creates geometry.[4] John's cymatics machine has a thin copper disk about 25 inches in diameter, which has a copper rod through the center. The copper rod is vibrated by various tones being tuned up or down—raising or lowering the frequencies. The disk is covered with a very thin layer of extremely fine sand (silica), and the tones generate geometric patterns in the sand according to frequencies. With each tone, the design alters dramatically. As we watched the sand flowing, it clearly moved according to geometric forms that have borders and vortexes of inner flow; we could see sound making geometry. This shows how sound creates geometry, which eventually replicates things in 3D. We witnessed 7D down through 3D in action.

The main developer of cymatics, Hans Jenny, M.D., used many different mediums, such as jellies and sand, to make the patterns of sound visible. He has made videos of how the changes in frequencies alter shapes in the mediums. Low frequencies create simple geometric forms, and high frequencies create very complex forms. Watching a cymatics experiment makes it possible to see that everything oscillates, vibrates, and undulates in nature, which results in organisms and things. Forms are all patterned by vibrational frequencies that lead all the way up to sound and eventually to light. This can only be observed through mediums that show frequencies in action; *frequencies are the basis of everything.* I've mentioned many times in this book that the Platonic solids are the basic geometric forms that make up all matter, yet this does not mean much until you see it in action.[5] When the sand in the cymatics machine responds to tones that vibrate the plate at a certain frequency, the geometry moves in, around, and through tetrahedrons, cubes, octahedrons, and so forth. We watched the Platonic forms being created by vibrations.

The mathematician and astronomer Gerald Hawkins has established that the octave scale is often the basis of crop circles.[6] The end tips of the forms can be used to draw large circles, while there are various circles within the designs themselves (figure 7.3). When he divided the surface area of the inner geometries by the areas of the outer circles, he found that they often show octave relationships—the diatonic scale. The octaves increase by ratios, which means this geometry is harmonic, or has pleasing resonance. Since many crop circles show the octaves, they are showing sound creating geometry, just like the cymatics machine. We can be sure crop circles are important because the Elite works so hard to debunk them (see chapter 10).

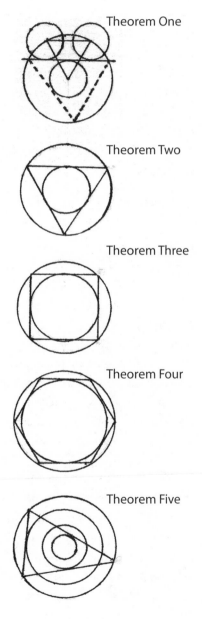

Theorem One

Theorem Two

Theorem Three

Theorem Four

Theorem Five

Figure 7.3 The basic theorems of Euclidean geometry: 1) tangency, 2) triangle, 3) square, 4) hexagon, 5) general. These show all the diatonic ratios.

Frequency ranges are measurable, and humans can see, hear, and feel a limited portion of the total range. By understanding how detectable frequencies function and knowing they increase exponentially by octaves and resonance, we can infer that high-frequency dimensions are real in the universe. We cannot know the "name" of God, simply because this frequency is way beyond language in our dimension—the *ineffable*—yet we can be sure God is there. By resonance, we *feel* divine grace; and the more we know this, the more we can raise our own frequencies in response. Physics has responded to this situation by birthing a new branch of study called string theory, which includes superstring theory, that is actually reaching for the ineffable. Although very complex, string theory operates in 7D and shows how the nine-dimensional system functions mathematically. String theory first gained wide scientific respect the same year *The Pleiadian Agenda* came out, in 1995, yet only physicists had access to its formula at that time.

Superstring Theory and a Variable Speed of Light

String theory catapulted to a new level in 1995 when one of the most brilliant physicists of all time, Edward Witten, ignited a second superstring revolution (the first revolution was from 1984–1986). Witten formulated *M-theory,* which unifies the five string theories, and created a context for *eleven* dimensions. The fundamental entities of string theory are incredibly tiny, vibrating strings that have spatial extent but no content. That is, the basic energy units of matter—quanta—are oscillating strings, not atoms or particles.

The observed particle properties (electrons, quarks, or neutrinos) are simply reflections of the various ways the strings can vibrate. Light waves are always traveling, and everything is vibrating. Just as a violin string vibrates and we hear specific notes, the vibrational patterns of the strings give rise to different masses and force changes. According to string theorist Brian Greene, "there is a direct association between the pattern of string vibrations, and the particle's response to the gravitational force."[7]

Gravity dictates the rhythm of the cosmic dance. The graviton (smallest particle of gravity) is one particular pattern of string vibrations. Just as an EM field (such as visible light) is composed of many photons, a gravitational field is composed of many gravitons.[8] Many vibrating strings are executing the patterns encoded in the dimensions as well as creating material things. The very fabric of the dimensions is a pattern of vibrating gravitons with different frequencies. The electrical charge, the strong and weak charge, and gravitational fields are determined by the precise ways the strings vibrate. Greene uses the poetic image of the strings as the "threads of the spacetime fabric."[9]

In string theory, the nature of all matter and forces is the same; what appears to be different particles are "notes" on particular strings. Everything in the universe exists by these oscillating, vibrating strings. Many physicists are seeking a unified theory of the micro- and macrocosm, and Greene notes that string theory is a "cogent framework for merging quantum mechanics; general relativity; and the strong, weak, and electromagnetic forces."[10]

String theory is building a beautiful bridge between the microcosm and the macrocosm by discovering that the properties that distinguish one particle from another—mass, force, charge, and spin—are the same as the properties that distinguish one black hole from another. Greene comments that "black holes might actually be gigantic elementary particles."[11] This leads to the idea that there is a potent transmutational relationship going on between the oscillating massless strings and the gigantic vibrational patterns of black holes. These ideas give support to theories of dimensional structures that can hold such energy and structures.

String theory equations are unbelievably complex, and few people comprehend them, yet their laws are being aggressively pursued. Greene notes that the actual shapes of the extra dimensions (imagined as Calabi-Yau shapes; see figure 7.4) determine whether the configurations appear as black holes or elementary particles.[12] String theory has a very different interpretation of the microcosm from quantum mechanics, and it works perfectly well in the micro- or macrocosm.

String theory opens the doors to understanding 7D because it explains the nature of *movement* in the universe in the smallest and largest realms. Nonscientists who have contemplated EM frequencies and the visible light spectrum can sense out string theory. The strings vibrate by all the forces, including gravity, since their energy comes from vibrations and windings, such as the knots in topology (see chapter 5).

As we move up the vertical axis and wander into some very high dimensions, the physics gets extremely complex, which is accurately reflected by string theory. The *structure* that has emerged since 1995 in string theory—eleven spatial dimensions—is so close to the Pleiadian system that it is basically the same. I will cover a few aspects that have to do with dimensionality.

Take M-theory, for example: Its integration of five different string theories means that string theorists are describing five different views of one grand theory. The five string theories are each equations that describe nonextended dimensions that "curl up" into this dimension. For the last hundred years, the laws of physics have been associated with symmetry, a property of physical systems that enables them *not* to change when the system is transformed in some way; a sphere is rotationally symmetrical, since it looks the same when you rotate it. As physicists and mathematicians have probed ever deeper into nature, the importance of symmetry has been growing, and now it appears that everything in the universe is operating by exquisite supersymmetrical laws.[13]

In the latest superstring theory, the incredible energy inherent in the vibrating strings requires eleven dimensions in the universe.[14] The laws of physics are always the same everywhere, from the smallest to the largest things, yet things do not look the same because of vibrations and dimensionality. Considering eleven dimensions for a moment, there are three extended spatial dimensions (which the Ps describe as 1D through 3D), and then string theorists consider eight more. But, where are they?

Figure 7.4 6D Calabi-Yau spaces on a 3D grid. Adapted from *The Elegant Universe*, Brian Greene, p. 208.

Figure 7.4 shows six-dimensional geometric shapes—called Calabi-Yau spaces—on a 3D grid, as an example of what physicists create for visual assistance to imagine how nonextended dimensions ("subtle" in the Pleiadian system) might interface.[15] To describe the dimensions, string theorists use a concept called *branes* (the latter half of *membranes*), which are planar, two-dimensional objects and not just flat. A one-dimensional brane—one-brane—is the basic vibrating string itself; a two-brane is the membrane of a dimension; a three-brane is an extended object with three spatial dimensions; four-brane is space-time; and it goes up to nine-branes. The idea is that maybe we live on a three-brane—a huge three-dimensional membrane to which a time dimension is added—and we're stuck in it and can't see out of it.[16] Considering figure 7.4, we *are* stuck in 3D and can't see out of it, yet all the higher dimensions are imagined interfacing with us via Calabi-Yau shapes on a 3D grid.

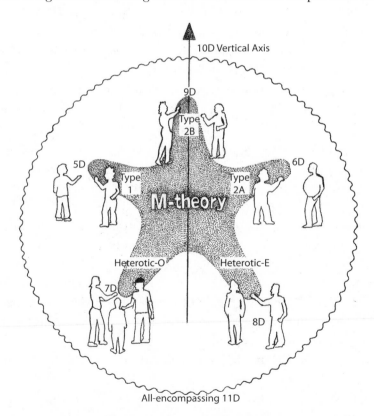

Figure 7.5 A hypothetical imposition of the nine dimensions into Edward Witten's M-theory. Adapted from *The Elegant Universe,* Brian Greene, p. 287.

The M-theory illustration (see figure 7.5) is Witten's model of the unification of the five theories, in which the branes are on equal footing. For readers who know something about M-theory, the illustration takes a stab at placing 5D through 9D into brane theory. The first four dimensions are contained within the starlike figure; the next five—5D to 9D—are noted; 10D is the vertical axis; and 11D is supergravity, or the all-encompassing fabric. I made my own judgment on where to place 5D through 9D by considering the connections between the five theories, since nobody understands what these equations really describe. The branes sound exactly like the nine dimensions, and the string physicists add a vertical axis, which is actually 10D in the Pleiadian system, while 11D is the container.[17] My main focus is how all this relates to the vertical axis model; and remember, the Ps said we are now developing the capacity to understand *nine* dimensions, not eleven.

What first made me think string theory might be the 7D hard science is that string theory also offers a scientific basis for the 7D Pleiadian "galactic information highways of light." Obviously, the galactic highways of light are some kind of high-energy transportation system in the Galaxy. Physicists study cosmic strings—hypothetical objects predicted by some particle physics theories—that are "long threads of concentrated energy extending across the universe."[18] Portuguese physicist João Magueijo, who has proposed important theories for a variable speed of light (as opposed to Einstein's constant), has written equations that show that the speed of light could become much faster in the vicinity of these cosmic strings, as if "a coating of high light-speed enveloped it. . . . This would create a corridor with an extremely high speed limit extending across the universe."[19]

Magueijo realizes that these corridors would mean a space traveler could move at very high speeds, which some people, such as some physicists and the explorer Jacob Atabet,[20] can do with their minds. I think these corridors (galactic highways of light) suggest that there are three speeds of light in the universe. I suspect that Einstein's constant—186,000 miles per second—is the speed of light for 1D through 3D; a second speed of light governs 4D through 6D; and 7D through 9D are moving even faster.[21]

Just to speculate a bit, what could be traveling in these corridors? Muons—the quintessential higher-dimensional light frequencies—vibrate in the light spectrum as the background particles of cosmic radiation that stretch time.[22] Maybe the highways are muon bands? Magueijo and a colleague investigated connections between a form of geometry in which space-time appears atomized, as well as M-theory.[23] They discovered that high-frequency photons speed up, and the speed is color-dependent. Physicists are actively pursuing a color-dependent variable speed of light, which I think will be the key to detecting scientifically the structure of the dimensions. Even though these concepts may seem very difficult to us today, thousands of years ago our ancestors were in divine communion— through sound—with the tiny and potent vibrating strings and cosmic black holes that end up manifesting bodies that spin and orbit in the universe.

Stone Age Soundtracks and Megalithic Music-Makers

The British archaeologist Paul Devereux recently studied the acoustical properties of Paleolithic caves and megalithic structures in France and Spain. These caves, which were used 40,000 to 12,000 years ago, have beautiful paintings; those who painted them were very sensitive and intelligent. Many have tried to get into the mind-set of these ancient ones, and Devereux offers his own theory. He has discovered that the caves have acoustical properties, and the cave people probably maintained an artistic culture thousands of years before the Twelve-Tribe Nations (see chapter 6) *by using sacred sound techniques.*[24] This, of course, is another form of Michell and Rhone's enchantment.

I will consider these cave people first and then will follow up with early use of sound during the Neolithic era. This discussion is based on the main thesis of my book *Catastrophobia* (2001), which posits that a great cataclysm that occurred in 9500 B.C. ended the Paleolithic era. Survivors of the cataclysm were afflicted with collective trauma, and ancient science seems to have been lost over a long span of time. Paleolithic and Neolithic people understood sound in ways that we have long since forgotten, which may have been caused by the trauma our ancestors experienced at that critical time in our collective history.

The key Paleolithic caves have various red ochre and black dots, lines, and symbols that mark the acoustical properties of stalactites and stalagmites as if they are vaulted acoustical pipes (see figure 7.6). The marks indicate where the dominant resonances in the caves are located, and most paintings are located in places of the greatest resonance. Devereux calls the musical stalactites of Dordogne Cave, France, *lithophones* and speculates they were used for "cave concerts."[25] Musicians and singers have experimented with using these caves as gigantic instruments, and they have noticed that the markings indicate where the human voice has optimal resonance,[26] as well as which cave features make sound. Imagine being in one of these caves in utter darkness, or possibly with torches lighting the paintings, and in the shadows of the stalactites, music *emerges*. Imagine the resonations in the minds of our ancient ancestors, who may have realized that their brains were frequency-receiving organs.

Figure 7.6 Lithophones! The Paleolithic Cougnac Cave, France, with stalactites and stalagmites that appear to be vaulted acoustical pipes.

There is much evidence in hunting symbology and magic indicating that the ancient ones used their minds very intentionally. In modern times, the Hopi of Arizona make rain by using frequencies in their brains to alter frequencies in the air.[27] The mind can alter events by intentionality if a person absolutely believes he or she can change reality with the mind. I think the people who worked with sound frequencies in Paleolithic caves used their brain frequencies—coupled with attunement to 2D Earth forces—to manage their lives and get what they needed. For example, the hunters could go into an altered state and experience hunting down an animal, and then when they went on the hunt, they *knew* where to go and when to act. Most people have forgotten how to do this, although I've often seen fishermen using these skills, and I think this is why modern people continue to hunt and fish. The film *Winged Migration*, mentioned earlier, shows birds operating on these levels.

We have few remains of the Paleolithic people except in the ceremonial caves. In those days people mostly lived by the sea, which rose hundreds of feet after the 9500 B.C. cataclysm and destroyed their living places. Their ceremonial caves were inland and higher than the rising sea. Archaeologists and anthropologists have assumed the people were primitive and undeveloped based on the assumption that they *lived* in the caves. Instead, these caves were their temples, not their dwellings, and they give evidence of a very advanced sound technology.

Following the cataclysm in 9500 B.C., there is evidence of advanced acoustical science among the megalithic cultures starting around eight thousand years ago. The megalithic people in the British Isles and on the western coasts of France and Spain built circles of standing stones and various interior stone temples, such as beehive and passage cairns. Devereux did an extensive study of the radial and horizontal acoustical standing waves (wavelengths) in these structures.[28] By generating and analyzing sound waves in various locations in cairns, he discovered that they were constructed to enhance the adult male vocal range—90 to 120 Hz.

Devereux worked extensively in Newgrange, which is a gigantic passage cairn in the Boyne Valley of Ireland.[29] Newgrange was built to capture the light of the Winter Solstice through a roof box above the passage, which projects the Sun's rays onto spirals carved in the back of the inner sanctum (see figure 7.7). Great standing waves of 110 Hz were generated by male chanting, which would have sent otherworldly tones out through the roof box as the Winter Solstice sunlight came in. Singing and oracular sounds are very enhanced in this chamber, and the ancient ones left even more evidence for what they were doing there.

Figure 7.7 Newgrange, the great passage cairn in Ireland's Boyne Valley.

When the wave frequencies are graphed, they make patterns like a seismograph, and there are similar notations for sounds. Devereux noticed that five-thousand-year-old spirals and patterns on the walls looked similar to his own modern sound graphs. The wall symbols look like sinusoidal arrangements of alternating nodes and antinodes. He concluded that the carvings illustrate the sound waves that were generated during the rituals. *The ritualists at Newgrange could see sound waves!* Devereux proposed they might have induced *synaesthesia*—sound-induced experiences of color—such as the shamans seeing shimmering colors while taking ayahuasca[30] (see chapter 6). He also proposed they might have used smoke or incense during their rituals as a medium for revealing the patterns of the standing waves.

Following this idea, researchers made sound waves in a dark cairn, and as the rays of the Sun shone through the mist, patterns of standing waves became visible. Newgrange may be a megalithic cymatics machine with smoke as the medium![31] Whatever the megalithic people were doing, they knew a lot about wave frequencies, which have only been rediscovered in the last one hundred years. They knew how to construct devices to feel and see the waves, which was important to them for some reason. Of course, the capacity for synaesthesia may be related to the potential human ability to detect the color-coded variable speeds of light; that may be what projects our minds into very high dimensions.

Carnac as a Great Seismograph

Carnac and the stone complexes in and around the Gulf of Morbihan in France's Brittany (the whole complex referred to as Carnac) comprise the largest and most complex megalithic site on the planet. The standing stones of Carnac are set in ten to twelve rows that run parallel to each other for about five miles, and many of these stones weigh 50 tons (figure 7.8). The Grand Menhir Brise, which has fallen, is 350 tons and once stood 65 feet tall! Gerry and I visited Carnac during the Fall Equinox of 2002 after reading about the research of a French engineer, Pierre Mereaux, who had studied Carnac for thirty years.[32] Mereaux wanted to know why anyone would go to all this trouble. Why were they built? Why in this location?

Figure 7.8 The great avenues of huge standing stones at Carnac, France.

Mereaux began with an analysis of the geology, fault lines, the effects of granite and quartz rocks, seismic activity over time, magnetic and gravitational anomalies, as well as the local myths and site names. His first conclusion was that the rows of standing stones had to have been directed by a scientist—a priest in those days—for a reason. Some stones are inscribed with scientific-looking hammers, cup marks, and lines. The region is very seismically active, and Mereaux thinks this action occurs because gigantic volumes of tidal water rush into the gulf and suck back out. The weight of the water is the cause of the numerous earthquakes, and the greatest effect is during certain times of the year. This zone has great seismic activity because of many geological faults, the thinness of the crust, and the enormous amount of water flowing in and out. The thin neck of the gulf makes the volume of water into a periodic reservoir.

Dolmens are constructions that have huge flat balanced rocks resting on the points of standing stones, with a corridor leading into a chamber. The flat capstones oscillate when the ground moves, which is frequent in this area of Brittany. Over ninety percent of the dolmens and their corridors are oriented in the same direction along fault lines running through the region. The standing stones and dolmens mark the fault lines.

Reviewing thirty or more significant quakes in the twentieth century, Mereaux found that the epicenters are usually in the faults; he also found that where there are no megaliths, there are no quakes. The quakes mostly occurred between the fall and spring equinoxes, but not from late March to early September. Also this region responds strongly to the new and full moons, which cause a tidal effect. He studied the many carvings of so-called "axe-plows" (figure 7.9) in various strategic locations, and concludes they are megalithic seismographs that measured the strength of quakes. He made one of his own as a model, and it worked! Mereaux has made a strong case for the possibility that Carnac was a *megalithic geological university* where a priestly elite taught students about Earth vibrations, a site where 2D was very active and generated powerful periodic forces.

Model of Type A   Etching from Pen Hope

Figure 7.9 Model of an "axe-plow" made by Pierre Mereaux from a drawing of an "axe-plow" found etched on a wall at Pen Hope, Gulf of Morbihan, France. Adapted from "Carnac, Stones for the Living: A Megalithic Seismograph?" Roslyn Strong, *NEARA Journal*, Winter 2001, Vol. 35, No. 2, p. 68.

I agree with Mereaux and think Carnac is loaded with acoustical properties that could be used to create standing waves for mental enhancement and healing. Regarding the conditions six thousand years ago, the magnetic field of Earth was much stronger than it is now. This might mean that the ancient people knew more about how to exploit magnetism. The human body is an electromagnetic apparatus that is extremely affected by EM fields, and Mereaux found much evidence that the ancient people were experts at detecting magnetism. There must have been a reason for measuring quakes at this complex site.

Mereaux believes the people were very advanced healers using magnetism. He suggests the stones were erected because of their field effects on the human body; I have often felt energy in standing stones.[33] Often it is stronger according to cycles such as solstices and equinoxes. More specifically, Mereaux wonders if some of their research was for fecundity—the ability to reproduce—which may have been a critical issue six thousand years ago after the earth changes.[34] Did they know how to create sound waves that could heal DNA or enhance reproduction? Given the drastic drop in fertility rates in Europe and North America, we may soon need to recover this science.

The reason I agree with Mereaux that Carnac was a healing center is because of an experience I had in John Beaulieu's sound-and-healing seminar. John taught us how to heal with tuning forks. Tuning forks, properly calibrated, can instantly harmonize our physical bodies. Organs that are out of resonance move back into harmony by being vibrated at their specific frequency by means of the tuning forks. This actually works; however, clients tend to avoid these sessions, probably because the healing is *so* fast! For example, when a person gets his liver reharmonized, instantly all the emotions that caused the imbalance in the first place must be faced. Tuning-fork frequencies also may unlock ancient trauma.[35]

Our species is suffering major post-traumatic stress syndrome, and our organs are holding much archaic pain and fear. When this gets released, we ripple with the force and then are forced to do a lot of heavy clearing. Perhaps the people at Carnac six thousand years ago had greater difficulties with trauma locks than we do, since the cataclysm was closer to them in time. Within the Carnac region, the crust was moving a lot when the seas were rising, and the land was rising as the weight of the ice lifted. Their teachers must have known (judging by the lengths they went to build these complexes) that the people needed to raise their vibratory fields to release this trauma. The regular quakes would have created incredible standing sound waves that would have caused the stones to oscillate strongly, like huge tuning forks.

The people probably came to Carnac during new and full moons, and fall and spring equinoxes, to experience this huge vibrational sound complex for healing and knowledge. *We* are the ones who are not developed enough yet to detect their science. The land must have sung to the stars and balanced the people as they bathed their bodies in the sound waves. They knew a lot about how sound receives light; it is we who are only beginning to remember.

EIGHT

The Eighth Dimension:
The Divine Mind

Opening Meditation

Find your breath. Find a column of light following your breath, from the top of your head to the bottom of your spine. Take your time, and let the light find you, as you find the light inside yourself.

Let your gaze be soft, and using your inner sight, see yourself as a column of white light. See your whole body as light. See yourself relaxed, and whole, and radiant. This is your light body. This is your Higher Self.

Place your tongue lightly on the roof of your mouth. Breathe. See yourself as transparent, as pure energy. Stay perfectly still, and relaxed, and continue to breathe in even breaths. Notice you are able to observe yourself as you do this.

Place your attention on the crown of your head. Let your next breath enter your body through this area. You may feel sensations at your crown. Simply notice them, and continue to breathe gently.

Now, using your senses, take notice of what is around you. Do you see something, or someone? Do you hear anything? What is it telling you? Can you taste or smell anything? What is it? Honor your senses; they are here to assist you. Take your time. This is like prayer. It goes on until it is done. This message is just for you.

Ask your Higher Self, what is the teaching here? What teaching is there for my light body today? See if you can get a message, a sensory image. You will know when it is completed. Now, put your focus back on your light body, and the column of light, with each breath. Let your eyes begin to focus on the space around you, and return to your awareness of yourself in your physical body and the room where you are sitting.

The eighth dimension is the realm of the Divine Mind—Light—that manifests through the visible light spectrum in 3D. The frequencies of 8D are actually much faster than the sound waves of 7D in the galactic photon bands, which is why mystics report being "blinded by the Light." The eighth dimension is the organizational field of Light, where the energetic spin dynamics of sacred geometry originate; these dynamics then step down by octaves into 7D sound, before configuring as geometric light forms in 6D. The all-encompassing energetic realm of 8D is the reason we feel the love of God as a constant energy source in our lives.

As energy moves down through the dimensions to the iron core crystal, each dimension becomes more dense and material. And as we move up through the dimensions to the Galactic Center, the planar fields get larger (see chapter 5, figure 5.2). The planar fields become larger and more filled with space the higher up we go, and finally their diameters become limited by the increasing number of creations within them. The first dimension is incredibly dense, while the 8D geometric forms hold the vertical axis.

Even though 8D generates 7D sound that forms 6D geometric configurations that eventually flow down into 3D creations, the Ps say the only way we can directly contact 8D is by entering the mind of the Sun.[1] Praying to the Sun attunes indigenous people to solar wisdom, especially during the equinoxes and solstices. Sacred geometry and gravity are the forces that hold the planar fields on the vertical axis, while the vibrating strings in all matter hold the frequency ranges of the different dimensions by resonance. This is why most people intuitively know that the Divine Mind is real and omnipotent. Yet, because of this awesome connectivity, it is easy for clever manipulators to use "God" as a program. I do not like the word "God" because of the prevailing programs run by organized religions, so here I will define this 8D force simply as the Light, or the Divine Mind.

The Ps say that 8D is managed by the Galactic Federation, a group of great intelligences that we can actually work with in 3D. The Federation manages many libraries in the Milky Way stars, such as our Sun and Alcyone. The Federation inhabits the dark nuclear center of the Galaxy, the womb of pure creativity, and it emanates thought by means of sacred geometry. Within the potent dark vortex, the Divine Mind expands and contracts by waves of time as our hearts send out incarnational timelines from the darkness inside our bodies.

To get a new understanding of 8D frequency ranges, we must first thoroughly understand the God-Poison Program, which is used by the Elite to control humanity (see chapter 4). This program always describes the Light in terms of 4D entities. Any dimensional description of the Light that is lower than 8D is false. Personification of the Light, such as Yahweh, blocks our access to the Light; defining the Light in history mocks this great Mind.[2] No one knows anything about the Light except what each one feels in the silent recesses of his or her heart. Such consciousness cannot be identified or described with words or concepts; it can only be experienced.

The Light is not the same as any god or mythical being that has ever interacted with any human, since historical gods operate at the 4D level. Their dramas are like human dramas, such as the antics of the Greek gods and Yahweh's wars. The Light simply guides the quality of existence for all beings in all dimensions by emitting frequencies; these frequencies then become sound, which forms geometry that emanates worlds. The Light shivers in ecstatic creation, which can be felt in nature. The Galactic Federation organizes access to the Light, and we can learn how to access the Federation as well as the Sun. As with any cooperative adventure, how well we know our cohorts enhances this process, thus beings and gods can help us access the Light, which is a higher frequency than they are. Indigenous people have conscious relationships with the Sun and many advanced beings, such as the Manitou.[3]

The Federation works with the plans and desires in our minds because we were created in the solid world to reflect consciousness back to the Light; we are mirrors for the Light. When our desires are ethical, pure, and all-knowing, they carry high-frequency ranges. Since 1998, when the Sun moved into the Photon Band, the high councils of the Federation are open to any human who cherishes life and is wise. All we have to do is ask for divine assistance. This is the quintessential moment for Earth. Many souls are here now because Earth is no longer just a place to learn from our experiences. Instead, Earth is a Galactic Federation School from 1987 through 2012. This means each one of us is reaping our karma directly. A rich timeline is ending, and our personal incarnational timelines are awakening in our hearts. By denying the feminine, humanity has split reality, and since 1998 collective humanity is functioning in a reality split. Two operative worlds exist right in 3D, as if two movies were running simultaneously; what each individual contributes is of cosmic significance. Those who are working with the Federation to transmute Earth's biology are experiencing Earth's ascension—nine dimensions opening simultaneously in 3D. Those who do not cherish life are experiencing the Apocalypse described by Saint John of Patmos in Revelation.

According to the Ps, the Keepers of 8D are the beings in the Orion star system, which is seen as "the great hunter" hovering over the equator. It is one of the most beautiful constellations in the night sky. Due to Earth's $23^1/_2$ degree tilt, Orion moves very high and low on the horizon.[4] If Earth's axis tilted only 11,500 years ago, as I speculated in *Catastrophobia*, then Orion is now at its highest position in the sky since the catastrophe of 9500 B.C. According to ancient Egyptian sacred science, when Orion rises high, humans become wise. The Ps say the most exciting thing about Earth's ascension will be that each one of us will be able to feel the frequencies of all the lifeforms, even our own!

As we learned earlier, the Amazonian shamans can see the molecular essence of life. Someday, scientists will invent instruments that can detect frequencies forming matter. Just by loving matter and organic life, we can feel these frequencies. What do you feel, for example, when you watch tadpoles oscillating in pond water as they absorb their tails and grow their legs?

By teaching workshops that explore nine dimensions, Gerry and I have found that many students have difficulty contacting 8D because they live in a world controlled by the New World Order, which has collapsed the higher dimensions into 4D. Our students often work in schools, hospitals, government, and industry; yet because America's ethical standards have deteriorated in the last fifty years, many of them function in jobs that do not serve the greatest good. They are often asked to carry out orders that contradict their beliefs. The antidote to this is to understand how the citizens of the United States fell under the control of the Global Elite in the first place. America was originally founded by people who traveled across the oceans to escape imperialism and religious persecution—and most of all, to be free.

The Business of America Is Business

The United States became a significant economic player on the world stage in the mid-nineteenth century, when its aggregate of business and agricultural wealth became large enough to influence the world. These Americans were an industrious lot. There were many opportunities; people came from all over the world to build businesses and begin new lives. America's agenda *was* business. Once there was enough money changing hands, people in power adopted the *pyramid,* a system that was invented by European aristocrats and has been described well by British researcher David Icke.[5] Pyramids are used to organize large systems, such as banks, corporations, schools, and governments (see figure 8.1) because the pyramids take on a life of their own once they get started. Pyramids force people to do what the Elite wants and make it very hard to see "who is running the show" when you are in the middle of them—yet it all becomes obvious once the pyramids are exposed.[6]

The bottom of the pyramid is occupied by the workers. The workers are supervised by lower-level managers, who keep their jobs by obeying orders. The lower managers get their orders from middle managers, and they must do as they are told. If a middle manager tells a lower manager to make the workers do something that is dishonest or evil, such as putting the workers in dangerous or unpleasant working conditions, the lower manager has to obey these orders or risk being fired. Consequently, that manager becomes ill-tempered, unhappy, and eventually sick.

The middle managers are given their orders by higher managers. They may not like these orders, but they must send them down through the lower managers. The higher managers get orders from officers in the company, who get orders from the executive branch, who get orders from boards, banks, corporate owners, and politicians. Everybody struggles in the pyramid system to keep their jobs, and the person at the very top reaps the profits.

People working in the highest levels of the pyramid make the most money, and they have the most to lose by not obeying their higher-ups. People in the middle and high ranges are forced to dress and live in a

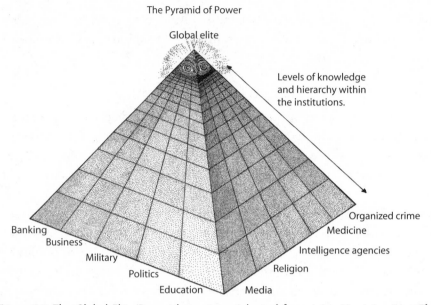

Figure 8.1 The Global Elite Pyramid structure. Adapted from *I Am Me, I Am Free: The Robot's Guide to Freedom,* David Icke, p. 18.

manner befitting their position, and they are usually in debt and cannot quit. It is easy to force them to do things that are unethical because they are supporting their families. People working in the lower levels are dispensable, and they often quit or get fired. They can collect unemployment and move on to another low-paying job, which ensures the low-level working pool. Poor ethics, greed, and control disseminate from the top down, and anybody who does not agree can always quit.

Everybody is in debt except the people at the very top, who have huge amounts of money; however, these people can be kept in place by blackmail. Data on their private lives is collected, just in case it will be useful later. Anyone who gets honest and tries to change the system is a threat. Whistleblowers, who often lose their jobs and sometimes their families, are in great danger. This self-perpetuating system gives great control, financial rewards, and freedom to the people at the top, who are then controlled by political and financial systems that support their companies. Through pyramids in corporations and large systems, the Elite runs America. This is why the dollar has a pyramid with an all-seeing eye at the top.

Occasionally, people at the top create a *fleecing,* when a pyramid is collapsed and the resources are moved elsewhere, as occurred with Enron.

This often happens when the whistle-blowers appear. The people at the very top of big pyramids, such as the Federal Reserve System, are given orders by a few of the richest families in the world. This system is what perpetuates the outrageous level of human disempowerment in the world today. The reason most people get stuck in meaningless jobs (and lives) is because they follow orthodox belief systems.[7] In my life, I've watched many people disempower themselves by *seeking* the divine, instead of just finding it in nature or in other beings by loving them. Everything is arranged so that the most people get sucked in and trapped, since they are always seeking things and answers instead of just experiencing life. Let us leave the pyramid concept for a moment to consider 8D science.

The Science of the Eighth Dimension

We've already learned about the piano keyboard and how octaves double until we are out of the audible frequency range. If we keep on doubling these vibrations, eventually we get to the visible light spectrum (VLS), which vibrates at much higher frequencies than sound. When we see a color, we are seeing a frequency that vibrates by millions of hertz (Hz). Since we *hear* sound and *see* color, and science has exactly measured the number of pulses per second that create these things, then we have the capacity to imagine very high dimensions by doubling the octaves, even though we rarely perceive them by our senses. Regarding the whole hertz range, there are no pulses at the bottom, while the highest frequency is white light that travels at 186,000 miles per second. The electromagnetic spectrum chart of hertz frequencies *defines the edge of 3D as the speed of light.*

There are many other things going on in 3D that we cannot see or hear but that we can *measure,* such as radio waves and gamma rays. Therefore we can be sure of the existence of very high vibratory ranges, as well as the possibility of the Light. Recently, scientists have measured light at higher frequencies than Einstein's constant; for example, at three hundred times faster than the normal range of white light.[8]

Of course, going faster than the speed of light takes us beyond "light as the edge of 3D." What could that be? We have to think about this even to have a context for what is going on in 8D. As I said in chapter 7, some scientists have been speculating that there may be three speeds of light.[9] Light in 3D would be the slowest speed, and this opens up the possibility that each of the three groupings of nine dimensions—1D through 3D, 4D through 6D, 7D through 9D—functions by increasing speeds of light. This might explain why we can perceive the lower dimensions easily, yet why we struggle so hard to go beyond them.

The VLS represents a range we can perceive, and the 2D ranges are much lower but measurable. For example, infrasound, which travels under the surface, is below the human audible range, and the 1D core vibrates at 40 Hz. Considering 4D through 6D, the light frequencies that oscillate the 6D geometric light forms must be vibrating much higher than 3D light, since we cannot see these geometric forms. Yet they replicate patterns in 3D that evidence the 6D geometry. The geometric vibrations flow down into 5D pulsations of love, which are experienced but usually not seen. Moving down, the 4D dualities and polarities of our feelings are so palpable that they run most people's lives; however, feelings cannot be seen, except by some as auric fields. Since we humans recognize the traces of higher dimensions in nature and we live by intense feelings, we can be sure higher realms are there. However, when we consider 7D through 9D, nothing we commonly experience leads us into these realms.[10]

Recently, astronomers have been tearing down this perceptual wall by studying the nuclear processes of stars. As I've been seeking analogs for the incredible frequency ranges in the 7D galactic photon bands, the 8D Light, and 9D time waves, science has been heading in the same direction. I am beginning to think *The Pleiadian Agenda* came in as a full-blown cosmology in 1995 because it was the same year that string theory successfully related the microcosm to the macrocosm.

The higher three dimensions *must* function by very high speeds of light, which helps us grasp the nature of the Divine Mind. Each dimension is a *wave plane* or *planar field,* and our minds (whether we know it or not) are receiving devices for *all* these waves, as if our brains were vertical-axis radios. We greatly underestimate the power of our minds, especially as we wander into high-frequency bands, where most of us get spacey and ungrounded. The antidote is to think of sacred geometry imbued with 8D force, since *geometry and gravity hold the dimensional wave planes in form.*

How might 8D organizational structure and 1D gravity function as the forces that hold the dynamics of the vertical axis? We've already looked at how 6D vibrating forms replicate as lifeforms in 3D, yet a short recap is needed. The nautilus shell always grows by the Fibonacci spiral, as do the sunflower and other similar flowers. The Golden Mean (phi) math ratio of 1:1.618 determines the spiral, which is the basis of materialization. At the subatomic level, spin generates primal movement, which begins any materialization. By 8D movement, these factors of spirals relate the material world to the world of geometric forms. We can even see the Golden Mean in the spiralic bones in the human ear!

According to science, the Golden Mean spiral spins energy from one state to another by shifts in frequency ranges. A simple geometric form, such as a circle or square, vibrates at a lower frequency, while a more complex form, like a spherical icosahedron made of twenty triangular faces, vibrates faster. The traces of these phase transitions can be seen with cymatics machines. Each frequency range generates different geometric patterns, which explains how there can be so many designs that become more complex.

The most successful way to envision the Light is to contemplate the Fibonacci spiral—the Golden Mean known geometrically as phi—because it shows how geometric fields can grow and contract in size. It is possible to fit geometric shapes inside one another, giving them a nested look, as I described earlier in regard to the holographic monad that birthed *The Pleiadian Agenda*. The only way you can execute this process is to trace how the *nodes* (the tips of the Platonic solids that touch the encasing sphere) move relative to each other. The way to trace the movement from node to node is with a spiraling line, specifically the Golden Mean, which is related to musical frequencies through mathematics. Chapter 10 shows this principle in action by means of crop circles, which by their appearance each summer in fields in England are making the Light more and more comprehensible to all of us.

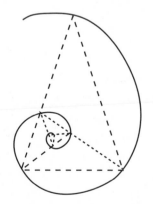

Figure 8.2 The Fibonacci spiral.

Here I will drop to a simpler level by offering two visuals that show in a very subtle way how things expand by the Golden Mean. The first visual (see figure 8.2) is a drawing that shows how the Fibonacci spiral works with the Platonic solids. Notice first that the two-dimensional spiral makes huge expansion possible; then as drawn with a few curves, follow it out with your eye by its phi ratio—1:1.618—and move it off the page. Next, notice that in light of the spiral's geometry—the triangles—it appears as a cone; this three-dimensional spiral is called a *conical helix*. Herein lies the path to imagining the breadth of the Light.

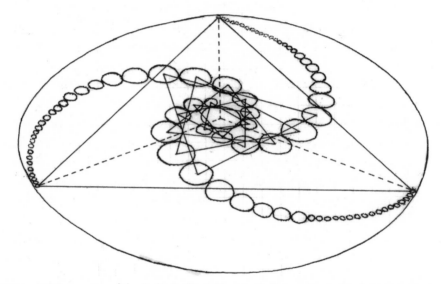

Figure 8.3 Expansion of the "Julia Set" into its spherical aspects via tetrahedral geometry. Adapted from a drawing in chapter 13 of ascension2000.com/ConvergenceIII/c313.htm.

The next visual (figure 8.3) opens our minds to this idea. The two-dimensional aspect is a drawing of the "Julia Set," an exquisite triple-fractal crop circle that was 1,000 feet in diameter and appeared in 1996. The visual makes the Julia Set into a three-dimensional form by adding its spherical component and its tetrahedral geometry, which pulls the spiraling arms into dancing cosmic waves. We will be contemplating the tenth dimension—the vertical axis itself—by studying crop circles as visual manifestations of the Light in our times. This spherical, ratcheting expansion of tetrahedral geometry along fractal-based spiral pathways is a painting of the Light in Gaia.

When light interacts with gravity, the rate of its molecular spin slows down.[11] This is how the form and color of objects and organisms are determined. The 3D frequency waves generated from oscillating 6D configurations are held at a certain level by gravity. That is, *ideas step down into reality as gravity emanates waves through the dimensions*. It is a fact that gravity holds together Earth, solar systems, galaxies, and the universe. Yet, because its effect is so minimal at the subatomic level, scientists are puzzled by it. Also, the 8D geometric force vibrates within each string at the microcosmic level. Thinking of gravity as the force of Light in nature, gravity is the weakest yet most directive force in 3D. Imagine its immensity and power in the lower dimensions where its molecular spin is much slower due to density than it is in 3D. Imagine its gigantic reach and inconceivable huge spaces in the higher planes.

In 1998, three physicists suggested that if some of the extra dimensions (according to superstring theory) were as much as a millimeter larger, this could explain why gravity is such a weak force. They went on to suppose that *gravity is comparable to the other forces in nature* (strong and weak nuclear forces and electromagnetism) *because it is diluted by propagating through the extra dimensions,* while the other forces are confined to 3D.[12] Science may never measure gravity at the subatomic level because it steps down so far, yet it is a connective force as the dimensions ascend by frequencies to 8D. Gravity is the macrocosmic energy that holds the universe together; therefore gravity is a real force at the subatomic level, which the string theorists are describing. Meanwhile, our students report many direct experiences with the 8D Divine Mind by detecting it in their 3D lives. How to do this emerges by considering the pyramid structure again.

Collapsing the New World Order Pyramids

Many of our students have been changing their lives with a simple technique that enables anyone to work directly with 8D. However, using this technique can totally alter your life. For example, you might quit a job or change a partner. Be very aware of these possibilities when you consider this information. It is best to work at the 8D level intentionally, only when you are certain you can accept whatever changes come in your life. This is the technique that gives each of us our vote in our world, since it collapses the pyramids that cull our personal power.

You have been living with a dilemma in your life. You are working in a group, factory, company, school, or hospital, and things are happening around you that are wrong or even abusive that you are forced to participate in. You have been losing energy and feel bad. The excellent work you could be doing is seriously compromised by the system you work in. You *know* there is a better way, yet you know you could lose your job if you take action. You have reached the point where you have to do something or you'll quit, lose your mind, or stress out your partner—possibilities that are not a solution. You want to change this in spite of the consequences. Here is what you can do.

Go to your altar or someplace where you will not be disturbed. Have paper and pencil in case you need to make notes or draw pictures. Sit in your space and go into a deep place of contemplation. Consider all the parts of the dilemma. Who are the people and what are the roles and games? What are the related conditions, such as budgets, community influences, working conditions, and history of the situation? You may need to make drawings. Once you have a firm grasp on all the elements that are involved, enter into a deeper state of contemplation.

Now that you have a firm grasp on the whole field, without thinking of changing any person or thing, or implementing any particular solution, bring yourself forward in the situation. As you come forward, tune in to what you can feel is the highest potential resolution for this dilemma. What would be the very best way for this situation to resolve itself so that meaningful change could come? Do not limit your opinions! Remember not to think of any specific person, such as your boss taking a long holiday, or any specific thing happening, such as the building burning down. Once you can see the best result that you can imagine, picture it in your mind. Imagine seeing it all happen, then breathe awhile and let it all go. Forget about this, and soon you will probably notice things changing around you.

Pyramids function by the thoughts and actions of all the people involved in them, as well as the direction set by the higher-ups. This technique gives each person in the situation *the same amount of power as the person at the top.* There are many more people at the bottom than at the top, and often the people at the bottom think alike in the culture. If enough people at the bottom get clear about what they want, then the top breaks down and change follows. This principle has been amply demonstrated by people's groups that have changed realities.

The Ps say our world is changing because the Galactic Federation has direct access to us now because a significant number of us want to function in higher orders. And we are approaching the end of the Mayan calendar. Our personal intentions to live in a more ethical world are forming potent and massive group intentions; the mist for a humane world is thickening. Our ability to feel the power of our minds is greatly enhanced by learning to *manifest,* which is an 8D skill. Manifestation teaches us how to access the 8D potency in nature, which is a very high order of life.

Manifestation

Just by being born in Gaia, you have the right to create the realities you want. The Light simply emanates energy so that each being can experience life. I believe the solution to our current dilemma is for each of us to realize we have a vote and to use that vote. The voting machines in America are programmed by the Elite now that they are computerized.[13] If you want to have your place back as a person who lives the way you want, practice this technique and watch what happens. Again, with a pad and pencil, go to a quiet place where you will not be disturbed. Make a list of three to nine things you would like to have or create, and state clear timelines and circumstances around these desires. For example, if you ask for a cleaning lady, make sure you have a salary limit, how soon she should manifest, and whether you will drive her to work or not. Be specific, otherwise you might get one you have to drive for miles!

It is simply not appropriate to use such high-dimensional techniques to manifest nonessentials like Cadillacs, fur coats, and diamonds. But, if you need a car or coat to get to work, go for it! You cannot ask for a specific person, only a partner, and you can specify which gender. You cannot manifest things that manipulate other people, since that takes their vote away. Once you have your list, do the following technique for each item on your list:[14]

1. Put the image of the thing you want into your mind and make sure the time, conditions, and probable changes in your life are very clear. Once you have it firmly in mind, imagine it actually happening in your life, and then ask yourself the following question, "If I could have it, would I take it?" You may be surprised to discover that sometimes you don't want something. Knowing what you do *not* want clears your mind of the

junk that keeps you from knowing what you *do* want. When your mind is littered with desires, the Light can't penetrate the shadows.

2. With your wish in mind, do three visualizations of scenes that portray the manifestation happening in your life. For example, see the cleaning lady knocking on the door, cleaning up the house with a smile on her face, and leaving the house with her money in hand. Never see this person as a specific person because then you would be influencing another person with your mind. This is against the laws of karma, it does not work anyway, and it can really mess you up; it is *conjuring*.

   As you sense the proper visualization for each scene, close your eyes and see the first image in your third eye (the place between and above your eyebrows). Once it is clear in your third eye as a little picture, then transfer the image to the back of your skull to the place where your neck connects with your skull (medulla oblongata), and see your medulla as a television screen.[15] Hold the image on the screen and strengthen it visually as much as you can, make it crackle, then go onto the next scene, and do the same thing again.

3. Once you have visualized all three scenes, then say, "So be it!" Do the same technique with the other wishes, then end your session and forget all about it, but keep your list. In a few months or a year, check your list, and you will be amazed how often things happened in the time frame you listed. Use the technique again when you feel like things are not moving along, when you feel stuck.

The more you create your life with this simple manifestation technique, the more you will learn the power of your mind and experience the magic of God. You literally can create almost anything. *The Divine Mind does not assist you unless you ask.* Things may not manifest the way you think they should because 8D beings use 3D in a way that works from a much greater perspective. For example, I remember a young woman (not my student) who manifested the love of her life. Instead of a man, she got a daughter when she was single. That little girl turned out to be the love of her life. You may not realize you've actually created things for many years until you see how things come magically to you. Often how things work out is miraculous.

According to *The Pleiadian Agenda*, the Moon has a huge influence on what we want because the Moon reflects our desires to the Sun, where our access to the 8D library is located. There are some great lunar techniques for using the power of our minds, which add the solar power. First, let us see what the Ps have to say about how the Moon influences our world.

The Moon Reflects Our Feelings

The Moon reflects the collective thoughts of humanity, our *feelings*, back to us. The intensity of the Moon's light is proportional to human feelings. Our personal mastery is based on dealing effectively with our feelings, so knowing about the lunar influence is very helpful.[16] We are "sensitive" during the New Moon, our feelings intensify during the Full Moon, and we are especially affected by lunar eclipses. The surface of the Moon is almost devoid of electromagnetism, so that its vibrations are very ethereal. Because the Sun is four hundred times larger than the Moon, and the Sun is four hundred times farther from Earth, visually the Moon appears to be the same size as the Sun. The influence on us by the Sun and Moon are balanced and equal, although different. The Sun vibrates solar-wind frequencies as resonant waves, which it uses to read the locations and angles of the planets in the solar system. The Moon captures EM energy from the solar wind, which it can read, and it mixes the solar data with our feelings. In our dreams, the Moon transmits these luminescent, ethereal frequencies containing the records of our subconscious mental banks.

Humans, animals, and plants magnetically draw consciousness from the Moon. Compared with the polarized interactions of our reactive patterns bathed by the potent solar force, these lunar vibrations are very subtle. The Moon simply emanates memories to us that modulate our responses to everything. Since we cannot develop our emotional bodies without memory, the Moon holds our soul memories lifetime after lifetime. When we become ill because of negative emotional patterns, the Moon transmits healing information to us. This makes it possible to feel what is wrong and know what to do about it. For those who value such acute sensitivity and cull this information, Bach Flower Remedies and aromatic oils can heal instantly. When we totally open up these lunar feeling receptors, we never need doctors or people to protect us. Whenever we have a lifetime on Earth, we can consciously work with our lunar subconscious memory banks to clear trauma and blocks—that is, process our feelings. We can be lighter, more harmonic, and happier by doing bodywork and spiritual therapy to clear these negative imprints. These old memories exist in our minds as belief systems that cause us to run inner tapes, such as "I can't have this," "I can't do that." All these negative conclusions about ourselves are stored in the subconscious, which receives the lunar light.

When we use manifestation, we can override negations and go straight for the positive outcomes. The Moon plays a strong role in our emotional lives, which is obvious in police records that report heavy societal stress during full moons. Therefore intentionally working with the Moon and Sun offers much potential. For twenty years, I have taught techniques for working with the Moon, solstices, and equinoxes. I've discovered that the seasons and lunar cycles hold us in intense communion with the Light when we direct our lives by manifestation. The Moon waxes and wanes, as it emanates the records of our experiences by sending us dreams that trigger feelings. The Moon sends Earth a new seed every month at the New Moon, when the Moon hides from the Sun behind Earth. Out of the solar light, very high etheric potential bathes Earth, which can be analyzed by studying the New Moon chart every month. By intentionally working with the lunar cycles, we can greatly accelerate the quality of our emotional lives and our health.

The Sun Directs Our Intentions

The big solar cycles—equinoxes and solstices—are the best calendar to live by to craft our lives in harmony with the Light. For most indigenous people, the New Year is the Spring Equinox, and *that* is the time to manifest! The first three months of the new year up to the Summer Solstice are the time to receive and actualize things. The next three months up to the Fall Equinox are the time to develop these things, and the three months up to the Winter Solstice are the time to complete what we have been creating. The final three months in the winter up to the next Spring Equinox are the time to go into deep contemplation about the larger meaning of these creations.[17] Then the new Spring Equinox is the time to create new manifestations for another whole year.

If you choose to manifest for the year exactly at the time of the Spring Equinox, things may change so powerfully and quickly that you may be shocked, so be very careful about what you choose.[18] When you create intentions at the Spring Equinox that you plan to work on for the year ahead, you go on the accelerated path. Pay attention when your consciousness tells you that you do not want to manifest something. Eventually, you will notice that what is in your mind is creating the realities all around yourself. If you could see the frequencies in your head—the movies in your mind of all the scripts waiting to happen—each one of you would clean up your mind. You are in divine communion when you own your own mind, which is an exquisite way to live. Once you really see all the potential you have, ordering your life by the seasons and the lunar cycles and using manifestation become essential.

Now it is time to investigate the 9D timelines that emanate out of the 9D Galactic Center, since these are the timelines of all the potential manifestations on Earth.

NINE

The Ninth Dimension: The Black Hole in the Center of the Milky Way

Opening Meditation

Center yourself. This means pull all your energy to your center. Like a magnet attracting little metal filings to itself. Let your midline, your energy column, be that magnet.

Feel yourself like a magnet, pulling all the parts of your body toward your center. This means your thoughts, your feelings, your past experiences, your future experiences—they are all drawn inward, toward your center.

Now, close your eyes, and see this process in action. See all the parts of you being drawn energetically to your center. See them speeding to you, all of them. Do this until there is nothing more to draw to yourself. Be patient; this may take a while. The goal is to get to a place where there is no more, where there is only silence.

Sit in the silence of yourself. Sit in this emptiness. Sit in this completeness, this sense of the whole. Empty but whole. Hear these words in your head. Notice what's going on around you.

You might like to put your fingers together; either have all five meet all five, or just have the index finger and thumb on each hand touching each other. Experiment; do what makes you feel whole.

Now, become aware of your breath. Feel the breath coming inside you, and going outside yourself. Let the space outside of you do the breathing. Be breathed by the space outside of you. Go ahead. Try it. Notice the difference between breathing . . . and being breathed. Just notice.

Now expand your consciousness way outside the room you are in. Let your consciousness go out into the stars, into the galaxies outside our planet. See if you can find the center of our Galaxy. Let yourself be drawn to it, like to a magnet. The magnet inside of you will help. Find that place that attracts you the most, like a giant magnet.

Stay with this feeling of attraction. Notice what it feels like. See and feel and hear what else comes along. Stay perfectly still, and breathe evenly, as you do this. Notice that you are still seated, yet you are light-years outside yourself.

Now, become aware of the room around you. Become aware of how the energies in the room come into you, and how the energies in you come into the room. Notice the circulation of energy. Picture the Galactic Center in your mind, and then picture this room. See how they relate. Simply take notice.

Now, take a deep breath, and open your eyes. Stay with your breath. Take whatever time it takes for you to feel fully present in this room. Thank Galactic Center for attracting you, and know that you can travel there anytime, at any moment. It is always there.

The ninth dimension emanates out of the black hole in the center of the Milky Way. A black hole is an object formed in the collapse of a large star, with such intense gravity that light cannot escape from it. According to the Ps, this black hole is the source of time in the nine-dimensional vertical axis from Earth's iron core crystal to the center of the Milky Way. They describe the black hole as a spinning gravitational nucleus that manifests itself in time waves. These waves create events on Earth reflective of the Light in nature. These waves of thought in our dimension are felt by us in fascinations that attract our attention, such as seeking the Holy Grail; these time waves draw us into questing—seeking spirit in the material world.

The Milky Way is the entirety of the ninth dimension that contains the mysterious 9D black hole, which is continually receiving the force of creation generated out of Earth's core in the vertical axis. According to physics, everything in the universe is omnicentric, which means realities unfold from centers.[1] In our omnicentric evolutionary universe, reality unfolds from the beginning, always centered upon itself at each place of its existence. Just by being alive, we are at the geocentric center of this complex whole, which is expanding. The center we exist in connects us to everything because it is where the vertical axis of consciousness is located, and our nervous systems are designed to feel the cosmos via the axis. Since they know about the axis, which is imaged as the Sacred Tree, Native Americans always honor the seven sacred directions when they pray—the four directions plus above, below, and heart (self). This awakens omnicentric sensitivity in 3D and opens doorways to the subtle worlds where the Ancestors live.

The Great Mystery is that the full potency of the black hole is now activating our bodies and minds. This is happening because the plane of our solar system intersecting the galactic plane is closely aspected by the Winter Solstice Sun—the galactic Winter Solstice.[2] This galactic infusion of high-frequency energy (caused by the brief alignment) is pulsing down into the vertical axis, which is a tunnel (wormhole) into the black hole. The Ps insist that what is left of Earth's biological intelligence in 2012 will pass through the black hole, which will be a biological singularity. This winnowing of life that is valued by human love prepares us for the next stage of human evolution. The possibility of a biological singularity is a concept that is being thought about by scientists.[3]

The black hole is a world of awesome, dark nothingness, which is filled with some of the most dense matter in the universe. Lately, reality seems strange to us on Earth because we are struggling to encompass this potent force changing our world, and few people understand what is going on. We all live in a truly amazing moment in time: Earth's scientists are entering our Galaxy, which is important because realities do not actually exist unless they can be imagined or visualized. While many of us are being distracted by other stories being dished out by the media, astronomers and astrophysicists are quickly becoming the great adventurers in the Milky Way, the cosmonauts of the dark universe questing for the secrets of the universe.

The Ps describe the Milky Way as a jellyfish of light having orgasms that make eternal waves and pulsations in its field of attraction. The Galaxy evolves in time and creates in space based on the intentions of the Divine Mind. The Ps define the "future" as any past memory that is still potent enough to allure us in the present moment—the now. Spinning on its axis, the Galactic Center shoots out 9D galactic synchronization beams that are torqued by axial spin. These beams and axes, plus the planes and belts already discussed, manifest agendas by means of the 8D intelligence system—Galactic Federation—in time waves, which are creative projects coming out of the Galactic Center.

The Galactic Center is always receiving beams from other galaxies—the connectors of the intergalactic system. The Milky Way received the big galactic Synchronization Beam on Harmonic Convergence, August 16 and 17, 1987, which was joyously awaited by millions of humans who had heard about the Mayan calendar.[4] The Ps say that this beam caused the Photon Band moving into the solar system to attain new dimensional frequencies, while the funnel from the black hole was already directing high frequencies into Earth. The beam shifted the whole Pleiadian system into setting a new intention for Earth's next biological stage of evolution beyond the reptilian mode.[5]

The Galactic Center exists in eternal samadhi or bliss. High frequencies are slowly building in Earth, especially in 2D, which is transmuting humans in 3D into silica-based (instead of carbon-based) creatures.[6] The Ps say that the Galactic Center pulses out waves of energy that are nuclear, and the 7D galactic information highways of light are the receivers of these pulsations. As humans, we can attain samadhi by opening our crown chakras. The Ps say that as of 1998, samadhi waves have been increasing exponentially on Earth, which is radically altering nature. Higher dimensions observe our world becoming radiant, yet many humans cannot comprehend such pure high energy.[7] Attempting to cope with this unseen force, many individuals and groups are becoming obsessed with apocalyptic beliefs. This response is dysfunctional because the real need today is to value life and its powers of transmutation.

Time Waves and the Mayan Calendar

The most unusual thing about the Pleiadian view of the Galactic Center is the time waves that influence 3D, such as the twenty-five-year galactic synchronization from 1987 to 2012. We comprehend time waves by exploring events, such as human dramas in history, and by considering myths and nature. The signature of the Light can be detected in what fascinates us. All other versions of time in other dimensions, such as 3D clock time, are faulty shadows of the real nature of time. Time creates realities, which means time *is* the Creator by love and intentional thought. To organize cycles on Earth, the great being in the Galactic Center—*Tzolk'in*—created the Mayan calendar to orchestrate Earth's evolution. Calendars are formats for spiritual masters who orchestrate specific time waves by working with the Keepers of all nine dimensions.

Tzolk'in, the Keeper of 9D, is orchestrating events on Earth for this twenty-five-year period.

The Mayan calendar is the Big Game that supersedes other plans. The Elite is well aware of this game, since its agents, the Conquistadors, plundered most of the Mayan calendars four hundred years ago while sending a few back to the Vatican archives. They are doing everything possible to divert our minds to dead-end time waves, such as rebuilding the Temple of Solomon in Jerusalem or occupying ancient Sumer (which is now Iraq). According to Tzolk'in, around 26,000 years ago we humans discovered the vertical axis and found the story of our past as galactic citizens. Once we saw the bigger picture, we experienced a feeling of acute awareness in the present moment: We could see how to craft intentional futures with our minds since our brains are wired to function in the vertical axis.

In those days long ago, we experienced healthy bodies, open hearts, wise minds, and activated spirits. Limitation was not part of our lives until the great Earth changes 11,500 years ago, when we became afraid of living on Earth. Tzolk'in heard our anguished cry and crafted a time wave designed to teach us how to process the fear. This is an arduous process, because the horrific experiences of the cataclysm and subsequent survival period must be sorted out. Each memory in our brain has depth charges that can pull consciousness into regions that are not part of the primary time wave. These past time waves were useful as temporary training tools for survival, but now *we are going beyond survival.* Soon we will be flying in the Galaxy with no fear in our bodies.

Tzolk'in crafted a game called history for us to be players in so that we could attain brain synchronization. The joke is: Brain synchronization is all it takes! The Maya, a brilliant stellar culture, were selected as the guides for this learning process. They agreed on the condition they could move in and out of 3D at will, since they were not willing to be trapped in 3D clock time. The Maya can and do appear in 3D at will, as do the Pleiadians and many other beings. By managing our crown chakra, we also can move in and out of 3D at will, yet few of us have attained this skill. Most people move out into nonphysical realms by means of their mental bodies to gather information.

We are coming to the end of this long game, when the activation in the Galactic Center opens our crowns. The rest of our time through 2012 will be truly memorable, and working with our minds is where we already have the most skill. Now we need to discern—and master—frequencies.

As science begins to describe beautifully the Milky Way—and enough Mayan masters have time-jumped into 3D to teach us the game—humanity is beginning to enter the Galaxy. Since the Galactic Center is connected with all the stars of the Milky Way, and our minds are wired into the center, beings from many dimensions are unifying their consciousness with us as we process the past trauma in our bodies. We are solid and can hold any frequency that arrives here, and all beings want to experience our story. The Ps say we can benefit from this *interdimensional merging* by knowing the qualities of the nine dimensions; most importantly, learning how each one *feels*. Feelings are 4D through 9D fields that resonate in our nervous systems. Think of the range of complex intelligence on the nine-dimensional vertical axis, including the potent black hole. We are all feeling the intensification of the 2012 time wave. This process began for me in 1982, once my elders contacted me so I could help to prepare for the Harmonic Convergence celebrations in 1987.

The Mayan calendar has now become the operating manual for human potential, and it is one of the few things in 3D that makes any sense. It is a huge time wave that functions as an attractor in the sky that is sucking us into a new stage of development, the apotheosis of Earth's biology. We are the pinnacle, and the transmutation of our reptilian minds will send us into the stars if we can learn to respect our planet. In *Biocosm: The New Scientific Theory of Evolution: Intelligent Life Is the Architect of the Universe* (2003), science writer James N. Gardner presents his "Selfish Biocosm hypothesis": The cosmos is selfishly focused on its own self-replication.

Similarly, Gardner cites the astronomer Edward Harrison, who theorized that our universe was once designed by minds like our own. Gardner posits that life and mind arise in the universe so the universe can regenerate and reproduce itself.[8] Some physicists and mathematicians have been studying emerging dynamics on Earth that seem to express the stated end of time in the calendar. The concept of *chaotic attractors*—advanced forms of order that influence less organized states—is considered to be a factor that could pull these states to an end point.[9] The amazing thing to me is that, as we get closer to 2012, it becomes more obvious that thousands of years ago the Maya described the date of our emergence in the Milky Way in their calendar.

Considering the Selfish Biocosm hypothesis, are the Maya "the minds like our own" who designed us? Is that why the Maya knew the date of our emergence? Life on Earth will not end: Instead, Earth will expand into the Milky Way, which the Selfish Biocosm hypothesis predicts; "Baby Universes" will be intelligently designed and sent out to populate the universe.

The Science of the Ninth Dimension

With the astronomical discoveries of Galileo and Giordano Bruno only four hundred years ago, humans began to think of themselves as inhabitants of a planet that orbits around the Sun with the other planets. Before then, they thought of themselves as people who lived on Earth in the center of the universe. There is much evidence that people thousands of years ago understood that Earth is in orbit around the Sun, yet used geocentric perceptual systems. What we are interested in here is our recent emergence from the so-called "Dark Ages," during which the Church tried to suppress the new astronomical theories by burning Giordano Bruno at the stake in 1600 A.D. Now, as we are beginning to truly explore the Galaxy, the Church champions the big bang theory, as if Yahweh were the originating explosion!

Regardless of the contentious arguments about the big bang, physicists, astronomers, and astrophysicists have been successfully mapping the universe since the 1950s. They have penetrated the real nature of our Galaxy and our place in it, possibly just in time for them to anticipate the 2012 singularity. Physicists are planning to turn on the Fermilab or the CERNS Large Hadron Collider with seven times more energy in 2007, which will produce (if superstring theory is correct) miniature black holes![10]

More and more people know that we live on Earth, which orbits around the Sun, which orbits around the Milky Way. Others are beginning to realize that the Andromeda and Milky Way galaxies are the largest in our local cluster, which orbits around the Virga Supercluster, which is not moving at all. All the other superclusters are moving away from us so symmetrically that we've discovered that *we are in the center of the cosmic expansion.*[11]

Even though many more discoveries are happening, we already know an amazing amount about our place in the Galaxy, regardless of how old it is. Until 2002, Andromeda was thought to be twice as large as the Milky Way, but then a new outer ring of Milky Way stars was detected in 2002.[12] This ring is estimated to be ten times thicker than the rest of the Galaxy and 120,000 light-years in diameter. (A light-year is the distance light travels in one year, which is 5.88 trillion miles.) Thus the Milky Way is by far the largest galaxy in our cluster, and more mysteriously, all the other galaxies are moving away from us. A strange exception, Andromeda is moving rapidly *toward* the Milky Way; the two galaxies are dancing with gravity like giant twins in the sky.[13]

As an astrologer, I spend many hours visualizing the location of the planets orbiting around the Sun. Now as I struggle from my vantage point on Earth to visualize the galactic landscape with myself inside it—what a mind expansion! Consider this: We can see millions of galaxies around us and ascertain whether they are disks or spirals, as well as their size, age, and star populations. Yet we will probably never be able to look at our Galaxy from the outside; but it could look like figure 9.1. Whenever we look out into the night sky, we can look one direction toward Sagittarius and peer into the Galactic Center; or we can look in the opposite direction through Gemini to gaze through our own spiral arm (the edge of the Orion Arm) out into the universe; or we can look above or below the edge of the Orion arm to see beyond the thickness of the disk we travel in. Yet we cannot see the whole Galaxy. For a long time, the Milky Way was thought of as a spiral galaxy, like Andromeda, and the latest thinking is we are a barred galaxy, that is, the arms of the Galaxy are more like bars than spirals.[14] We may never know; meanwhile, *we are in the center of everything.*

Figure 9.1 How the Milky Way might look from space.

The center of the Galaxy is a huge bulge, and the arms radiating out from the center have a thin center plane with a thicker region above and below. Our solar system is located in the old area of the thin disk approximately 27,000 light-years from the center. At the present time, we are near *perigalacticon,* which is our closest point to the Galactic Center during our approximately 225-million-year orbit around it.[15] As we make this approach, the solar flare cycle is changing. In November 2003, the Sun exploded with the largest flare ever recorded, yet the period of 2002 to 2010 was expected to be a dormant one for solar activity.[16] Also, we can now peer into the Galactic Center and study it, although there is a lot of interstellar dust in the way. We have a pretty good idea of our solar system's location in relation to the other stars in the Galaxy and beyond, yet we have a hard time seeing into the galactic beast we inhabit!

The Milky Way Black Hole

At the opening of this chapter, the Ps noted that the Galactic Center is a black hole that is the source of time on the 9D vertical axis. It is a "spinning gravitational nucleus that manifests itself in time waves, which create events on Earth." The Ps said the full potency of the black hole is activating us now, and we are struggling to comprehend such high energy. They say that we are being forced to process deep trauma and go beyond just survival because the vertical axis is transmitting intense energy waves from the black hole. When all this information

Figure 9.2 A fanciful depiction of the vertical axis energy shooting out of the black hole in the Milky Way.

came through me in 1995, I had no idea what any of it meant. I studied astrophysics, and I became more and more mesmerized by the black hole in the center. Scientists have been suspicious for twenty years or so that a black hole was lurking in the Milky Way center, but it was not confirmed until 2002.[17]

Sensitive X-ray images captured the Galactic Center flaring with intense eruptions every day. The exact center is located astronomically at 27 degrees Sagittarius. From this center, radio waves are emitted out of the "Sagittarius A" black hole, which has more mass than the Sun, but is not especially large. A cluster of blue stars named IRS 16 (infrared source) lies above the black hole. This cluster hurls material into the hole, and the ejecta blasts a nearby red super giant star—IRS 7—causing its gaseous surface to flare into a tail, like a comet. This complex of stars flares at least once a day for about ninety minutes, erupting with X-ray bursts ten to forty-five times more powerful than the Sun's energy, and these short-term flares are apparently unique in the Galaxy.[18]

To comprehend these powerful images, we need to know more about black holes, which science struggles to imagine because they do strange things with time. A black hole forms when a large star experiences a rapid gravitational collapse and gets sucked down into a funnel, which is shaped by the curvature of space-time. It gets steep as the density of matter increases (figure 9.3). Once matter is sucked into this funnel, it is crushed into intensifying density, yet since matter is energy, it becomes a *singularity*—a point of zero size—and then it reappears in a "different universe." Itzhak Bentov—one of the greatest minds of the last century, who walked out of kindergarten and never went back to

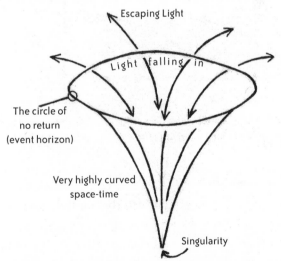

Figure 9.3 Matter sucked over the event horizon into the funnel of a black hole that becomes a singularity. Adapted from *Stalking the Wild Pendulum*, Itzhak Bentov, p. 136.

school—says that what happens in the "different universe" is a white hole, which he conceives of as a *new universe*.[19]

From my own research and teaching, I have arrived at the thought that we are going to be propelled into a new universe in 2012. This idea is supported by James N. Gardner's hypothesis of the Selfish Biocosm. And if physicists do create miniature black holes in particle accelerators in 2007, what will that do to the 3D fabric of Earth? Our students are having kinesthetic responses to this idea, as if they sense it in their bodies.

It is difficult for us to imagine such an idea, just as it was for scientists to find ways to describe black holes, yet Bentov imagined a similar concept way back in 1977 (figure 9.4).

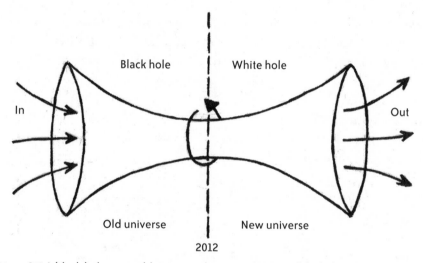

Figure 9.4 A black hole as an old universe that emerges in a white hole as a new universe. Adapted from *Stalking the Wild Pendulum*, Itzhak Bentov, p. 136.

Bentov notes that with this model, once we have a black hole, we have a white hole (since matter is energy), and he calls its nexus point a *nucleus*, which I've marked as 2012 on the diagram, the end of the Mayan calendar. This nucleus is a reference point for when time begins, and from there we can best describe the development of matter from radiation to atoms and galaxies. In this model, time is simply a measure of distance, a dimension that overlaps our three spatial dimensions. This model works well with Einstein's relativity model, yet it allows for many dimensions beyond four.[20]

Bentov notes that time does not flow anywhere, it just is; *matter is what moves along.* In the nine-dimensional model, the dimension that emerges out of the nucleus is the top of the vertical axis. What fascinates me is that Bentov's model describes time in a similar way to the Pleiadian concept. Bentov notes that as we move in space, we are also moving on a time axis, which is exactly what the Mayan calendar time wave is.[21] Bentov notes that what is expanding is our space-time, and the greatest rate of expansion occurs at the point when matter reverses direction in the nucleus connector of the black hole and white hole.[22] Scientists call the outside edge of the black hole funnel the "event horizon," which is the boundary beyond which light cannot escape (figure 9.5). Once matter crosses it, it is sucked down the hole. They say that once sucked in, if you could look back you'd see the future history of the universe flash before your eyes, yet once inside you'd be unable to communicate anything you saw back to anyone outside it.

Falling In:
If you fell feet first into a black hole, the difference between the gravitational pull on your head and your feet would be so strong that it would instantly stretch you out like spaghetti.

Event Horizon:
The black hole's gravitational "boundary" beyond which light cannot escape. Once crossed, there is no return.

Looking Back:
If you could look back as you fell, you would see the future history of the universe flash before your eyes. But once inside the event horizon, you would be unable to communicate anything you saw back to anyone outside it.

Oblivion:
As you neared the singularity at the center, you would feel yourself being torn apart atom by atom.

Space and Time:
The grid denotes the distortion of time and space.

Singularity:
At this point, everything we have ever known about the universe breaks down.

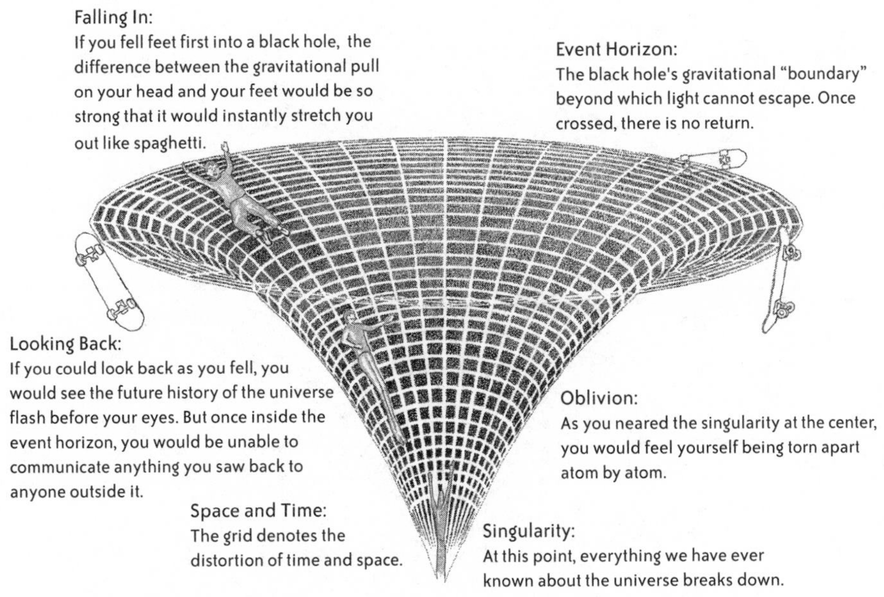

Figure 9.5 Falling into a black hole. Adapted from *Secrets of the Universe,* TM International Masters Publishers, AB, Card 14.

As you approach the singularity, the point when you come out in another universe, you'd feel yourself torn apart atom by atom. Then, at the singularity, everything we've ever known about the universe breaks down. Scientists came to that conclusion because they are hopelessly hung up on the Vatican-certified big bang theory. Meanwhile, Bentov has got it right; a new universe is created as it always was, eternally. This is why there is little to fear about 2012, and even less reason to take the violent big bang theory seriously.

The renowned theoretical physicist Kip Thorne notes that the black hole's gravity pulls atoms of gas from all directions of interstellar space toward the center of the black hole (figure 9.6). These atoms speed up as they approach the center—going faster, then extremely fast, then almost as fast as the speed of light. Far from the hole they produce slowly oscillating electromagnetic (EM) waves (radio waves); then, closer in, the EM waves are the color range from red to violet, like a radial rainbow; then they vibrate very fast as X-rays; and finally, as they speed up even faster, they produce gamma rays.[23] Let yourself visualize the superhot atoms streaming into the absolutely black hole. *That* is the radial 9D energy vortex that generates the 10D vertical axis in Earth that is intensifying our consciousness now.

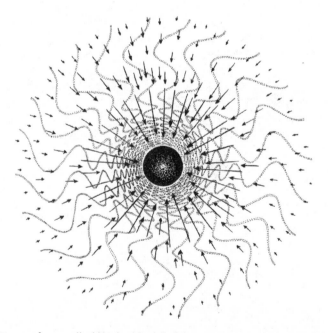

Figure 9.6 Atoms of gas pulled by the black hole's gravity streaming toward the hole from all directions. Adapted from *Black Holes and Time Warps*, Kip Thorne, p. 24.

Time Waves and Gamma-Ray Bombardments

Recalling what the Ps had to say about time and the Galactic Center, they say it emits time waves that create events on Earth that reflect the Light, or the intelligence of the Divine Mind. We humans explore these time waves when we follow our fascinations, which incite us to seek spirit in the world. Indigenous teachers instruct us that we can find our center—the source of spirit in the world—by praying to the seven sacred directions. The Ps say centering with the sacred directions creates direct access to the nine-dimensional vertical axis; this is the only way we can handle high-energy forces. We *must* be centered in 3D. The logical implications of these connections and of centering are that we have the ability to travel in the Milky Way, in Andromeda, and anywhere else in the universe. This is absolutely true, yet the more astonishing implication of drawing all these complex threads together is that Earth is being activated by the galactic nucleus point from 1987 to 2012 when our world will emerge in a new universe.

Another startling thing the Ps said was that in 1998, 9D samadhi waves would begin to alter nature radically. To my astonishment—even though I was barely aware because my son Matthew had just died—what the Ps said was confirmed. A tremendous X-ray and gamma-ray bombardment from a magnestar (a collapsed star believed to have greater mass than the Sun, and that is compressed in a 12-mile diameter) blasted Earth in August 1998.[24] For ten minutes the sky was writhing with light, which shut down ordinary scientific instruments, yet was seen by many people in the early-morning sky. More significantly, this moment was the first observed physical change to our atmosphere from a star other than our Sun. On August 27, 1998, at 5:22 A.M., EDT, the blitz caused our ionosphere (upper atmosphere) to shrink from its greater nighttime height to its smaller daytime altitude! *It turned night into day.* Amazingly, Earth's resilient atmosphere shielded its surface from being fried by gamma rays. Scientists noted that similar X-ray cosmic blasts closer to Earth might have been the cause of Earth's species extinctions in the past, which also often correlate with fast stages of new evolution, such as the beginning of the Cambrian Period 540 million years ago. I am comfortable suggesting that we humans experienced a jolt of high energy evolution in 1998 that may end up being viewed as the initiator of a new stage of evolutionary consciousness.

In 1996, cosmologists also discovered that the expansion of the universe is speeding up, which foils the big bang theory. In 1998, they proposed that the cosmic acceleration may be an effect from another universe.[25] Then in 2002, astronomers announced that all of a sudden in 1998, Earth's gravity field began getting stronger at the equator and weaker at the poles. A mysterious bulge formed at the equator during 1998, which is a significant change.[26] And in 1998, physicists suggested that gravity is comparable to the other three fundamental forces because it is diluted by its propagation through the unseen dimensions.[27] Something big was going on in 1998, just as the Ps had said in 1995.

These concepts are mind-boggling because their implications are startling and very new. While teaching this material and watching for scientific news, I have struggled to comprehend these things myself.[28] My work from 1995 through 2003 has also involved research on crop circles. When I sat down to write this book many months ago, I found I could not even begin to describe the nine dimensions until I first was able to explain how and why crop circles are being created in our times. In the fields of grain, mostly in England, crop circles have been demonstrating the nine-dimensional model year after year in ever-more complex patterns. My next chapter, which begins part 2, will consider the crop-circle phenomenon and how it relates to the nine dimensions.

PART TWO
EXPERIENCING THE
NINE DIMENSIONS

You now have a basic understanding of dimensional codes, and of how science explores seen and unseen realms. While science and the Pleiadians have been prodding us to stretch our minds out of the solid world that seems fixed in space and time, the makers of crop circles—the Circlemakers—have been painting the fields (mostly in England) with astonishing nine-dimensional geometry, as if Pythagoras has somehow learned how to fly! Interacting with the Pleiadians and the Circlemakers can be a parallel journey; nothing on this planet in modern times offers so much knowledge about the nine-dimensional form as do the crop circles.

The nine dimensions penetrate our world and inspire us to expand our consciousness, and a good way to do this is by exploring crop circles and mind-body healing. Notice that while the Circlemakers have been awakening the living Earth, a great wave of mind-body healing has been occurring. Millions of clients and thousands of healers have been exploring ancient techniques that teach us to use our minds and higher selves for health and well-being. The nine-dimensional model greatly facilitates mind-body healing, and that is why healers are always present during our Activations.

The final chapter is Gerry's exploration of healing and the nine dimensions, since we each must start with our own healing and our own personal journey with this material.

TEN

Crop Circles and the Nine Dimensions

"Crop circles are the big news on Earth while black holes are the big news in the Galaxy."

—Barbara Hand Clow

Crop circles are the most mysterious phenomenon happening on Earth right now, as geometric symbols are appearing in the fields of wheat and rapeseed in four counties in England known collectively as Wessex, and all over the world. These complex symbols often resemble megalithic art, such as the Newgrange spirals, and more recent indigenous art, such as that by the Hopi, Australian aborigines, and the Dogon. Some crop circles are based on complex fractal geometry and the Golden Mean proportions.

Crop circles are deeply connected with the downloads of information I've been receiving from the Pleiadians since the early 1980s, as well as with my research into the latest superstring theory. In the Pleiadian model and in string theory, the tenth dimension (10D) is some kind of vertical activator of the first nine dimensions, and this structure also elucidates much about crop circles. Keep in mind that the Ps say we are ready to activate *nine* dimensions within our bodies, not ten, eleven, or more. For me, 10D is the vertical axis rising from the center of Earth into the black hole in the Galactic Center; that tenth dimension *generates* the nine dimensions that we *can* perceive.

I'd like to share my personal connections with the Circlemakers, spelled with a capital C because I think of them as the Light. Contemplation of the circles has greatly enhanced my ability to under-stand all nine dimensions, and the circles have become progressively more complex and multidimensional since 1995, the year when Edward Witten correctly described string theory. Recent complex trigonometric and fractal circles have been astonishing researchers, and decoding how they are made has actually been accomplished. Crop circles are the big news on Earth while black holes are the big news in the Galaxy. Researchers have been deciphering the crop circle messages and, based on a lot of experimental data, have formulated specific scientific theories describing how the crop circles form.

How do I dare say who I think is figuring out this great mystery? Because of my relationship with the Pleiadians, I believe I understand exactly what is going on.

The Circlemakers have been deeply involved in my writing from the first. Whenever I have written a book, once the feeling of it arrived, I made a sculpture or a series of symbols to help me bring it into 3D. For this book, I have been using an altar with a record crystal, the five Platonic solids, a carving of Krishna, and pieces of spiral coral that exhibit the Golden Mean. While I was writing *Heart of the Christos* (1989), *The Liquid Light of Sex* (1991), *Signet of Atlantis* (1992), and *The Pleiadian Agenda* (1995), some of the symbols I used for writing these books appeared at the same time in England. I will describe just a few of these remarkable synchronicities, such as *Signet of Atlantis* and the "Barbury Castle" circle (see figure 10.1). Years after this 1991 synchronicity event, I realized that the Barbury Castle crop circle was a demonstration of nine-dimensional geometry, which I will analyze with Freddy Silva's assistance based on his monumental *Secrets in the Fields* (2002). Barbury Castle was a quantum leap in circle design back in 1991, when its subtle complexity impressed everyone.

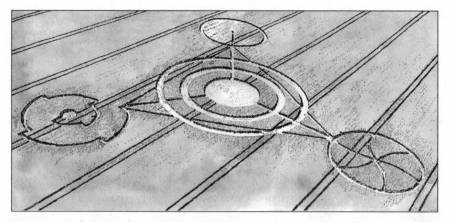

Figure 10.1 Barbury Castle tetrahedron (1991) near Barbury Castle hill fort, near Swindon, Wiltshire, England.

During this journey, I've often wondered who is teaching whom, and rationally my connection with the phenomena does seem unbelievable. Luckily, I taught at a few crop circles conferences, where I was able to demonstrate and test these links in public, which were later verified by experts. At a Power Places Tours crop circles conference in England in 1997, my students and some of the faculty meditated with symbols I'd designed, and then versions of them appeared on the fields three times in the next few weeks (see chapter 11). Nobody was more amazed than I! These events were witnessed and confirmed by key crop circle researchers Colin Andrews, John Michell, and Teri Weiss. By sharing this experience, I am adding to the growing body of data proving that the Circlemakers communicate directly with some researchers.[1] My story adds key information to the astonishing conclusions described in this chapter.

I know that many of us have been receiving these exquisite crop circle transmissions in our consciousness. When new symbols are transmitted from 8D Light, all the people on Earth are transmuted by them as Gaia herself rejuvenates. Indigenous people work with calendars to predict times of revelation, so they can watch for the 8D symbols that can reawaken their cellular memory and remake the human bridge to the subtle worlds. Our times have been very dark since September 11, 2001. In 1989, my Mayan sisters and brothers frequently told me I had no idea how dark it would get, and they were right. Often the Circlemakers have kept me from utter despair.

Harmonic Convergence: August 16–17, 1987

The Circlemakers are orchestrating the progressive initiatic awakening of our species, since we are the Keepers of Gaia. This awakening is timed by the mysterious Mayan calendar, which was recorded in stone in Mayan temples in Mexico and Guatemala thousands of years ago. A key turning point in the calendar occurred on August 16–17, 1987—galactic synchronization—which was the shift point into the last twenty-five years of the calendar. José Argüelles and indigenous teachers called for a planetary ceremony—Harmonic Convergence—so that we humans could receive high-frequency transmissions from the center of the Milky Way.[2] Argüelles believes that in 1987 humanity began vibrating in resonance with the center of the Milky Way, which pulses with gamma rays. This is the same thing as saying the 10D vertical axis from the black hole quickened the 1D iron core crystal.

Gerry and I were deeply involved in the ceremonies in 1987 with more than 100,000 native peoples at Teotihuacan, Mexico. Ceremonies during equinoxes and solstices have since been faithfully carried out by the Maya, as they will until December 21, 2012. There is a total news blackout on this significant cultural phenomenon, yet each year a million indigenous people jam Teotihuacan and the roads leading to it to attend ceremonies during the Spring Equinox![3] During the 1989 Mayan Initiatic Ceremonies with Hunbatz Men, we traveled from Palenque to Chichén Itzá and met with the tribal elders in each region. During the culmination at Chichén Itzá, it was prophesied that Quetzalcoatl would appear in the sky as the serpent descended the Pyramid. As the pipe ceremonies completed at the foot of the descending serpent, and the full Moon rose while the Sun set, Asteroid 1989-A zoomed over 40,000 people in an air-imploding roar and crashed into the sea just off the Yucatan Peninsula. This was the expected return of Quetzalcoatl, the sacred serpent. Astronomers, but not Hunbatz Men and the Maya, were surprised by this close asteroid.[4]

Because of this incredible experience, I have been watching ever since for changes on Earth that are being caused by our resonance with the Galactic Center; crop circles are the most important and consistent signs of this progression. The first simple crop circles began appearing in the late 1980s, although there have been occasional reports of simple ones since 1680. Soon after Harmonic Convergence, they became more complex, and they have become extremely complicated since 1998.

According to astrophysics, in 1998 the plane of our solar system moved into alignment with the plane of our Galaxy. This caused an extreme frequency shift (see chapter 9), which is being documented by the Circlemakers. Freddy Silva notes: "During the 1998 and 1999 seasons there was a mood swing, as if a new type of energy had lodged itself within the Earth. This energy was reflected in the crop circles: They seemed more agitated, some more disruptive to the body than usual. In others, the veil between the seen and the unseen felt thinner than ever. The mood among people, particularly the competition among crop circle 'experts,' was abrasive, confrontational, and more polarized than ever. A new wave of crop circles appeared whose designs fit neither the recognized hand of humans nor the will of the Watchers. What changed?"[5]

Consciousness researchers have taken Harmonic Convergence seriously, because so many predicted changes have actually happened since 1987. Researchers have also been attempting to comprehend what might happen at the end of the Mayan calendar in 2012. Strangely, few Mayan calendar researchers have paid much attention to our solar system's alignment with the Galactic Center in 1998. Ironically, hardcore scientists report that Earth exhibited bizarre changes in 1998,[6] and they are so enthralled with galaxies and black holes that they are turning into mystics! Meanwhile, crop circles are actually describing the changes in the unfolding galactic alignments, as if they are the handwriting of the Mayan calendar.

This is an exceedingly complex topic, since it involves both symbolic and astrophysical phenomena. However, the story of our awakening to the Galactic Mind is best understood by studying crop circles because the symbols integrate many worlds. The Maya say God—*Hunab K'u*—is *Movement and Measure,* which the Circlemakers are demonstrating. We achieved galactic *synchronization* in 1987, galactic *resonance* in 1998, and we will be offered galactic *citizenship* in 2012—provided that by this time we have attained multidimensional consciousness as a species. Since 1998, we have become resonant with very high frequencies, and by 2000, the Circlemakers started to deliver circles based on the laws of trigonometry and spherical geometry.

As we proceed on this quest, you might be wondering why most of the circles appear in England and not in Mexico? The Ps say that the central vortex of patriarchal ignorance is located in England, while the Mexican people already know what is coming. Also, the Salisbury Plain has very unusual geomantic features, which have been utilized for consciousness enhancement by humans for thousands of years in sacred sites such as Stonehenge.

The most comprehensive and insightful book I have read to date on the circles is Silva's *Secrets in the Fields*. Based on his review of the scientific research that has accumulated over the past twenty years, and his study of human interaction with the circles, Silva theorizes that the circles are activating Earth's power grid and sacred sites. I will summarize his theories on circlemaking, and I will also compare some of Silva's conclusions to my own experiences. I will focus on what the Circlemakers are communicating about the Mayan calendar, since it ends in less than ten years and because crop circles are intimately connected with it. The Circlemakers are transmitting geometric codes that inspire us to open our consciousness according to the timing of the calendar. Contemplation of Tzolk'in—the Mayan God of Time who gifted the Maya with the calendar—is quintessential mystical bliss. The Maya come into our dimension during special times to share the Light with us. Receiving it tests our human ability to wake up when the Universe tells us we are ready.

How Crop Circles Are Made

When it is time for the Circlemakers to communicate with Earth, a great tube of light comes down from high in the sky, which is visible for only a few seconds. These tubes have been seen and photographed a few times, and Silva has a good photo of one in his book.[7] The tubes usually appear between 2:00 A.M. and 4:00 A.M. when everybody is asleep, which is also when Earth's magnetic field is the lowest. The walls of these tubes could be visible because they are formed by the outside edges of billions of vibrating spirals of light that form the Golden Mean, the math ratio that determines spiral action (see chapter 6).

The Circlemakers actually create physical imprints in the fields, which is what all the uproar is about. Since the same geometry can easily be seen in shells and in skeletons, no one should be surprised. The visibility of these tubes of light and the numerous spirals in crop circles are analogs to the visibility of spirals in nature. Materialization occurs by the spin or motion of spirals, and the crop circles are material things. Once the great force is drawn down to Earth, the tubes of light imprint a crop circle where it enters a plane—the field of crops—where 2D interfaces with the curvature of the surface. The actual circle is made in seconds.[8] Scientists are penetrating the deeper mysteries of the Golden Mean these days, as the Circlemakers are constructing ever-more complex expressions of it (figure 10.2).

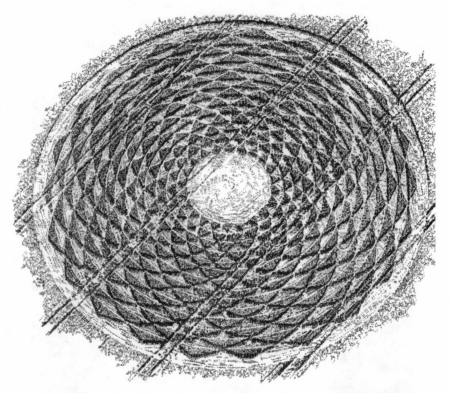

Figure 10.2 Sunflower (2000), Woodborough Hill, near Alton Priors, Wiltshire, England.

The Golden Mean spiral spins energy from one state to another by shifts in frequency ranges.[9] Simple geometric forms, such as a circle or square, vibrate at lower frequencies, while more complex forms vibrate faster. Each frequency range generates different geometric patterns, which explains how there can be so many designs that are becoming increasingly complex.[10] Scientific tests show that there has been an exponential increase in high-frequency circles since 2000, and it is more difficult to test them using current technology. I believe this rising complexity is in direct proportion to human awakening. These extraordinary circles prove that hoaxing represents only a small percentage of them—although hoaxing in 2003 appears to have returned with a vengeance.[11]

To summarize, the tube of light is a mass of spiral energy that enters Earth from the sky, the geometry of the mass is determined by frequency ranges, and the design of the circle reflects the spherical geometry of the frequency ranges. The crop circles show creation in action, and the nine-dimensional system sheds much light on these processes, just as they suggest a context for superstring theory.

Figure 10.3 Tube of light intersecting a field, creating a vibrating light sphere. Adapted from *Secrets in the Fields*, Freddy Silva, p. 242.

When 8D light steps down into sound in 7D, sound occurs in the tubes of light; many people have heard this and recorded it. Often, high-frequency trilling is reported, while some describe exquisite celestial chords.[12] These sounds are usually just below or higher than the human audible range, and the ability to hear them passes in and out. Sometimes it is very irritating. In the circle where the light tube penetrates the field of crops, the sound generates a vibrating sphere of light, in which a resonating plane of light energy then creates the crop circle. This is a classic example of the transmission from 8D light to 7D sound to 6D geometry. Those who know the laws of spherical geometry can use the planar geometry on the field—the crop circle imprint—to deduce the geometry of the sphere.

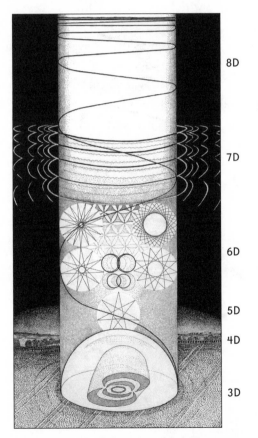

Figure 10.4 The higher dimensions of the tube of light generating a sphere in a field. Fanciful adaptation from *Secrets in the Fields*, Freddy Silva, p. 219.

To visualize how the crop circle forms, it may be helpful to imagine a plane of light forming within the center of the vibrating sphere of light. The sphere rests within the tube of light, with half the sphere above the ground and half the sphere below the ground. Gravity and magnetism draw this sphere down into Earth, and the 2D geomantic fields attract it to its specific location. Having read the chapters on 1D and 2D, you probably have a richer sense of the world beneath Earth's surface. You probably can imagine all the dense energy in the part of the sphere that is below Earth's surface.

Salisbury Plain in Wessex, England, sits on top of one of the largest chalk aquifers on Earth.[13] Chalk is piezoelectric and is interlaced with magnetite, the little iron slivers that are used to demonstrate the shape of magnetic fields (figure 10.5). This circle, the Magnetic Grid (2000), depicts a perfect magnetic field, which showed Colin Andrews, a key researcher working on magnetic-grid analysis, that he was on the right track.[14] This circle appeared the day after he was up all night thinking about magnetic grids! Because of the chalk aquifer, Salisbury Plain has a very low magnetic field, which makes it the world's largest conductor of electricity. This level of conductivity probably creates the means for the geometric design of the sphere to bend and weave the wheat or rapeseed plants into a specific design on the surface. Silva thinks that reversed magnetic fields of varying frequencies bend and weave the plants—and remember that the circles are made in seconds, basically instantaneously.[15]

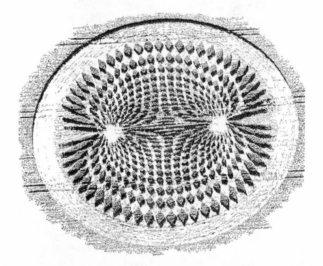

Figure 10.5 Magnetic Grid (2000), Avebury near Trusloe, Wiltshire, England.

On a parallel track, scientists have been investigating physical manifestation. They think that matter may form when energy is spun from a vacuum where consciousness has been integrated with gravitational forces and electromagnetic fields.[16] There are other fascinating reasons why so many crop circles occur on Salisbury Plain. Around five thousand years ago, the megalithic people constructed complex systems of stone circles, cairns, dolmens, and henges all over the low-magnetic field in this part of England, and eventually they built Stonehenge. Like Carnac, this megalithic technology marks the places where 2D energy is the most potent. Wessex is unusual today because it still has the original field divisions on the rolling hills over the aquifer, which may be enhancing the 2D energy. This is one of the few places left where plants still thrive within potent telluric energy fields, and the Circlemakers seem to need to use this activated biological field. The fields of Salisbury Plain are the perfect painter's canvas for the Circlemakers, who may be commenting about modern farming by emphasizing the ancient field system.

In the mid-1980s, I received images of a Druid initiation in the Avebury complex and of Silbury Hill being first constructed. This seems to have caused my mind to become deeply involved with the Circlemakers.[17] Yet, my first insight about the Circlemakers came out of an experience I had in Egypt with my teacher, Hakim, in 1994. Back then, few people understood much about crop circles, and I was very curious about them. In March of that year, while leading a group to sacred sites in Egypt, Hakim and I were walking between Sakkara and the desert, and we were talking about the ancient days in Egypt. Hakim, an Egyptian archaeologist, preferred to say little about what he knew, and he would listen to see if I intuited anything myself. If I *did* figure something out, then he would share his great knowledge.[18]

I was looking out at the rolling sand dunes, and through a time warp I saw a vision of golden fields of wheat. When this happens, the air in front of me becomes a screen showing a movie of the past or future. Since Sakkara is such a major sacred site close to the Great Pyramid on the edge of the desert, I asked Hakim if the hieroglyphs first came here as crop circles on fields where the desert now exists. In those days, I did not know that five thousand years ago this area was rich cropland due to more rainfall. Hakim answered by telling me that the hieroglyphs were a divine language given to the ancient Egyptians to accelerate their consciousness.

They arrived on the fields in this location, and the Pyramid of Unas was built for their first inscriptions.

Archaeologists controlled by the Elite say that suddenly the hieroglyphs appeared from nowhere around 5,500 years ago. They may be more accurate than they realize! Unlike the British today, the Egyptians were ecstatic to see divine revelation arriving on the fields. The sacred symbols were transcribed in limestone, even though they first were passed from one initiate to the next, possibly for thousands of years. Maybe someday a similar monument in stone inscribed with the authentic crop circles will be erected as close as possible to Avebury Circle and Silbury Hill in Wiltshire (part of Wessex).

Wessex still has fertile fields, while the land near the Great Pyramid and Sakkara is now a desert; thus southern England is receiving the majority of the circles. The circles are intimately involved with the megalithic system, which was built to enhance telluric energy when people were much more in touch with Earth and used geomancy to align their consciousness with these forces.[19] Since Earth responds to stellar patterns, the arrangement of the megalithic system was also determined by alignments to star patterns. The stars are related to human awakenings by specific cycles, such as the Mayan calendar. The stone alignments and the crop circles charge telluric forces, enhance Earth's energy grid, and activate human consciousness. The grid is a geodetic system that exists because of water flow and crustal geological characteristics that change by the cycles in the sky. As a net of lines and nodal crossings where energy flows, it is very much like the blood veins and lymphatic systems of our bodies.

Megalithic monuments are like a system of acupuncture needles that moves energy through the telluric realm—the Earth's blood—and crop circles are charging this system. These days, in most places, Earth is devitalized because geomancy has lapsed; yet geomancy is how humans can interface with the telluric as it responds to stellar cycles. For the most part in the West, people have not interacted with Earth at the sacred sites for hundreds of years because of religious repression (see chapter 2). Christianity taught that being in tune with Earth invites possession by the devil, which in turn taught people to fear Earth. However, this link is our access to higher intelligences that can interface with us and encourage us to become free people again. Western religions have enslaved the people, and religious and government authorities are debunking the crop circles because the information in the crop circles threatens their agendas. Regardless of the current human oppression, *the Circlemakers are reenergizing the geodetic grid,* and their work is enhanced when individuals interact with them.

This awakening is not a repeat of the megalithic experience. For us, the new geomancy is being expressed by light, sound, and geometry, since we will be responding to galactic resonance as a species by 2012. The megalithic awakening was solar because humans needed to learn how to deal with axial tilting,[20] and stone was the ideal material thousands of years ago because it resonates with the iron core crystal, which pulses at 40 Hz. These low-frequency ranges have been healing human cellular memory of deep trauma from the ancient catastrophic experiences 11,500 years ago. This cycle is completing itself. This activation of the telluric realm and our 3D world is toppling world religions by drawing power abusers into sexual abuse. We are recovering from deep trauma and learning how to unify our consciousness so we can be masters of the 4D archetypal realm of feelings and the collective consciousness. When people in every country are involved, the Global Elite's pyramid systems crash. Our relationship with Earth grows now in our hearts as the Galaxy spins us wider and faster.

We are vibrating with some extremely high frequencies, like the frequencies generated by great gurus and spiritual teachers. If you watch ordinary people, they have no idea what is happening, and their biggest challenge is to stay in their bodies. These are the same frequencies seen when Christ transfigured and became white light in front of his disciples as described in the Bible. He showed the Light to show us all the way. People handle these complex resonances better when they understand what is happening, especially when repressed trauma gets stirred up. The crop circles are showing us a path through the darkness in the middle of mind-boggling change at the end of the Mayan calendar.

The Dome of Light and the Druid

I first connected with the Circlemakers while doing past-life regression sessions in 1982–83 in Chicago. Such "past lives"—whether they be lives in the past, parallel existences, or genetic or racial memory—are certainly fragments of my operative consciousness, since once I retrieved them, I changed in current time. I recorded these early sessions[21] in *Eye of the Centaur: A Visionary Guide into Past Lives,* the first book of my Mind Chronicles trilogy. As you can see in figure 10.6, a Druid (around 600 A.D.) is using his hands to generate energy in a standing stone. He is standing in "The Sanctuary" near Avebury Circle, which is connected to the main complex by a long winding avenue that once consisted of hundreds of pairs of huge standing stones. No stones remain today in the Sanctuary, yet a few still remain along the avenue.[22]

Figure 10.6 A Druid raising energy by working with stones in the Sanctuary of Avebury, Wiltshire, England. Drawing by Judibeth Hunter and Christopher Clow.

The Druid is activating telluric energy in the Sanctuary stone circle by using his consciousness to vibrate the stones to alter their frequencies. He does this by feeling the telluric energy below the circle in his body, while he "hears" the stellar vibratory pattern in his higher brain centers—the hypothalamus and pineal gland. Using his own body frequencies as a connector between Earth and sky, he feels the lower frequencies like quaking waves and the higher ones like very high frequency tones. When his higher brain centers feel like they are spinning, he sends energy out through his hands into the stones, and a spherical dome of white light, half in the ground and half above, forms within the circle of stones. For a few seconds, an exquisite celestial sound permeates the sphere, like the sweet elixir of divine consciousness in his brain. He is ecstatic as his body flows with Earth density and sky toning, and he charges his body with electricity. This causes piezoelectric flashing in the crystals in the stones, and currents of snakelike energy shoot down the avenue and into Avebury Circle. The Sanctuary seemed to be an electrical switch for Avebury Circle, and experiencing it altered my whole neurological system.

I experienced this very explicit regression in 1983 when I knew nothing about Avebury, light technology, spherical geometry, domes of light, or electromagnetic energy in our bodies. Wherever this Druid scene came from, I experienced wild sensations in my own body. This was so amazing to me as a wife and mother of four that I did not want to lose this subtle and intriguing thread in my body from the past, especially since the American culture around me was so vacuous. I guarded myself from ridicule or judgment from others by not discussing these revelations with anyone outside my immediate family. My therapist specialized in retrieving themes and initiations from past lives. Then he used the material his clients retrieved to help them utilize the information in their current lives. He believes that ancient cultures did this to progress instead of regress, and judging by what's going on now, he is right. During this delicate time, I did not consult outside sources on the Druids because I sensed that this regression probably contained more real information about the Druids and Avebury than any modern source. Before publishing this material, I researched archaeology, geology, and topology of Wessex and the global megalithic system.

While I was doing this work from 1982 through 1985, simple crop circles were occurring more frequently around the Avebury complex and the Sanctuary, but I did not hear about them until 1986. Soon after the Druid regression, I accessed a lifetime as a young Avebury priestess from around 5,200 years ago, and my connections with Avebury took a quantum leap. Her clan was the Owl Clan, which had served Avebury since the Paleolithic era, as the Maya serve their sacred sites today. Her life offers clues on plants as keys to dimensional access—one of the great mysteries with crop circles.[23]

Figure 10.7 Owl Clan priestess in 3200 B.C. bringing sod into the chalk chamber in the center of Silbury Hill, Avebury, Wiltshire, England. Drawing by Judibeth Hunter.

The Owl Clan keepers of Avebury were in tune with a sacred stone placed there by their ancestors thousands of years before the megalithic era. These ancestors buried a river-tossed egg stone to mark this as a *sacred center* by the River Cunnit, which flows out of a spring dedicated to the goddess. The white-quartz stone was brought from a river flowing into the sea where it was polished in the gravel, and the same stones cover the face of Newgrange temple. When the Owl Clan buried it many years ago, there was a land ridge between Wessex and the Continent. Her clan still retained this memory, and now it is 3200 B.C. According to the cycles in the stars, a resonator (Silbury Hill) must be constructed to enhance the power of the sacred stone, which guards female procreative powers. In the illustration, the priestess began the project by building a chamber made of cut chalk blocks that was initially open to the sky. She carries in blocks of soil teeming with moist living plants, while a man raises energy elsewhere in front of a great standing stone. Later, they sealed the chamber with chalk on the top, like an igloo. After this, Silbury Hill was constructed over the chalk dome with layers of carefully chosen stones, chalk, and mud to enhance Earth frequencies. As seen from the sky, Silbury Hill's form is a pregnant goddess.[24] It emits Owl Clan records that by symbols announce the time of human awakening.

I could not imagine what this session meant, yet when I heard about the circles appearing in the fields all around Silbury Hill, I began to understand what was happening, and it changed me. I became absolutely imbued with the urgency of Earth's ecological crisis. All I knew was I had to get to Avebury as soon as possible. Being mostly Scots-Irish by birth and only one-eighth Cherokee, perhaps I could connect with Earth in the old country, too.

Gerry and I went to Avebury in 1986, which is when I discovered in the site museum that archaeologists had tunneled into the center of Silbury Hill looking for the tomb of some ancient chieftain. Instead of finding buried treasure, they found a simple chalk chamber filled with *living plants and organisms* in the center! Arriving in Avebury, we marveled at its deep Earth resonance within the circling stones and the openness to the sky that invites all the stars. Like the circle in the Sanctuary, the Avebury henge holds the edge of a great spherical dome of light. Silbury Hill is alluring as it projects geometric lines of light that interweave and wave outward; at the same time, a magnetized green etheric force sucks into the ground through the Owl Clan stone beneath its chalk dome. Early crop circle researchers were around in the fields and in the pubs, and I wondered if the circles were Owl Clan symbols. We just meditated with the stones as if they were grandfathers and grandmothers telling us stories.

Today I have become certain that the main henge and stone circles are drawing the Circlemakers close to the whole complex and they move miles out from it through Wessex, especially around Stonehenge. Since a high percentage of each year's crop circles arrive here, Avebury would appear to be a consciousness center for the West through 2012, just as it was as long as eight thousand years ago. This force can break down the Anglo-American pyramid system that grips our present world like an Eastern despot. The Western logical mind requires too much proof before being willing to respect the unseen world, yet human interaction with the Circlemakers is changing this.

More about Harmonic Convergence

During my regression research, I was also the co-owner and editor for Bear & Company in Santa Fe, and I also began to do ceremonial work around the world. I looked for books that could help prepare people for the coming changes, especially after August 1987. This time of galactic synchronization was secretly awaited in indigenous circles, and Tony Shearer had announced the dates in his book *Lord of the Dawn: Quetzalcoatl and the Tree of Life,* which was first published in 1971. In November 1986, the visionary artist José Argüelles walked into my office with *The Mayan Factor: Path Beyond Technology,* which describes the full powers of the Mayan calendar and emphasized the importance of August 1987. We rushed it to press by spring of 1987, so there would be enough time to create various campaigns to publicize the need for worldwide meditations on Harmonic Convergence. In February 1987, José shared pre-ceremonies with a group that included Gerry and myself in the Courtyard of the Nine Lords at Palenque. During the ceremonies, Supernova 1987A exploded in the Large Magellanic Cloud, and in the few seconds of its death, it released more energy than all the Milky Way stars in a year. This supernova explosion also had great significance for Earth because for the first time *stellar* neutrinos (versus *solar,* first observed in 1967) were detected roughly three hours *before* the first optical sighting of Supernova 1987A.[25]

This event brought together previous theories and speculations into a complete and correct description of neutrinos and supernovas and their cosmic implications. Neutrinos (weak-force particles) have no significant attraction to other matter except on cosmic scales; matter is completely transparent to neutrinos, and they are passing through Earth and us all the time, usually from the Sun. The more deeply that photons (EM particles) penetrate matter, the more they harm living things. Neutrinos and photons both have the same dual nature of particle and wave, yet neutrinos are not made of oscillating EM fields. Since the optical sighting was after the neutrino detection, human interaction with the neutrinos was *faster* than the speed of light, yet nobody has any idea what they do to our brains and bodies. For me, neutrinos were cosmic messengers from Supernova 1987A.

A few months later, White Eagle Tree, my Cherokee medicine brother, and I helped lead the ceremonies for Harmonic Convergence at Teotihuacan, north of Mexico City. Gerry and I brought our son Matthew with us, who was multidimensional from birth, and what he saw the night before the Convergence was a direct link to the Circlemakers. He went out near midnight on August 16 and climbed the Pyramid of the Sun to study the sky. Around 3:00 A.M., as he walked down the avenue approaching the Citadel, he saw a rising light to the left of the long avenue between the Pyramid of the Moon and the Citadel, just as he passed by the front of the Pyramid of the Sun. Sensing he could interact with it mentally, he held his ground and breathed deeply as he felt the potential energy disturbances that often come with high-frequency transmissions. He saw a huge, vibrating, complex geometric sphere of light rise slowly out of the ground and shoot straight up into the sky; it was humming, pulsating, and seemed organic. When he woke me up shortly thereafter, he was glowing with very high frequencies. The sphere of light he saw was very much like the ones described earlier by Freddy Silva and the Druid. This is how things work when extremely high frequencies interact with Earth's surface. We cannot see the whole nine-dimensional vertical column, but some can see the sphere it generates. Most other people in the area probably could not see the sphere, just as most do not see the spheres at Avebury. They vibrate at frequencies faster than those in our dimension, and only people who can detect the vibrations in their higher head centers can sometimes see them.

Synchronistically, in August 1987, there was a huge explosion of crop circles in Wessex, and the researchers reported huge magnetic disturbances in them. This was when I became sure the communications from the Circlemakers are progressing by the cycles of the Mayan calendar. In my book *Chiron: Rainbow Bridge Between the Inner and Outer Planets* (1987), I explored the wounded healer complex ruled by Chiron, the newly discovered planetary body. This informs us that systemic and permanent healing of trauma complexes can be accomplished by means of accessing and clearing the originating basis. Chiron sensitized me to unresolved trauma, and I began to see varying energy frequencies in people's bodies that greatly reduce their comfort zones in 3D. Trauma complexes vibrate at low frequencies, while ecstatic states vibrate at high frequencies, such as the Druid charging the stone or Matthew seeing the sphere of light.

During this time I was doing past-life regression work with Chris Griscom of the Light Institute in Galisteo, New Mexico. Chris remarked that most people's emotional bodies vibrate at lower frequencies than their physical bodies, which is abnormal. As a result, they are not fully present in their physical bodies, which greatly diminishes energy access. We are designed to be fully located in our bodies at our lowest frequency where we access energy from many dimensions.

Crop circle researchers were offering various theories and publishing them, public curiosity was rising, and the circles became more complex. When I was working with Griscom in 1988 and 1989, we often noticed that we both could feel what the Circlemakers were communicating. *Heart of the Christos,* the resulting book, was published in 1989, just as I became more deeply involved in ceremonial teaching. The crop circles of 1990 seemed to be responding to the 1989 Mayan Initiatic Ceremonies described at the beginning of this chapter. As you can see from these images (see figure 10.8), these are pictograms—the same symbols picked into rock surfaces and painted on drums and pots for thousands of years in the Americas. Pictograms are a sacred language that represents specific ideas, such as energy radiating off two connecting circles in the illustration. This language is understood at the intuitive level, and it is revealed at the conscious level during auspicious times by indigenous scribes. By 1990, the Circlemakers were part of our ceremonies to heal Earth, and we began translating them when appropriate. In 1991, some astonishing crop circles appeared, including the Barbury Castle tetrahedron, more pictograms, a broken DNA sequence, and even a perfect Mandelbrot Set, which is the most complex computer-generated fractal. This was the first summer I experienced direct contact with the Circlemakers in 3D.

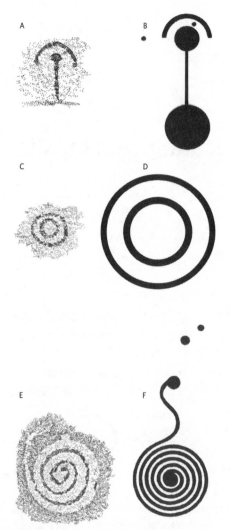

Figure 10.8 Native American pictograms that resemble crop circles. (B) From a selection of crop circles from 1991. (C) Paintings in Mogollon Red Style near Reserve. Concentric circle is 6 cm in diameter. Photo by Karl Kernberger. (D) From a selection of crop circles from 1970 to 1990. (E) Blanco Canyon, Largo Drainage, NM. Photo by Curtis Schaafsma. (F) A crop circle formed in 1990 in Bratton. Images A, C, and E adapted from *Rock Art in New Mexico*, Polly Schaafsma, figs. 59, 35. Images B, D, and F from *Secrets in the Fields*, Freddy Silva, pp. 6, 25, 29.

E L E V E N

Communicating with the Circlemakers

Barbury Castle (1991)

During a hot Santa Fe morning on July 15, 1991, I was in my writing office drawing symbols to help me start the third book of my trilogy, *Signet of Atlantis,* and I drew this odd symbol (figure 11.1). It felt like it was *Signet's* energy field, so I began the book. Meanwhile, *Eye of the Centaur* and *Heart of the Christos* were being translated into German, and I was in communications with my German publisher, Lutz Kroft of Zweitausendeins. On July 17,
Kroft faxed to me an image of the Barbury Castle crop circle, which had appeared in England during the night of July 16, when the power went out in a nearby military base and town.[1] He was very excited, since the Barbury Castle circle expresses complex tetrahedral geometry.

Considering that I cannot draw, I was stunned to see that what I had scribbled on the

Figure 11.1 Author's drawing of symbol similar to the Barbury Castle tetrahedron.

174

morning of July 15 (a half-day *before* the glyph appeared in Wessex) strongly resembled the Barbury Castle tetrahedron (see figure 10.1 for a comparison). Obviously, my mind was working with the same symbology; Kroft seemed to have intuited this by spontaneously sending it. So, the Barbury Castle image is on the title page of *Signet of Atlantis,* which came out in 1992, and I first wrote about this synchronicity in *Signet*'s introduction. Somehow my creative mind was flowing with the Circlemakers, although I was not paying much attention to them yet.

I thought it was incredible that I would draw this symbol just before it appeared as a crop circle in Wessex. I did not understand the geometry, which I'd forgotten about since the ninth grade. In those days when somebody said "tetrahedral," I smiled knowingly while I had no idea what they were talking about. In 1991 and 1992, Gerry and I were teaching in Bali, Mexico, Egypt, and Crete, and we could not get back to England. I continued to be mystified by Barbury Castle, and then finally in 1993, Power Places Tours invited me to go to England for a crop circles conference with some of the key researchers, including Colin Andrews and John Michell.[2] I was also offered the golden opportunity to teach with John Michell for a week after the conference. John has been an avid crop circle researcher from the beginning, a master teacher of sacred geometry, and the author of many wonderful books. My job was to lead ceremonies with the students at sacred sites, such as Glastonbury Tor and various stone circles out on Cornwall, and then John and I were expected to dialogue with the students.

When I arrived, John and I had not met before, and I was sure he thought he'd gotten stuck for the week with a typical American New Age airhead. I went about my work with the students, we had some great dialogues that at least indicated I'd done my megalithic homework, and then John retired with a book whenever ceremonies happened. The farther we traveled down into Cornwall, the more curious he got about what we were doing, but he stayed away.

The last ceremony was on a high cliff overlooking a churning gorge near King Arthur's Castle and Merlin's Cave at Tintagel, where my medicine brother Heyoka Merrifield was to do a pipe ceremony with me. The energy of our group was very joyful, and I noticed that John was curious about Heyoka's panther cloak. So I said, "John, this is the last ceremony. Please join us, we would be so honored." He smiled and sat down on a rock amidst the students. Heyoka smoked his pipe while I led a guided meditation into the center of Earth. Eventually, we all came out of it, and John was still sitting on the rock in a totally altered state. We waited quietly for a while, since a fall into the gorge would be deadly, and then we woke him up. His eyes fluttered, and he said, "Thank you, finally I have experienced real meditation." This was interesting because I often find that people who have never known good meditation often have powerful experiences if they are first taken into Earth. John Michell, of course, is a skilled mental traveler—another form of meditation.

After the work was finished, John and I enjoyed a great evening in the pub with some students, and *in vino veritas* John said one of the most meaningful things anyone has ever said to me. He said (from notes I took that night):

> You must read my *Twelve-Tribe Nations* that I wrote with Christine Rhone. In it we show that Wessex and other centers in England are sacred centers divided up into twelve spokes on a wheel. Each section is a district under a sign of the zodiac, and the people in each district express the characteristics of their sign as their clan. Each clan maintains its character by having appropriate ceremonies and mystery plays while using the right music to preserve the land's *enchantment*. When the Sun is in a certain section—Aries, for example—the Aries clan would go round the whole wheel and entertain the other clans to teach them about the ram. After working so hard with Christine to describe this sacred landscape, often I wished I could be there just once long ago during one of those ceremonies. Oh, to hear the music just once. You and your group have given me the greatest gift. During this week as I watched your group, I realized you were doing exactly what the ancient people did to preserve the character of the sacred land. Thank you.

Then a friendship began, and John has helped me more than any other researcher, other than Freddy Silva, to comprehend the crop circles.

From 1992 through 1994, there was a lot of tension in Wessex. The media allied with the hoaxers and downplayed the real truth about the phenomena to keep the public from realizing the importance of the circles, while serious researchers were outrageously debunked and harrassed. The Circlemakers outwitted the hoaxers and their media lackeys by creating circles that no human being could have ever made, especially those laid down in less than a minute. Only a fool, a lackey, or a liar could think otherwise. In 1993, the circles were so complex that open-minded people could be sure most crop circles were real.

Many of the 1994–95 circles were very astronomical, with circles and crescents around planets and moons, and were messages about the state of our solar system. Neptune conjuncted Uranus (i.e., lined up in the same place in the sky) in 1993, which occurs every 180 years. Neptune conjunct Uranus initiates a whole new cycle of spiritual awakening (to 2173 A.D.), and the Circlemakers celebrated this change. To see many images, you will need to get Silva's book, books by others, or go to the Internet (www.cropcircles.org), since there have been at least 3,500 genuine crop circles since 1985.

The circles also crafted images of two monumental astronomical events (figure 11.2). In July 1994, comet Shoemaker-Levy crashed into Jupiter and pummeled its surface with twenty-two hot fragments. Many people on Earth awaited the event and then watched it on television, but few realize that some crop circles that summer actually depicted the Jupiterian catastrophe. Jupiter's trauma reminded the public of times in the past when our planet has been hit by asteroids or comets, thus this event awakened hidden fear. In 1995, comet Hale-Bopp was bright in the sky all summer and fall, and again the circles that year were predominantly astronomical (see figure 11.3). All this affected me greatly because I'm an astrologer, and by late 1994 the Pleiadians came through me much more forcefully than ever before. Until this time, they had been guides who appeared sporadically, I had no alliance

Figure 11.2 A 1994 crop circle that seems to depict the twenty-two fragments of comet Shoemaker-Levy crashing into Jupiter.

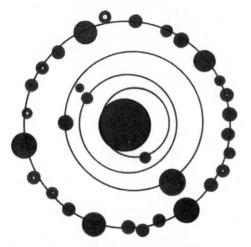

Figure 11.3 Astronomical circle in 1995 that suggests the Circlemakers were depicting our solar system during the summer when comet Hale-Bopp was visible nightly.

with them, and at the time I wished they'd just go away. Now that this present book has come forth, I am grateful for their forceful, urgent communications; I think the Pleiadians and Circlemakers are connected in some way, and I think together they will debunk the Elite spinmasters by 2012.

The Pleiadians and the Circlemakers

From 1992 through 1994, the military, government, and media were working together to debunk the phenomena, but why would they bother? Some of you may remember the "Doug and Dave Show," a pair of beer-soaked hoaxers who occasionally flattened the fields with ropes and boards to create "circles" which the media immediately displayed on the evening news. Considering the spiritual importance of the circles, the battles over fake and real circles and the disturbances in the fields by the fakes were distracting and heartbreaking. The Circlemakers virtually never injure animals, researchers, or plants, and their art is truly inspiring. Some wondered if the Circlemakers were extraterrestrials, possibly like the ones who reportedly abduct people. The way I come to terms with such thorny questions is to observe what comes into my life, and I have not seen any green men from Mars, yet.

In November 1994, as I reported earlier in this book, my ears began ringing incessantly, like having a telephone ringing in my head. Somebody was dialing me up, and I wondered if it was the Circlemakers, the Pleiadians, or both. The resonance felt familiar, and it felt like totally nonphysical higher-dimensional beings of light. For me, contact with the Pleiadians has never been about flying saucers and little green men. I called together a small group of people who wanted to ask questions of the Pleiadians while I channeled them. We taped the channelings, and the material for *The Pleiadian Agenda* was completed by March 1995. This moved me into total resonance with the Circlemakers, and I believe that a number of the 1995 circles are a direct response to *The Pleiadian Agenda*. The Circlemakers may be higher-dimensional frequencies of the Pleiadians, who are very fifth dimensional. Since 5D is the opening of the divine heart and the Pleiadians are a loving expression of this divine love, the more we can see how this works, the better.

The Nine-Dimensional Model and the Circlemakers

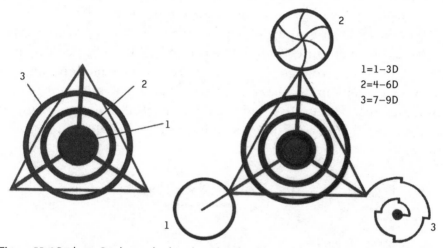

Figure 11.4 Barbury Castle tetrahedron (1991) with addition of nine-dimensional dynamics.

The Barbury Castle crop circle (figure 11.4) is an expression of complex tetrahedral geometry: Three strange circles form out of the tips of the triangle to create the tetrahedron's base; and within the base, the circle and two rings suggest the tetrahedral form by emphasizing the pyramid's raised point. Tetrahedrons are made of four equilateral triangles with one triangle on the flat with the three faces rising to the center point, and they are the primal bond of matter. The three circles form out of the top of the pyramid and radiate down, forming a cone. The large circle in the center is 1D through 3D, the second circle beyond is 4D through 6D, and the outer circle is 7D through 9D. As numbered in the illustration: *circle 1* with the line from 1D into its center is 1D through 3D, with the core indicated by the center point and 3D as the simple circle; *circle 2* is 4D through 6D with six morphic divisions that are moving by the wavy lines; and *circle 3* shows higher-dimensional 7D- through 9D-level changes with 9D in the center ratcheting down to 3D, which connects back into the tetrahedron. This perfectly models the nine dimensions based on the principle of threes: 3 + 3 + 3 = 9.

In other words, the Barbury Castle tetrahedron has taught me about the dimensional structure of the nine dimensions—yet it is the very circle I drew in 1991 *before* it appeared in the fields! The three circles in the tetrahedron show how the dimensions are nested and offer a sense of spin by the rising cone. The spinning circles increase in complexity by spin or torque, which may be the Circlemakers sending information about three different speeds of light. The three circles at the points of the triangle show three levels of how motion and spin activate matter out of geometric form. The third ratcheting circle intrigued me, because I sensed there was much meaning in it, and as you can see by my crude drawing in figure 11.1, I could not express it myself.

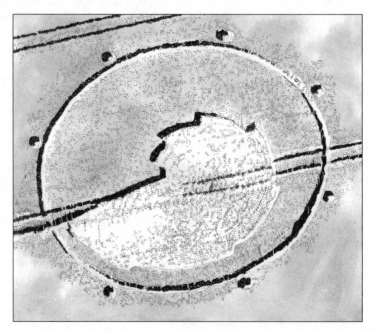

Figure 11.5 Ratchet crop circle (1995) near Stockbridge Down, Hampshire, England.

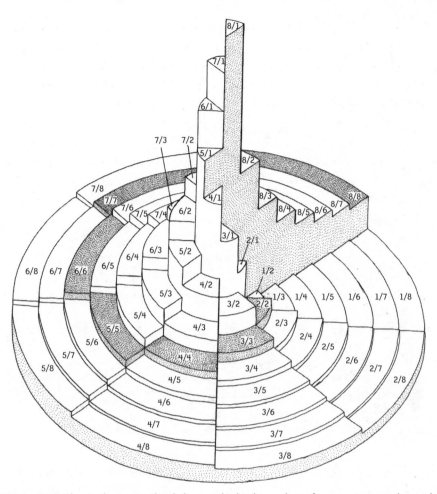

Figure 11.6 The Pythagorean lambdoma which shows how frequencies accelerate by octaves. From *Secrets in the Fields,* Freddy Silva, p. 211.

The Circlemakers made another version of the ratchet in 1995 (see figure 11.5). Back in 1995, I did not understand the higher three dimensions, and I thought this ratchet might clear my own fog, but I was stumped. Freddy Silva has figured out these 1995 ratchets based on Barbara Hero's research on the *lambdoma,*[3] a diagram that dates back to the Egyptian mystery schools (figure 11.6). The Pythagorean lambdoma exactly defines the relationships between harmonics in music and mathematical ratios. It expresses the principle of octaves and shows how frequencies accelerate (see chapter 7). It is a circular matrix that contains all the ascending harmonic proportions, and it offers wonderful feelings for the complexity and mechanics of ascension. The 1995 ratchet glyph has eight little circles outside the circle around the ratchet, just to make sure everybody knows we're talking about octaves! The Circlemakers were making sure the researchers would be led to the lambdoma, which explains how octaves ascend by mathematical ratios. The lambdoma also explains the three higher dimensions of the nine-dimensional form, and it shows how wavelengths (9D light) vibrate by octaves (8D order) creating harmonics that form 7D sound. That is, by showing how sound ascends by octaves to light, the ratchet translates how divine intelligence speaks. Finally, that one is solved!

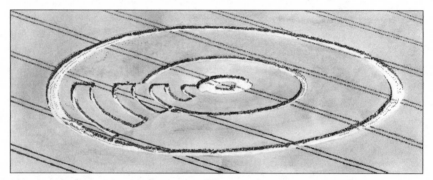

Figure 11.7 Cow Down (1995) near Andover, Hampshire, England.

When the heptagonal geometry glyph—Cow Down—appeared at Cow Down in June 1995, it felt like radar signals from the Pleiadians calling to me. This feeling was visceral and funny because the Ps always talk about how they are "the cow people who come down." When I saw it, I realized it is a version of a symbol the Ps gave to me while I was writing *The Pleiadian Agenda,* which is the second illustration in the introduction in this book. Compare figure 11.7 with figure I.2 in the introduction. My symbol represents the creation of matter by electromagnetism in nine dimensions, and I used this version (see figure 11.10) in a lecture at the 1997 Power Places Tours' crop circles conference to speculate on how crop circles are major agents of change and are awakening multidimensional consciousness. Freddy Silva amplified this connection by pointing out that researcher Paul Vigay registered radio interference over a Telegraph Hill glyph, and he sketched the path of it in his notebook.[4] The

Cow Down glyph also expresses his drawing. Thus both researchers had detected that Cow Down was an expression of electromagnetic forces and how they are involved in created matter. The Cow Down glyph appeared five days after I got my symbol from the Pleiadians, and seven days after Vigay's drawing in his notebook.

As analyzed by Silva, the hidden geometry of the Barbury Castle tetrahedron is pentagonal, hexagonal, and heptagonal (figure 11.8). The art itself, from Freddy Silva's computer drawings, is exquisite and mind-expanding, and in light of tetrahedral geometry, it shows that Cow Down is exhibiting some electromagnetic keys. By applying heptagonal geometry to Cow Down (see figure 11.9) as well as to Barbury Castle, our consciousness is encouraged to think of sevens. Of course, 7D is the world of sound that creates geometry, and Silva comments that seven represents the geometry of the soul.[5]

Figure 11.8 Barbury Castle (1991) with pentagonal, hexagonal, and heptagonal geometry superimposed. From *Secrets in the Fields*, Freddy Silva, p. 188.

183

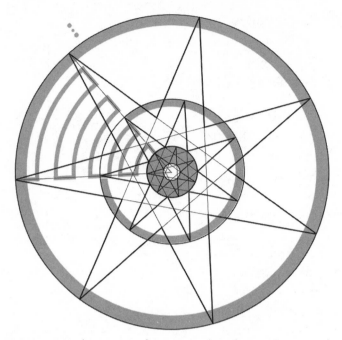

Figure 11.9 Heptagonal geometry of Cow Down (1995). From *Secrets in the Fields*, Freddy Silva, p. 189.

My first public interpretation of a crop circle was of Cow Down at the 1997 crop circle conference at Salisbury, England,[6] and I will repeat it here (see figure 11.10). I used dots and bars (Mayan system) instead of numbers for the nine dimensions, hoping the Circlemakers would create something with it in 1997. The glyph exhibits the principle of three by three circles, and the ratchet shows how the energy accelerates electromagnetically from 1D through 9D. The inner circle is 1D–3D, the second 4D–6D, and the outer 7D–9D. The ratchet begins out of the 1D–3D circle, and the 4D ratchet breaks the 4D–6D circle. This explains how 1D and 2D telluric energy determines 3D, and it shows we are very overlaid by 4D forces. The 5D through 8D ratchets are in the area between the 4D–6D and 7D–9D circles, and the 9D ratchet melds into the outer circle.

Cow Down may demonstrate how 5D–9D expands. It offers a sense of how all dimensions are contained by energy, and there could not possibly be a more perfect expression of how the dimensions interrelate. Cow Down may be showing us another way to conceptualize how higher dimensions

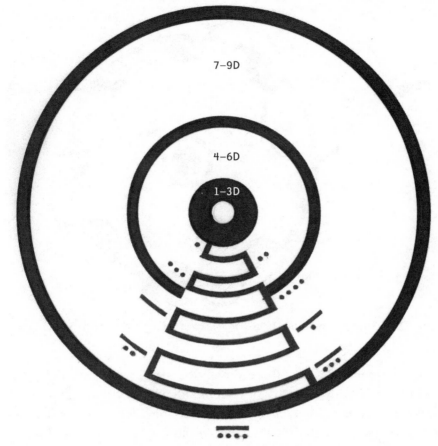

Figure 11.10 Cow Down (1995) with nine dimensions indicated by Mayan numbers.

enfold into the lower extended dimensions, which stretches our minds as do the Calabi-Yau spheres (see figure 7.4). The geometric relationship between the outer and middle rings is an equilateral triangle and tetrahedron, which hark back to Barbury Castle (see figure 11.4). The two combined show forms of the nine-dimensional dynamic, and they show how frequencies ascend by harmonics. It is fair to say that Barbury Castle appeared as a form in 1991 and that Cow Down activated it in 1995, which is typical Circlemaker humor. To better understand the nine-dimensional form, this circle shows how sound is a key to dimensional shifting. It graphically depicts how sound permeates all nine dimensions.

Another circle (see figure 11.11) appeared in 1995 that offers more information about the highest dimensions—8D and 9D—and it shows how opening the heart is the access to high dimensions. The small center

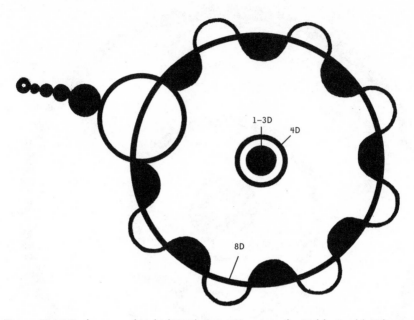

Figure 11.11 Darkness and Light (1995). From *Secrets in the Fields*, Freddy Silva, p. 152.

circle represents the first three dimensions, and the tight circle close around it is 4D restricting 3D, or the emotional body vibrating too slowly. Way out beyond, the next circle, which is 8D, has eight loops of darkness and eight loops of light. It shows that working with darkness and light is the way to access the Light; however, the Light is often administered by religions in our times.

Religions reduce subtle feelings, such as the play between dark and light, to dualized 4D collective mind-sets. Magnificently, a large circle of light penetrates the outer circle making space in 8D. The circle of light is a transformation of the smaller dark circle touching it, which is the 5D heart dimension of the string of five circles that propel the circle of light into 8D. This shows that the heart can always move us beyond belief systems that split us between dark and light. The way of the heart is always the most direct route, but Western mental complexity creates a need for many people to work with the nine-dimensional form. There are so many things I could say about other 1995 circles, since they are so deeply connected with *The Pleiadian Agenda,* but we must move along.

Koch Fractals and the Power of the Divine Mind

The circles in 1996 continued to lead the researchers on by making versions of complex fractals and DNA helixes. You've already had a taste of this in chapter 8 with the presentation of the Julia Set (1996), with its tetrahedral and spherical aspects superimposed. Consider it again in figure 8.3, and imagine how many pages I could write about it as an expression of $3 + 3 + 3 = 9$, and the spiral as the Golden Mean. The first Julia Set was a complex fractal 1,000 feet in diameter that appeared in broad daylight right next to Stonehenge, and the Triple Julia Set tripled the fractal spiral. What awesome beauty! Fractals are patterns that repeat their general features over a wide range of scales, so that without magnification, you see essentially the same pattern, such as the circles in the Julia Sets.

In chapter 10, I mentioned testing links with the Circlemakers at the 1997 Power Places Tours crop circles conference. I was so inspired by the Circlemakers that I wanted to see the world be inspired by them. The Western rational mind blocks most people from being able to appreciate these phenomena. I decided I could help spread the word by proving that humans can be in direct communication with the Circlemakers. As a lifelong astrologer, I am familiar with the pitfalls of *proving* that anything exists that can't be measured and verified. I created a symbol, presented it at a conference in public, showed students and some faculty how to imprint it in their brains, and then waited to see if a version or versions of my design appeared in the fields after that exercise. That would be a proof. And I would be taking all the risk if there were no response to our test, assuming the crop circle was too complex to be hoaxed.

The perfect occasion was the 1997 crop circles conference at Salisbury, especially since I'd teach with John Michell again and he'd enjoy the experiment. There were fifty people plus a few faculty present for the experiment. Each person was handed a copy of the symbol (see figure 11.12A); they studied it enough to get a visual memory; then I asked them to shut their eyes. They were asked to visualize the symbol in their third eye (the space between eyebrows), and then to transfer it onto an imaginary television screen at their medulla oblongata (the top of the spine at the back of the skull). The symbol is my design adapted for what the Circlemakers could do with

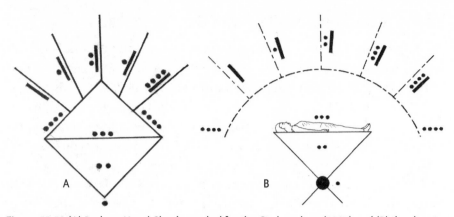

Figure 11.12 (A) Barbara Hand Clow's symbol for the Circlemakers (1997) and (B) the drawing of the canopy of light show how the Mayan dot and bar system reflects the nine dimensions.

the nine-dimensional form given to me by the Ps—the Canopy of Light. I sensed the Circlemakers might enjoy playing with it, since it is a double pyramid that shows how the human body receives and translates nine dimensions.

Compare my original design to the design for the Circlemakers. Now here is what happened. Our group imprinted this symbol in the morning on July 31. (In 2002, while reading Freddy Silva's book, I realized that the first Koch Fractal appeared July 23 beside Silbury Hill, but I didn't know about it at the conference, nor did anybody else as far as I know. It is intriguing that I drew the symbol for the conference handout around July 23, just before leaving the United States.) I left the conference after asking the faculty or students to let me know if there was a response, and then I got barraged by faxes in mid-August. On August 8, the Milk Hill fractal was obviously a version of my symbol (see figure 11.13). Next came the Strange Attractor on Hakpen Hill on August 18 (see figure 11.14), and Colin Andrews, who was present for the experiment, faxed it to me and said he thought it was a clear response from the Circlemakers. The facts are: Two Koch Fractals that are an expression of my symbol appeared just after our group imprinted the design, and the Strange Attractor is an especially remarkable expression of our group thought-form. It cannot be a hoax, since it had a reversed tetrahedral form woven into the standing pattern at the center, and its 204 circles each have a thin central clump.

Figure 11.13 Milk Hill Koch Fractal (1997), Milk Hill, Alton Barnes, Wiltshire, England.

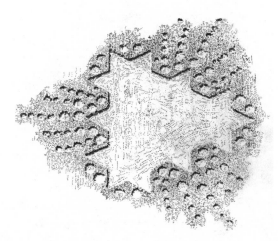

Figure 11.14 Strange Attractor (1997), Hakpen Hill, near Broad Hilton, Wiltshire, England.

Fractals are computer-generated images that are used to figure out where geometric order breaks down into chaos—such as stock-market crashes and turbidity and flow in water—in order to understand *changes of state*. It was impossible to observe these complex dynamics before computers and the crop circles. The most complex fractal that has been created so far is called the Mandelbrot Set. The Circlemakers created one with a 1,000-foot span in 1991 at Ickleton, near Cambridge! Since the circles have progressed by number and complexity in tandem with the proliferation and complexity of computers, there must be a relationship between how they both affect our minds.

When Silva analyzed the body (with the recessed, woven, raised tetra-hedron) of the Hakpen Hill glyph, he saw that it exhibits the Pythagorean *tetractys,* which is a triangle (tetrahedral face) divided by ten equidistant dots, and the dots also form a Platonic solid cube inside (figure 11.15). According to Pythagoras and the esoteric traditions, the tetractys expresses the Ten Words of God.[7] Since my design was originally inspired by the Pleiadian Canopy of Light (see the introduction)—which shows how our bodies translate nine dimensions of consciousness—then our bodies are the vehicles for the Ten Words of God! The ten dots show the musical ratios and the octaves as well as the three elements of light that govern creation itself. This geometry is most easily seen in this fractal, which also most resembles my symbol.

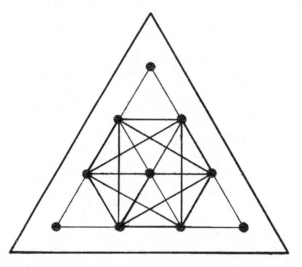

Figure 11.15 The Pythagorean tetractys related to the Strange Attractor. From *Secrets in the Fields,* Freddy Silva, p. 186.

The symbol is probably loaded with 10D information, which I still barely understand. Certainly, it also shows why people like to go bowling. The ten bowling pins are the tetractys! Humor aside, the dots or circles emanating off the twelve pyramids of the Strange Attractor (see figure 11.14), with the big spray in rays off the three sides, are an expression of the nine-dimensional system and how it relates to changes of states in nature. Taking a central pyramid on one side, six circles for 6D run off the apex, five circles off each side, and again five circles off the rest of one side between the bases of the pyramids. At the three tips (which are three pyramids), there are only four circles surrounding them. Just as with Egyptian symbology and hieroglyphs, all this is totally intentional. This glyph is showing that the potent power of the 10D tetractys is held in stable form by the 6D morphic field lines in the center of the sides surrounded by the 5D fields of love. The spherical contact points on the tips are dormant momentarily to hold changes of state on the 10D vertical axis. Responding to our desire to know the universe better, the Circlemakers showed us how biological forms will undergo changes of state. Letting crop circles go, with Windmill Hill as a last example, it is time to investigate the healing aspects of the nine-dimensional system. In our Activations, I primarily work with our minds, and Gerry works with our bodies and with practical applications of these teachings.

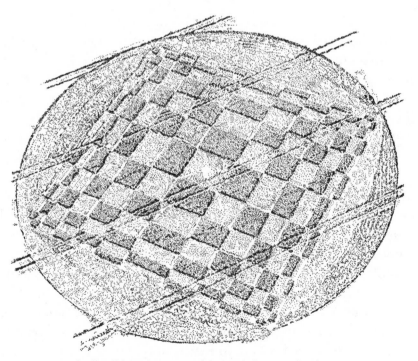

Figure 11.16 Windmill Hill (2000), near Avebury, Wiltshire, England.

TWELVE

Living the Nine Dimensions

By Gerry Clow

If you are like me, you probably have a lot of questions right now. Your mind is buzzing with all the information you have received: the nine dimensions and their scientific implications, followed by explanations of how crop circles connect to these dimensions. This is kind of like making a super milkshake: putting in all sorts of ingredients and blending them together. Now it is time to let those ingredients settle, to fall into place in your everyday life.

As I do this, part of me (my mind!) wishes to find out how these dimensions relate to all the other mysterious "levels" or "realms" we hear about from esoteric sources, such as the Bardos (Tibetan Buddhism), the Twelve Houses of the Duat (ancient Egypt), and the Kabbalah (mystical Judaism). John Beaulieu (see chapter 7) has a video entitled "Seven Levels of a Stillpoint," and it too touches on this esoteric realm, sourced from the work of Dr. Randolph Stone, who studied Ayurvedic wisdom in his later years. We also hear of the experiences of those who venture into the ecstatic realms visualized while under the influence of hallucinogens such as ayahuasca, LSD, and peyote. Finally, I think of Barbara's favorite teacher, Dr. Felicitas Goodman (the anthropologist who discovered Ecstatic Trance), who refers to how various peak and out-of-body experiences are received at "different brain maps" within us. Are the nine dimensions one such brain map?

I wish I could give you—and myself—an easy "road map" through this maze of understandings. I want an easy mental answer, and there is none, other than this: These nine dimensions, channeled through Barbara from the Pleiadians, are a clear contribution on their own. Perhaps all of the other "systems" and "road maps" were just preparation for this material. Perhaps these nine dimensions are our future, replacing or complementing earlier understandings from the past.

In any case, I will keep working on the connections to traditional or previous teachings, and I encourage each of you, from each of your own perspectives, to interweave these new understandings with those teachings you have received from other sources. Meanwhile, what's exciting about the teachings of the nine dimensions is how *alive* this material is; every time we teach it, we learn something new from our students. And as Barbara has shown, scientific discoveries continue to parallel these new awarenesses.

Having said all this, I want to move into a formal and firm closing for this book. Much as I would assist a client off the table, I am going to work with you to bring you back to your feet, back to today, back to the now. For many of us, the big AHA! is not enough. We get swallowed back up by our regular lives, and only rarely do we ponder the levels we found in ourselves during the time together. So even for those of you who have already "gotten it," and especially for those of you who, like me, are still integrating the work into your daily life, let me describe a helpful process for bringing the nine dimensions home.

Stabilizing Yourself

This process begins with a passage in a favorite book of mine. I discovered it during my classes with Matthew Fox, the former Dominican priest who embraced the mystical tradition within the Church and originally founded Bear & Company. Fox is an Eckhartian scholar (Meister Eckhart, ca. 1260–1328) and was the first spiritual teacher to bring this mystic's multidimensional work to the attention of spiritual seekers within, and outside, the Church. This little but powerful book is entitled *Meditations with Meister Eckhart,* and it is one of the first books we published at Bear. We were encouraged to read it by candlelight, in the spirit of how it was written.

My favorite passage from Eckhart is a question, and an answer. "What did the stable hand do when he had seen the face of God? . . . he returned to the stable." And that is what we do every time we have an ecstatic experience, a mind-opening, a big AHA!: We return to our stable. When I first heard these words, I was content just to get directions for what to do next. Today, having committed myself to the healer's path, I like the fact that in these words we have a place that is "stable" and a place of great fertility and power, from the rich nutrients in the manure and the vitality of the horse.

So, like the stable hand, having just walked through a "mindfield" of ideas, return to your stable, to your place of being stable. If your home is not stable, see what is making it unstable and make it stable. Your home is a direct reflection of your own body, of your own stability. A home can be a van, a tent, a mansion: All are worthless if they are not stable, and priceless if they are. From what you learned in the "class" of this book, all these sit on terra firma, *la tierra madre,* on Earth: All are subject to gravity, as you are, and all connect to the iron core crystal pulsating at Earth's center.

Now, your body. When was the last time you considered your feet, your hips, your shoulders? Are *you* stable? Are you walking around, sitting around, in a stable body? If not, what can you do about it? First, you can become aware of it. Look at yourself in the mirror: Is one shoulder higher than the other, one lower than the other? Touch your hips as you look in the mirror: Does one hip appear to "ride" a little higher than the other? What happens when you lie down? Are your feet even, or is one leg longer than the other? This is structure, and we kid ourselves by thinking we can go around with a structure that is out of alignment. What would happen to a building standing that way? Cracks would appear in the walls, and one or more of the footings would eventually settle and sink, causing the building to collapse. We shore up buildings, why not ourselves?

So, awareness first. Then, what to do about it. *Being aware* is the first step. The second, immediately after the first, is *not judging yourself.* Say to yourself: This is how I am finding myself today. That is what is called being neutral—not positive or negative, just neutral. Learn how to practice neutrality. And remember, all living matter carries three charges: positive, negative, and *neutral.* Neutrality is as much our birthright as is the process of taking and receiving. Neutral means no judgment, means just being.

Those of you with cars will know what I'm saying. Think of what it feels like when you put your car in neutral, N on the gearshift. Your car idles, it is settled, it feels happy, you and the car know you are going nowhere, even though you're ready at any time to resume forward, or backward, motion.[1]

The next step on the path to stability is giving energy to yourself. We sometimes call this "loving yourself," and this is a good way to express it, too. When you find yourself out of sorts, unbalanced, or if you injure yourself, you can judge yourself as not worthy and tell yourself this is why you are this way—or you can give yourself the love you often give to others and not to yourself. Consider the difference between sending loving energy to yourself, say, if you have cut your finger—versus cursing yourself as stupid, or worse, the finger for getting in the way! Which of the two solutions do you think leads to greater and faster healing? And would you be surprised to hear that medical studies have already proved that sending energy to an injury hastens the healing process? (Just read any of the work of Dolores Krieger, the brilliant cofounder of Therapeutic Touch, and you'll see what I mean; you might even take a course in it and share this skill with others!)

So how are you finding yourself today? Are you ready to address any imperfections you may find, with neutrality, and even with some self-love? Good. You are on the path to taking responsibility for your own wellness and stability. And if you find you need a helping hand along the way, go to one of those local healers or bodyworkers you have always said you'd check out but have never gone to see. Remember: They are there to facilitate your own wellness, not to become another crutch in your life. They want *you* to make *yourself* well.

Now, as to the revelations or awakenings in this book: How are you going to incorporate them into your newly stabilized body and life? I have a number of suggestions, and they mostly involve meditations. I also have a number of creative ideas of where you can go beyond these daily meditations, which I think you will also enjoy.

Nine-Dimensional Meditation (20–30 minutes)

Do you like to "tune in" before you have to get out of bed in the morning? Do you ever wake up twenty minutes before the alarm is going to ring, and feel like you don't want to get up, but you're not sure what to do? Or, can you take 20 to 30 minutes sometime in the day to tune in to the dimensions? To do so, I suggest you initially follow the meditation described here, and then let it inspire you to create your own process, your own meditation. I also suggest that you do this meditation in the following manner.

If you are lying down, increase the clarity and effectiveness of your meditation by placing your hands behind your head in what I call the Tom Sawyer pose. Overlap your fingers at the base of your skull, where it joins the top of your spine; see if you can find a place that seems to "pressurize" your brain a bit, to make your head seem a bit "fuller." (This is *not* recommended, however, if you have any current or recent head or brain injury.) Experiment with the pose, until you feel yourself slowing down and are able to "see" things going on in your life more clearly. This will assist you in experiencing each dimension in this "active" form of meditation.

Or if you are seated, let this meditation be an active form of "Inner Work."[2] As you begin to experience each dimension—as something you primarily see, hear, or feel—let it expand in your awareness. It is best to amplify whatever is bothering you—or inspiring you—so that you can see it clearly, in all its details. Therefore make your awareness of each dimension as large as possible. In doing so, you begin to see how it connects to you, how you connect to it. As a result, you are able to integrate it into your life in a way you would not otherwise.

Make yourself comfortable. Take your time, and remember what you have learned so far about becoming comfortable, about settling. Let your gaze become soft; keep only enough focus to read these words. Find your breath, and find your feet. Return to your body, let your mind slowly let go of the dance of words and ideas you have been holding inside your head.

Take a deep cleansing breath, and feel the air move along the inside of your skull, opening a space between your brain and your skull. Let your shoulders drop as you do this, and take another breath, doing the same things one more time. Notice how good this feels, after your brain has been working so hard.

Find your midline, the column of energy that runs top to bottom through the center of your body. Let the energy of your next breath follow your midline, all the way down to the base of your spine. Experiment: first a soft breath, and then a deeper one. Place your attention on this centering space within yourself, the place where life force, the liquid light, moves up and down your body.

Now feel how you are seated, how your bottom touches the chair you are in, or the surface you are lying upon. Take that same attention down to your feet, and see how they are planted, how they are in contact with the space below you. Let your next breath travel all the way down your body to your feet. Just notice the energy, feel how long your body is, how much energy there is in your feet.

Now let your attention drift down through the floor, down through the foundation of the structure you are in, and into the ground beneath. You can picture this ground as dark yet still alive. You can see rocks and minerals and water and tiny organisms. Continue deeper and deeper, and see and feel and hear what's around you. Continue even deeper, and begin to feel the vibrations of the giant iron core crystal deep within the center of Earth. It is safe to travel down this way, down to our home at the center of our planet.

Now begin to feel how this deep place resonates within your own body. Feel the vibrations of the iron core crystal at the base of your body. Feel the vibrations traveling through your feet and legs to the tip of your spine. Feel these vibrations held at your root, and cradled by your hips, one on each side. Feel these vibrations at your sacrum, that hand-shaped bone at the base of your spine, and at your pubic bone in front. Feel the sense of wateriness at this cradle in your body. Feel the sense of being fully present in our world, our world of 3D, and anchored safely here at the cradle of your hips and spine, at your bottom.

Hold this space. Notice that you are holding three dimensions in this space: the iron core crystal (1D), the telluric (2D), and linear time and space (3D). Take your time; there is a lot of information here. Take all the time you need to integrate these sensations into your body.

Now move your attention to your navel. Notice how vibrant and alive this area of your body is. This is where you were connected, long ago, to Mother, Nourishment, and Life. Take a deep and long breath through this opening in your body; feel yourself expanding. Notice all the power you have here in your body. This is your drum, your belly brain. This is what helps you take action when you need to take action, including running if you need to run. You have power and primal wisdom here. This is the source of your power. This is the connection to the archetypal realm (4D), the realm of collective feelings and story.

Now move your attention to the center of your chest. Take a big breath here, and feel your ribs expanding, and your diaphragm letting go. Feel the air circulating in your body from each new breath. This is where you expand to receive and to send out. This is where you experience ideas and love and joy. Let your heart expand with each breath, and feel yourself becoming lighter and lighter. Welcome to the realm of unconditional love (5D).

As you take your next breath, let it come through your throat. Let this breath come in through your open throat, like through the mouth of a baby bird receiving nourishment from its mother. See how open you can make your throat: Feel how all the joints in your body relax as you do this, starting with your shoulders, then moving through your spine, your hips, your knees, your ankles. See how open and loose and relaxed you can make your body. This allows your perfect form, the idea of you, to become whole again. You are creating the realm of your very own sacred geometry (6D). Tune in to your structure, and visualize the perfection of your form if you can.

Now place your attention on your third eye, the space between your eyebrows close to the middle of your forehead. As you place your attention here with your breath, you should begin to feel some heat, a place of recognition. Stay calm and take your time; sometimes it takes a few breaths to "heat up" this sacred space in your body, this window of sight and vibration. Feel it open, and feel and see the sight it allows. Pretend you have eyes behind this space, and look out. What do you see? Let your sight go far, to an imaginary horizon, and see the Sun setting or rising. Focus on this distant spot, and continue to feel your third eye pulsing. You are entering the galactic highways of light (7D). See what comes to you today, whether as feelings, sights, or sounds.

Now place your consciousness, and your breath, on the top of your skull, and just above it. Feel as if you have a hand above your head, warm, inviting, and not touching. Just there, beckoning. Let your energy flow to this hand. Let your consciousness rush up here, as you take each new breath. Feed this hand with your breath, as it feeds you with warmth and guidance. You are entering into the realm of the Absolutes, of the Divine (8D). See what's here for you today. Take your time. It may come as a sight, a sound, or a feeling. See if the Divine has a message for you today.

Finally, you are ready to take your consciousness far from your center, to the center of our Galaxy (9D). Picture the energy streaming up your body from the iron core crystal, up through your crown, and on up to Source. This Source is the black hole, the attractor, at the center of our Milky Way. It is as much a part of you as is the iron core crystal; you are both iron core crystal and black hole. This is your matrix, your full expanded self. Stay with this feeling, and with this realization, as long as you like. Breathe softly and easily; your journey is complete.

Now, as you become aware of your 3D self, your conscious self, let your breaths become quicker and deeper. Take three strong breaths, one after another, and open your eyes. Remember where you have been, and know that you can return there any time.

Welcome back to your everyday world, and let this day be filled with new understandings of what it is like to be fully alive.

Experiencing the Dimensions through Your Four Bodies

Another technique, which complements Inner Work, is to see how you receive new awareness at each of your four bodies: physical, emotional, mental, and spiritual. To do this, you must have a good working sense of each of your bodies. Learning how to "read" situations through your bodies is a bit like learning how to tune in to your chakras. Just as you can tell yourself to tune in to any of your chakras at a moment's notice: your solar plexus . . . your third eye . . . your root chakra . . . , you can tell yourself to tune in to any one of your bodies: your physical body . . . your spiritual body . . . your emotional body . . . your mental body. . . .

Barbara has discussed the four bodies earlier in this book (see chapter 6, for example), and I'm sure they're a concept with which you may already be familiar. A new way to look at them is through the recent work of the biologist Joseph Chilton Pearce, who writes about the four brains: reptilian, mammalian, human, and neocortex.[3] Each of these brains controls a different part of our perception and personality. The reptilian brain definitely connects us to our physical bodies, to our ability to connect to the elementals. The mammalian brain contains flight-or-fight codes, which connect us to our emotional bodies. The human brain is noted for reasoning, which connects us to our mental bodies. And the neocortex or higher brain connects us to our spiritual bodies. By tuning in to one aspect of our brain or another, we are connecting to one or another of those four bodies. Being able to "find" the four bodies is a good starting point in finding multidimensional consciousness.

More Nine-Dimensional Meditations

Seated meditation with Tibetan bells or chimes: This nine-dimensional meditation is designed for a seated pose. Please remember to make yourself comfortable in your pose; often a pillow is needed to lift you off the floor a bit to ease pressure on your sacrum and tailbone. When you are comfortable and settled, call your attention, out loud or in silence, to each of the dimensions in succession; when you call out each one, say, "I call my attention ('our' if you are doing a group meditation) to the first dimension," and ring the bells or chime. Let the resonance of the instrument fill the room, and let your body feel the fullness of the dimension you have invoked. You can do this in ceremonies, at sacred sites, or with a partner. You can add words, such as ". . . the first dimension, home of the iron core crystal." You can call on the Keepers of the dimensions. Be creative. Let yourself experience the feeling of each dimension. Each one is an aspect of each one of us. This meditation can take ten to twenty minutes, and longer if you wish to enter into silence following the invocations.

Standing, on-the-run meditation (1.5 minutes): Sometimes we are in constant motion during a day, and we have little or no time to "meditate." Here's an idea of how to take just ninety seconds and make contact with all nine dimensions. For those of you who do yoga, you'll find this to be familiar territory: How many times does your instructor remind you to breathe, either while you're concentrating on a pose or as you are out in the world, having a hectic day? Yes, just *breathe.* As our favorite yoga master Kali Ray says, "Stay relaxed and the benefits of practice stay with you!"

The meditation is simple, yet powerful. Stop whatever you are doing and simply take a series of nine even breaths. Inhale for five seconds, filling your lungs and your body, then exhale for five seconds. Each time you do this, think of each dimension in succession. First breath . . . first dimension. Second breath . . . second dimension, and so on. Ten seconds per breath cycle times nine dimensions equals ninety seconds. See what you feel like afterwards. Wow! Nice to stay in touch with the big picture, don't you agree? And notice how this calms down your central nervous system—just by taking your attention off outside stimulation and switching to the internal ones. Good work, and keep on doing it! Once a day at least at the beginning, then whenever you find yourself getting off track, unfocused, and needing to "re-source" yourself.

Journey to the nine dimensions using music: The incredibly gifted composer Michael Stearns created his own interpretation of the nine dimensions through twenty-four tracks of composed music, recorded voices, and natural sounds. We play this CD, which we entitled *Journeys through Nine Dimensions,* during all our Activations, and most of our students now own it. (Information on how to order the CD is at the back of the book.)

We recommend that you lie down, be comfortable, and do your best to stay awake. Let your body respond and flow with the music. Keep a tablet handy, and when the CD is over, immediately jot down any special things you remember about any or all of the dimensions. Keep in mind your experiences with the dimensions will change over time; they are never the same. This is an ongoing process. Keep the notes handy, and if you are doing the meditation with a friend, compare notes. If you're doing it in a class, form a circle and tell your experiences, one by one, around the circle. Someone else's experience will often ignite memories of your own. Weave a story of the dimensions as a group.

Use the nine-dimensional CD during a healing session: This can be done while you are receiving a session from a bodyworker, or when you are giving a session yourself. Keep in mind that it is probably best to turn off the CD after it finishes the ninth dimension; track ten is a blend of the dimensions, which can be integrative and good to listen to later. For now, you just want to tune in to the nine dimensions, one by one, which the music does beautifully. If you are a bodyworker reading these words, keep in mind that this is powerful music, not designed for everyone. Become familiar with it yourself first, then offer it when the time is right for the right client. For instance, if a client is working on grounding, it can be an excellent tool for helping that client be grounded, as well as higher dimensional. As a practitioner, I love to work with the CD, as it helps me pace myself, and I get to reexperience the nine dimensions in a special way.

Live one dimension for the whole day: This exercise is fun. It does not have to interfere with your day at all. All you have to do is set the intention on which dimension you wish to place your attention on that day—then live it. Take what you know of that dimension and watch to see what comes to you. For example, I wanted to have a fourth-dimensional day, to interact with the archetypal energies and see what synchronicities would teach me that day (i.e., what would happen outside myself that would confirm what I was thinking about or feeling). Within minutes, my attention was on the sound of the animals in the yard and my neighbor next door. I felt like I had walked through a doorway in my mind; I had placed my focus on my larger field, in which I was a player.

It was a very comfortable feeling, almost like imagining myself to be the Yaqui master Don Juan out receiving teachings in the desert landscape. I had a much broader, richer, interactive day. I still went about my business; I just had an additional "track" or "program" running in my mind. I did not lack for entertainment that day, nor will you. Open your heart and have a day of unconditional 5D love; watch the geometry and sacred order in all things on a 6D day; call on 8D and see what higher lessons are to be learned that day. The choices—and creativity—are endless.

Take a nine-day, nine-dimensional vacation: If you'd like to experience the dimensions one day at a time, over nine days, why not spend nine days of vacation somewhere nice and do just that! Your tenth day can be your return day, and let it be the day you integrate all that you have learned.

Create your own Activation: We encourage all the students who attend our workshops to teach this material to their own students, friends, and/or family, and to lead an activation. In the workshops, we do a Six-Polarity, Wheel of Twelve exercise with the students before we start the activation, much as Barbara described earlier in this book (see chapter 3). It is important, if you choose to lead a group in this work, to make sure your students are well grounded before they encounter the dimensions through the music (whether you use the CD or make your own, using a crystal bowl or other musical instrument). There is nothing more empowering than being the teacher, plus you get to relearn the material all over again yourself. We have taught over two hundred Activations, and they never are the same. The material only keeps growing and evolving, along with the music.

Exploring Your Home Dimension

A good way to complete this book, this process of awakening, is to go back through the dimensions one more time, this time with your body and mind more awakened, more empowered. What matters now is how *you* integrate this material in your life. It reminds me of leading a horse to water: It is up to the horse to decide whether to drink.

One way to begin this process is to ask yourself: What dimension (or dimensions) do I feel closest to? Is there one I feel is "home" to me? Do I naturally gravitate to one or another? This is an important concept to cover. This colors your feelings about all the dimensions and also gives you the power to discover more. Unless you have a personal interest, these dimensions are just concepts, however interesting or fascinating.

Maybe nothing resonated with you as you went through the dimensions the first time, or maybe one or two did. You either got excited, or ideas or images started popping into your head, or not. To get this far in this book, I'm assuming you did find one that particularly interested you. All I want to say here is: Embrace this dimension, get to know it. The meditations and practices I've described in this chapter are a start.

You will be able to go on a much deeper journey once you discover your dimension; you in effect become a teacher of that dimension. Think about the guides, the dreams, the awarenesses you have probably had throughout your life, and how they relate to your dimension. Barbara suggests you create an altar to that dimension; get a feeling of which direction it is most in resonance with, and place objects there that remind you of that dimension and its qualities. This becomes your tune-in place to that dimension, a mini-portal to that dimension.

To help you further, find others who share your dimension; I'm sure if you look around yourself, you'll find you already have many of them in your life. It is like realizing many of your closest friends also share your astrological sign, or are strongly aspected to it. Just as you might have a Leo party—or a Fire Sign party, for Leos, Aries, and Sagittarians—you might have a Second Dimension party—or an Even Dimension Party, for 2D, 4D, 6D, and 8D people (see more on this concept in the next section). The important thing is: Find out where you are centered, and move forward from there. Once you can "own" one dimension, you can begin to open up to, and work with, all of them.

Noticing "Neighboring" Dimensions and the Odd/Even Dimensions

One of the best ways to become more familiar with your home dimension is through the dimensions to either side of it. Take another look at figure I.2 in the introduction, and notice how the energy of one dimension "steps down" (or "steps up") into the energy of the next along the vertical axis. This will allow you to begin to feel the subtle differences between those dimensions on one side of the vertical axis or the other.

Barbara teaches—and many students have agreed—that as individuals we tend to favor the even dimensions as a group, or the odd dimensions as a group. This is probably because we are naturally linked to an odd or even dimension to begin with; that is, it is our home base (see the previous section) or one that we are working with or locked into at this time. The point is: We have natural inclinations, tastes, or dispositions. This is where we start, then we begin to move into all the dimensions.

The odd and even dimensions do have particular qualities. We tend to think of the odd dimensions (1D, 3D, 5D, 7D, and 9D) as highly conscious and conceptual—in other words, very comfortably received in our conscious minds—and the even dimensions (2D, 4D, 6D, and 8D) as emotional or structural—in other words, "felt" dimensions that we often take in through our unconscious minds. Personally, I feel that the odd dimensions have a lot to do with the mind, with the vertical axis, with above and below.

And the even dimensions have more to do with our feelings, with the horizontal planes, with being here now, with having form and boundaries.

A good way to reflect on these vertical and horizontal qualities is to picture a yoga pose, such as the seated twist; you feel this pose horizontally, but you can also feel it vertically. As you breathe into the pose, you twist further on the horizontal plane, but your breath also reminds you about the rise and fall of your spine, the distance from your sacrum to your crown. In any case, I like to use the word *movement* with the odd dimensions, and *containment* with the even dimensions. See if this strikes a chord with you, as you begin to work with the dimensions yourself.

Another way to look at the odd and even dimensions is via the right brain and left brain, or via the terms yin/yang, involution/evolution. If we notice the vertical axis drawn against the human body (see figure 1.5), all the even dimensions are on the left side, the side controlled by the right or intuitive brain; the odd dimensions are on the right side, controlled by the left or linear brain. The left side is akin to yin, the right side to yang. Using Dr. Randolph Stone's Polarity Therapy model, primal energy (energy from the Creator, or Source) moves down the right side of our body as involution, and back up our left side as evolution, in a continual loop of output and input.

Relating the Dimensions to the Chakras

The seven major chakras associated with our bodies are like seven energy bundles or energy centers into which our subtle energy systems are wired. They are like junction boxes in a house's electrical system, and they are very palpable (able to be felt and interacted with) to experienced bodyworkers. When I pass my hand over a client lying prone on my table, I can usually find the chakras as a change of vibration, sometimes with a feeling of warmth attached. I can especially feel the effect of what happens when I am holding that client with the other hand: an actual felt "current" passes from my off-body hand to the hand that is receiving. This tells me where that client is holding energy at that particular time, and is sometimes a clue as to where to work next.

For a long time, I kept looking at Barbara's (and the Ps') chart of the vertical axis (see figure I.2) and wondering how those nine dimensions related to the human body, and especially to our chakras. I have come to think of the iron core crystal and the Galactic Center as two additional chakras to which we are all communally related; in other words, they are shared by all. I also wonder if, as we become more sensitive and transparent (i.e., transfigured) as a species, our root chakras, located on our coccyx (some say, the remnant of our prehistoric tails!), will eventually become hard-wired to the iron core crystal.

In the same way, I wonder about our crown chakras, which are energetically connected to the tops of our brains: Will they too become connected energetically to the Galactic Center? Will we therefore "expand" energetically as a species, being intimately (i.e., all the time) connected to the Above and the Below? Is this what the end of the Mayan calendar is all about? And is this why the Pleiadians (via Satya in *The Pleiadian Agenda*) insist that they see humans with only five chakras connected to our bodies (i.e., they combine our root and sexual chakras and call them our sexual center)? Is it possible they see us as the humans of the future?

Meanwhile, back here in 2004 and counting, we are still getting used to being in the bodies we have. Here is how I relate our current, "felt" chakras to the nine dimensions; in parentheses, I have noted the element to which each of the lower chakras relates:

feel 1D at our coccygeal or root chakra (earth)
feel 2D at our sacral or sexual chakra (water)
feel 3D at both of these chakras (earth and water)
feel 4D at the solar plexus chakra (fire)
feel 5D at the heart chakra (air)
feel 6D at the throat chakra (ether)
feel 7D at the third eye chakra
feel 8D at the crown chakra
feel 9D at the crown chakra

This gives us a starting point. Each of you will have your own subtle interpretations of how you feel dimensional vibrations at your chakras. Write to us at our address shown at the back of the book; we'd like to hear your experiences. As I have said before, this work with the nine dimensions is a "work in progress," as are our bodies and our awarenesses of them. Keep tuning in to yours, and let us know what you discover! Good energetic bodywork is an excellent way to open up and learn about your chakras, particularly with a practitioner who has good verbal skills (i.e., communicates well with clients).

I love the association of the dimensions with our chakras and the elements. The chakras are electromagnetic and the elements are biological; all living things need the elements to perform the dance we call life, and the expression of that dance is felt at the chakras. And note, as I commented earlier, that our multiple connections to the Above (8D and 9D) and to the Below (1D and 2D) may evolve as we evolve. I'm looking forward to those next steps in our evolution.

Noticing the Dimensions Opening in Your Relationships

Bookstores are crammed, floor to ceiling, with all sorts of books on relationships. I hesitate to add much more to such a wealth of material. I'll just add one interesting tip. When you are relating to another person—whether it be a child, a parent, a friend, a lover—be mindful of what dimension you both are in before you engage in that conversation or action. We "think" we're all in 3D all the time, but consider those times you don't feel "quite here" or you are "out of it." Where are you? Where is the person you are relating to? Do either of you know North-South-East-West or what time of day it is? Are your feet on the ground? Are you conscious of your breathing?

Besides working on having both of you in 3D at the same time (or a whole roomful, if you are lecturing or speaking before a group), you can also do other dimensional work in your relationships, such as moving both parties into another dimension together. In other words, both choose to go into another dimension at the same time—and then see what happens between you. If you are a lecturer, this would mean moving the group's attention to another dimension, as well as your own. Just be sure you let others know where they are going, and where you're going as well! Meet you in the fifth dimension!

Noticing the Dimensions Opening in Your Workplace

At work we have many teaching relationships. Barbara says that is the main reason we all have jobs: to learn from one another. Relationships with fellow employees and the boss are important and often touch on power issues. Take what you have learned by relating to your friends and family dimensionally, and use it here, only this time, it is your job, your livelihood, your future we are talking about. When you have a hard time with someone at work, figure out what dimension he or she is coming from. Is this a fourth-dimensional takeover (i.e., the collective, cultural mind taking over), or is this just a difficult 3D conversation? See if 1D and 2D even exist in your workplace, as well as the higher dimensions of 8D and 9D. If not, seek ways to have those dimensions available. Taking crystals to work is a good start, and holding high intentions and backing them up through your actions is another one. I wish you well, in all ways, in your nine-dimensional workplace.

Practical Applications of Nine-Dimensional Consciousness

In closing, I'd like to share a few of the practical applications of the nine-dimensional work that we have seen taking place through our students. Here is a brief list:

- Teachers and parents who have experienced these dimensions have been able to open new dialogues with their students and children, who in their own lives are seeing these dimensions yet are unable and not encouraged to express them.

- Young people today want to be multidimensional, more than at any time in history; they are showing it in their body ornament, their dress, their language, their ability to take to the streets as mimics and mimes. Teaching them the nine dimensions gives them a much-welcomed road map to multidimensional consciousness.

- Office workers and those who work in business or the law, once they see the pyramid system and the power of the eighth dimension, are making clearer choices for themselves and their loved ones, which for some means leaving their work and for others blowing the whistle on those who are misusing power and position.

- Medical practitioners and healers are awakened to the roots of their power—the first and second dimensions—and to the canopy of the fourth that must be encountered and understood for the healing of themselves and their patients.

- Painters and artists have already sensed the nine dimensions and appreciate the clarification of their intuitions, allowing them to express the dimensions more freely in their everyday work.

• Meditators and spiritual teachers have appreciated the "road map of consciousness" supplied by the nine dimensions, allowing them to place themselves more easily in multidimensionality.

• And those who are simply curious and open to new thought have come away from the Activations with broader minds and a deeper appreciation of those who seek to find answers to life's biggest questions: Who are we, why are we here, what is our role on the planet?

Glossary

accretion: Increase of matter by external addition or accumulation.

acupuncture: Lightly inserting fine needles into the skin to alter energy flows.

Age of Aquarius, the Aquarian Age: The 2,160-year period from 2000 A.D. until 4160 A.D.

Age of Aries, the Arian Age: The 2,160-year period from 2320 B.C. to 160 B.C.

Age of Pisces, the Piscean Age: The 2,160-year period from 160 B.C. to 2000 A.D.

Aion: A planet in Andromeda that has a biology similar to Earth's.

alchemy: The art of understanding resonance and correspondences between dimensions.

Alcyone: The central star of the Pleiades, as viewed from Earth.

allopathic medicine: A system for maintaining health based on diagnosis, use of drugs, and surgery.

altar: A sacred space constructed in accordance with the laws of sacred science.

Andromeda: The huge spiral galaxy that is nearest to the Milky Way; together, these galaxies rule the Local Group. Andromeda is the Keeper of 7D.

animal totemic theology: Systems that explore how the gods act through humanity by showing characteristics in humans and gods that mirror animal traits.

anisotropies: Varying directional velocities within a field, such as Earth's core rotating faster than Earth's surface.

Annunaki: Sumerian gods from Nibiru, who the Ps say are the Keepers of 4D.

antiparticle: A particle of antimatter, which is matter that has the same gravitational properties as ordinary matter, but that has an opposite electrical charge as well as an opposite nuclear force charge.

apocalyptic belief: Any belief that the world is coming to an end.

aquifer: Geological structure that pools water.

Archea: The world beneath Earth's surface, which is a biosphere that feeds on primordial hydrocarbons.

archetypal dramas and stories: Mystery plays and games going on in 4D that result from human collective thoughts and feelings, which inspire or possess humans in 3D.

archetypes: Thoughtforms that shape reality, which may have existed before reality manifested and may even have precipitated reality; the primordial ideas.

astral energy: Emotional energy that bridges the physical and nonphysical, that can block contact with higher dimensions when it is polluted with fear.

astral influences: Desires of other humans and other beings to invade our minds.

astrology: The science of studying how the cycles in the heavens affect human behavior.

atmosphere: The area between Earth's surface and the ionosphere.

atom: The smallest particle in the universe; atoms are now being conceived of as tiny vibrating strings.

audible range: The field of air molecules vibrating more slowly than light (20 to 20,000 Hz) that can be heard and accessed by pianos, tuning forks, and other instruments.

auric field: The field of energy just off the surface of a living body.

autonomic processes: Functions of our bodies that are automatic, such as breathing.

ayahuasca: A hallucinogenic brew imbibed by indigenous people, especially in the Amazon region, to alter states of consciousness.

baby universes: New universes that are intelligently designed to be sent out to populate new universes.

Bach Flower Remedies: Minute potentized quantities of substances, from flowers, mixed in water that can change our frequencies and that are used on their own or sometimes with homeopathy.

bacteria: Live microorganisms that can cause infections.

big bang: A theory that the universe began with a big explosion.

biological singularity: When the codes of Earth's species pass through the Milky Way black hole to birth a new world of life in the Galaxy, according to the Ps.

biophotons: Photons emitted by DNA and which are its cellular language.

birdsong: The language of birds that comes from 7D, formulates Earth's blue band, and tunes Earth to high celestial frequencies.

black hole: An object formed in the collapse of a large star with such intense gravity that nothing, except possibly light, can escape it.

blood manipulation: Deformation of the human spirit caused by spilling blood in war and sacrifice.

blue band: A blue sphere around Earth where cosmic sound meets the outer boundary of Earth's gravity.

bodywork: Any form of therapy, such as massage or craniosacral therapy, that transforms our physical form by accessing our feelings and connections with spirit.

brain synchronization: The state of our brains when we have no fear, our crown chakras are open, and there is a balanced flow of energy between the left and right sides.

branes: Extended objects that arise in string theory and that correspond with the nine dimensions.

Caesar and Church: A coined term that describes the powers-that-be during the Age of Pisces—160 B.C. to 2000 A.D.

cairns: Megalithic stone chambers used for ceremony and sometimes burial; also refers to a mound of stones erected as a memorial.

Calabi-Yau shapes: Spaces in which the extraspatial dimensions required by string theory are curled up.

canon of sacred music: The music system that evokes the principle of enchantment, which enables humans to reattain the primordial vision.

canopy of light: The diaphanous 4D field that passes on higher-dimensional messages to us in 3D.

cellular memory: The memory of all experiences that is light-encoded in our cells.

chakras: Energy centers in our bodies that resonate with feelings and subtle-energy fields.

channeling: The ability to pick up messages from other beings and dimensions and transmit them in 3D.

chaos theory: Complex mathematics that explores how systems break down amidst order.

chaotic attractors: Advanced forms of order that seem to be in the future and influence less organized states.

Chiron: An astronomical body that orbits between Saturn and Uranus on a fifty-one-year orbit.

Circlemakers: The beings who are creating crop circles.

collective mind, world, or realm: The amalgam of individual thoughts and feelings that melds and weaves archetypal patterns, and into which everyone is plugged.

color spectrum: The breakdown of visible light into color ranges.

configurations of Platonia: The geometric structures of 6D that correspond to Plato's ideals.

conical helix: A spiral in the form of a cone.

conjuring: Using energy techniques on specific persons or groups.

conscious: Totally present in 3D with the ability to detect, learn from, and be guided by higher-dimensional intelligence.

cords: Strings of elemental forms that reach into our four bodies of consciousness.

Cosmic Restart Button: The arrival of Christ on Earth to seed Earth's biology with love.

cosmic strings: Long threads of concentrated energy that extend across the universe and stretch the speed of light.

cosmology: The contemplation of the universe in all dimensions.

creativity: Making art in 3D that is inspired by other-dimensional messages.

crop circles: Designs and patterns that appear instantaneously in fields of wheat, rapeseed, grass, and corn, most frequently in southern England.

cymatics: The study of geometric patterns made by sound.

cymatics machine: An apparatus that uses a medium such as sand to make sound patterns visible.

Dark Ages: The period from 500 to 1600 A.D., when the Church attempted to totally control the world.

dark energy: Negative and evil forces that come out of suppressed creativity and emotions.

debunking: Destroying the credibility of a legitimate phenomenon by making it appear to be false.

density: Weight and mass of objects.

diaphanous: Translucent.

diatonic scales: Octave relationships that increase by ratios.

dilemma: An unresolved situation.

dimensions: Realms in which physical or energetic realities manifest.

divine immanence: The 6D realm of geometric forms that directs nature.

DNA: Nucleic acids that are located in cells that are the molecular basis of heredity (replication); DNA's double-helix structure exhibits all the laws of sacred geometry.

dolmens: Megalithic constructions of huge flat stones that rest on three or more standing stones.

dreaming: Entering into, and traveling in, other dimensions.

drug: Any substance that blocks or enhances physical signals.

drugged: Possessed by substances that reduce or alter our health and consciousness.

duality: The division of an issue into positive and negative poles.

eclipse: When the Moon blocks the Sun (solar eclipse), and when Earth blocks the Moon (lunar eclipse), or when any body in space blocks the view of another.

ecosystems: Regions in which related systems of life can thrive.

eighth dimension (8D): The realm of the Divine Mind imaged at an organizational level, as run by the Galactic Federation. Orion is the Keeper of 8D.

electricity: The basic charge in matter.

electromagnetic (EM) fields: Energy fields generated by electricity in magnetic fields.

electromagnetic spectrum: The measurement of all the frequency ranges that manifest matter, such as our bodies, microwaves, and gamma rays.

electromagnetism: The force that binds electrons and nuclei.

electrons: Charged particles that cause the flow of electricity.

elementals: Radioactive, chemical, mineral, viral, and bacterial intelligences that maintain 2D and sometimes exist in 3D. The elementals are the Keepers of 2D.

Elite, Global Elite: The power group behind the military-industrial-energy-pharmaceutical-governmental complex.

emotional blocks/trauma blocks: Stuck areas in our bodies and consciousness that are the result of unhealed pain in the past and which disorganize our physical forms.

emotional processing: Any therapy that gets our feelings to speak, such as Jungian psychoanalysis and past-life regression.

enchantment: Using sound (chanting) and sacred geography to bridge Earth and sky.

enzymes: Catalysts for biochemical reactions.

erotic Christ: The cosmic progenitor of humankind; the alchemical male.

event horizon: The boundary around a black hole, from which nothing can escape.

fanatics: Individuals or beings who so totally believe in their own point of view that they will do anything to make everyone else go along with them.

Fibonacci spiral: The spiral that is determined by the Golden Mean or *phi*, which is the basis of materialization.

fifth dimension (5D): The realm of love held in form by the Pleiadians that expresses the energy of the whole universe.

first dimension (1D): The iron core crystal in the center of Earth.

fleecing: A technique used by the Elite to collapse pyramid systems in a way that enables them to take out the profits to set up a new pyramid system; the collapse of Enron in 2001 is an example.

four bodies of consciousness: Our physical, emotional, mental, and spiritual bodies that commingle within us.

four-directional altar or matrix: Any space on Earth that delineates how to receive the seven sacred directions—North, South, East, West, sky, Earth, and heart—in our bodies.

four forces in nature: Electromagnetism; the strong and weak nuclear forces; and gravity.

fourth dimension (4D): The realm of the human collective mind and feelings.

fractal: A computer-generated figure in which the same motif repeats on an ever-diminishing scale that shows where order breaks down into chaos, such as turbidity flow in water.

Frankenstein biology: Experiments on lifeforms, such as cloning, replacing body parts, and manipulating DNA.

frequencies: Electromagnetic radiation, such as radio waves and microwaves, that make matter visible in the visible light spectrum or detectable, as in a radio.

fundamentalists: Members of any religion who believe that their god is the only one and should control everybody else in the world.

Gaia: The spirit and ecosystems of Earth.

Gaia's biological codes: The primordial morphogenetic field of Earth.

Galactic Center: The center of the Milky Way, which is 27 degrees Sagittarius.

Galactic Federation: The organization, directed by the Orion star system, that runs 8D.

galactic highways of light: Huge 7D photon bands that structure the Milky Way that are the high-energy transportation system of the Galaxy.

galactic synchronization: Period from 1987 to 2012, when humans will learn to vibrate in resonance with the Milky Way.

galactic synchronization beams: The 9D beams that shoot out of the Galactic Center and are torqued by the axial spin.

Galactic Winter Solstice: The time—1987 to 2012—when the plane of our solar system intersects the plane of our Galaxy in close alignment to the Galactic Center and closely aspects the Winter Solstice Sun.

gamma rays: Very high-frequency waves that come out of black holes.

gauge symmetry: Mathematics that determines the effects of sequences of transformations of objects in time and space.

gauge theory: Experimental verification in physics.

geocentric: Viewing and describing the cosmos from Earth.

geodetic: Earth-measuring systems that determine the size and shape of Earth and exact points on its surface.

geomancy: The art of working with the powers of Gaia to harmonize ourselves with Earth's frequencies.

geometry: Spatial characteristics, such as angles and spheres, that arise out of measurement; since geometry orders the universe, it is where truth can be found.

gluons: Quanta of the strong nuclear force that bind quarks inside protons and neutrons.

God poison: A sickness caused by individuals and cultures that do not care for 3D because they are waiting for the gods to return and the end of the world.

God-Poison Program: Reducing divinity to the 4D level where it splits human thought, which makes it possible to get people to kill each other; using divine forces as tools to manipulate humanity.

Goddess Alchemy: Revealing all the secrets of spiritual science.

Golden Mean: The math ratio (1:1.618) that determines the curve of the Fibonacci spiral.

grace: A quality brought to humankind by Christ, which enables us to reclaim the sacred; Christ's blood flowing in our veins.

Grail: Celtic concept of the sacred that returns us to the primordial vision, which is the same as ascension on the vertical axis.

graviton: The smallest particle of gravity.

gravity, gravitational force: The weakest yet most ubiquitous force in nature that is more effective at greater distances than the other three forces.

grounded: Located consciously in your body, in 3D, and in the now.

hadrons: Quanta of the weak nuclear force that cause radioactive decay.

harmonic biology: Species with undamaged DNA.

Harmonic Convergence: August 16 and 17, 1987, when millions celebrated humanity's new resonance with the Milky Way.

harmonize: The process of modulating the frequencies of things so they resonate with each other, such as octaves on a piano.

healer: One who manifests healthy forces and assists others to resonate with these forces.

Heliopolitan Mystery School: The wisdom school in Egypt from around 3500 to 1500 B.C. that utilized the nine-dimensional system.

henges: Deep ditches with earthen embankments, such as around Avebury, which are generally circular.

heptagonal: Seven-sided.

hertz (Hz): Measurement of the number of wavelengths per second (named after Heinrich Hertz).

hexagonal: Six-sided.

hieroglyphs (Egyptian): Multidimensional writing system that was used in Egypt for thousands of years.

history: As defined by Julian Barbour, paths through Platonia and in the landscape in the mist.

hoaxers: In the case of crop circles, people who make artificial or fake crop circles and end up nearly blocking humanity's opportunity to receive divine inspiration.

Hollywood (Holyrood): The Elite media center used to mind-control the public.

holograms: Three-dimensional images projected into space with the aid of lasers.

Holy Communion: A Roman Catholic ceremony in which wine and bread are transubstantiated into the blood and body of Christ.

Holy Grail (hidden): The bloodline of Christ and Mary Magdalene.

hydrocarbons: Organic compounds containing only carbon and hydrogen.

hypernovas: Extremely large supernovas.

hyperspace: Dimensions beyond the physical in which light is faster than Einstein's light constant.

hypothalamus: The part of the brain that lies below the thalamus, forming a major portion of the ventral region that regulates vital autonomic functions.

Icosahedral Land: A limited, timeless, eternal world of icosahedrons that may generate the nine dimensions.

illuminated: A state of consciousness when we move out of our bodies into higher dimensions and fill with Light.

indigenous people, keepers, teachers, and elders: People on Earth who are dedicated to living in harmony with nature.

ineffable: Things that cannot be expressed in words.

inflated: When 4D forces get too potent because humans are not circulating them in 3D, which sickens the people and cultures that deny them.

initiations: Techniques that connect us with our formative nature.

inorganic: Not alive.

insanity: The loss of effective control and perspective in our 3D reality.

instants of time: According to Julian Barbour, real things that are experienced by us as dynamic and temporal.

interdimensional merging: Feeling all nine dimensions and unifying our consciousness with them.

ionosphere: The upper atmosphere of Earth.

iron core crystal: The center of Earth, which is a gigantic, hexagonal iron crystal that is about the size of the Moon, and is the Keeper of 1D.

Islam: The religious complex developed by Muhammad in 600 A.D. that utilized Hebrew and Christian wisdom and added more prophecy to it in the Koran.

Judeo-Christianity: The religious complex that has dominated Western culture since 1000 B.C. that is based on the Hebrew Bible and the Christian Bible.

Ka: The human spirit body that reads frequencies.

Keepers: Beings who keep dimensions in form.

Koch fractals: Fractals developed by Swedish mathematician Helge von Koch in 1904.

labyrinths: Advanced topological knots that we can enter, walk to the center, then walk back out, and emerge.

lambdoma: A Pythagorean diagram that defines the relationships between musical harmonics and mathematical ratios.

leptons: Quanta of the weak nuclear force that cause radioactive decay.

Light: Energy in the universe that functions as particles (photons) or waves (frequencies).

light-year: The distance light travels in one year, which is 5.88 trillion miles.

linear space and time: The extended solid world that operates by time.

lithophones: Stone devices used for making music—"stone phones."

lunar cycles: The waxing of the Moon from New Moon to Full Moon, and then the waning of the Moon—from the Full Moon to the next New Moon; eclipses; and the 18.6-year Metonic cycle.

lymphatic system: The vessels and glands that carry lymphatic fluid throughout the body.

macrocosm: The larger whole we inhabit.

maelstrom or whirlwind: Big collective insanity that has become so potent that it feeds on itself, and will run on out of control until it is consumed by its negative forces. Those who participate in it are destroyed by it, such as too many people believing the end of the world is nigh.

magnestar: A collapsed star believed to have greater mass than the Sun and that is compressed into a twelve-mile diameter.

magnetic fields: Gripping fields of energy that are size-determined by the amount of electrical flow.

magnetic grid: The structure of a magnetic field.

magnetic reversals: Periodic reversals of Earth's south and north magnetic poles, which may occur because the power of the core's magnetic field captures the magnetic field of the outer one and forces the outer field to correspond to the inner field.

magnetism: Fields of connective energy that result from moving electrical charges.

magnetite: Little iron oxide slivers that can be used to see the shapes of magnetic fields.

Mandelbrot Set: A complex fractal developed by Polish mathematician Benoit Mandelbrot in the 1970s.

manifestation: Using mental techniques to make images of things in order to cause them to appear in 3D.

Manitou: An energy force in nature; often great 8D guides are called Manitou.

Mayan calendar: The calendar that begins in 3125 B.C. and ends in 2012 A.D., which is the operating manual for human evolution during its phase.

Mayan Initiatic Ceremonies: A series of ceremonies led by Hunbatz Men, which are occurring at Mayan sacred sites calibrated to awaken humanity by December 21, 2012.

medicinal properties of plants: Compounds in various plants that can heal.

medicine laws: The indigenous way of life on Earth that works with the sacred laws of nature.

medium: A substance that makes vibrational patterns visible, such as a cymatics machine or the voice of a human channel.

medulla oblongata: A portion of the brain in the back of your skull, located near where your spine meets your skull.

megalithic system or science: Stone technology science of Earth from about 5000 to 1500 B.C.

messages: Impulses that come through our feelings that contain information from other dimensions.

Metonic cycle: Named after an ancient Greek, the 18.6-year cycle of the Moon that measures the location of the lunar nodes; the nodes are where the Moon's orbit intersects the ecliptic, which is the apparent annual path of the Sun in the heavens as seen from Earth.

microbes: Small particles that are alive.

microcosm: The small world we inhabit.

mist: According to Julian Barbour, the substance that permeates Platonia and which varies in intensity by the potency of the nows.

molecular biology: The study of living things at the molecular level, usually with high-powered microscopes.

monad: A holographic form that encodes everything about an idea; also a time capsule.

morphogenesis: The overall pattern that guides all growth.

morphogenetic fields, morphic fields (M-fields): Ideal forms that replicate life-forms in 3D.

M-theory: The theory that unifies the previous five superstring theories into a single framework that involves eleven dimensions.

multidimensional: Many dimensions, and referring to a person, one who can be aware of many of these levels.

muons: High-intensity particles that are produced when cosmic rays strike the Earth's atmosphere.

mystery plays: Dramas that express, contact, and interface with other-dimensional beings and scenarios.

Nephilim: The gods who came down and raped human females as reported in the Bible.

neutrinos: Uncharged, massless particles created by particle decay, which interact very weakly with matter.

neutrons: Uncharged elementary particles that have mass nearly equal to that of a proton and are present in all known atomic nuclei except the hydrogen nucleus.

New World Order: The Elite structure that is being used for the planned takeover of Earth.

Newtonian physics: The laws of physical causality that measure motion, weight, and forces.

Newtonian world: A mind-set that likens all living beings and non-living things to machines made of parts.

Nibiru: A planet reported in ancient Sumerian records (such as the *Enuma Elish*) that is the Keeper of 4D.

ninth dimension (9D): The Milky Way itself, a dimension that emanates out of its black hole. Tzolk'in, the Mayan spinner of time waves, is the Keeper of 9D.

node, nodal crossing: Either of two points where planetary orbits or energy streams cross.

nonrenewable resource: Substance that was made a long time ago that is no longer being made.

now: The unique moment in which we can craft our future from what we already know—the past.

nucleus: The nexus point of a black hole and a white hole where time begins.

octaves: Sequences of eight notes where the notes that open each octave resonate with each other, such as middle C to higher or lower C on the piano, because the frequencies are doubled.

omnicentric: Reality unfolding from centers.

omnipotent: Unlimited authority and influence.

omniscient: The ability to read the records of the collective mind in the past, present, and future.

orgone energy: The life-force energy in the universe that seeks orgasm.

oscillate: To swing back and forth like a pendulum.

Paleolithic mind: The memory within us of human life before the 9500 B.C. cataclysm, when we were not afflicted by collective trauma; we were global and ecosensitive.

Paleolithic period: Stone Age from 2.4 millions years ago until 9500 B.C.

palpable: Felt strongly at the physical level.

particle accelerators: Large apparatuses that impart high velocities to charged particles, such as electrons, in order to study their behavior.

particle/wave duality: The functioning of light as particles or waves.

past-life regression: A counseling technique that carries a person's consciousness into the past, present, or future.

paths: According to Julian Barbour, continuous events that are played out by systems and cultures.

pentagonal: Five-sided.

perigalacticon: The closest orbital point to the Galactic Center in the 225-million-year orbit of our Sun around the Center, which is occurring now.

Photon Band: A band of light (photons) that our solar system is entering and that is accelerating human consciousness.

photons: Particles of electromagnetism that have no mass and infinite range.

photosynthesis: Using photons to supply chemical energy, especially in the formation of carbohydrates in the chlorophyll-containing tissues of plants exposed to light.

pictograms: Symbols and pictures that are etched in stone.

piezoelectric: The ability to carry electrical charges, as is the case in quartz and human cell membranes.

pineal gland: A small conical brain appendage structured like an eye that seats the soul in the body.

planar matrices or fields: Dimensional fields held together by mind that are most easily thought of as planes.

Platonia: According to Julian Barbour, the universe configured of geometric shapes and all their relationships.

Platonic solids: Five geometric forms—tetrahedron, cube, octahedron, icosahedron, dodecahedron—that are the geometric basis of all matter.

Pleiadians: Beings from the Pleiadian star system, who are the Keepers of 5D.

polarization: The opposite ends of an issue that reveal the whole field and define its range, which we can use to develop our feelings.

post-traumatic stress syndrome: Feeling inner stress sourced in unresolved trauma that gets triggered unpredictably by outside events.

power objects: Things, such as crystals, that indigenous people feel have power or *manna,* which are kept and worked with because they contain information and ancient records.

practices: Any method used to align our consciousness with other dimensions, such as yoga, dance, and meditation.

Pre-Cambrian flora and fauna: Plants and animals that thrived before the Cambrian period—440 to 540 million years ago.

probabilities: Within a given situation, a predictable series of actions that will result.

proton: Elementary particle that is identical with the nucleus of the hydrogen atom and exists with neutrons in nuclei.

psychic: A person who has the ability to tune in to other dimensions and places beyond the physical.

psychodynamics: Interpretations of behavior and mental and feeling states.

pyramid: A model by David Icke for the method used by the Elite to control systems.

Pythagorean: Pertaining to Pythagoras, who promulgated sacred geometry and ancient sacred wisdom.

quantum mechanics (QM, or the New Physics): The study of the properties of light and the microscopic world of atoms (which may be vibrating strings) and molecules; quanta are the discrete units, and mechanics is the study of their actions.

quarks: Hypothetical particles that carry a fractional electrical charge that has neither structure nor spatial dimension, yet can be three different colors—red, yellow, and blue.

quartz crystals: Tools for detecting frequencies because they are hexagonal and excellent receptors, and they are piezoelectric.

questing: Seeking spirit in the material world.

radiation: Energy released as particles and waves. It is frequently used to describe the weak nuclear force that causes the nuclear decay of unstable elements, radioactivity.

ratchet: To raise up to progressively higher levels.

resonance: The vibratory response of frequencies by octaves.

resonator: Something that connects Earth and sky, such as Silbury Hill (in England) or the Great Pyramid (in Egypt).

sacred architecture: The science of building things on Earth that model 6D geometric forms, such as the Great Pyramid of Egypt.

sacred cultures: The flowering of inspired cultures in 3D by precipitating the mist of divinity.

sacred geography: Using features of the landscape to ground higher-dimensional forces.

sacred geometry: The system that determines the dimension and form of both human-made and natural structures from Gothic cathedrals to flowers and shells.

sacred sites: Places on Earth that possess special power because they are capstones of 2D forces and draw down higher dimensions.

Sacred Tree: A tradition in almost all religions that uses the tree—roots, trunk, and branches—as the ideal image for the lower, middle, and upper world.

samadhi: The realizable human experience of communion with the Divine.

second dimension (2D): The realm of life between the iron core crystal and Earth's crust, as well as the world of lifeforms inside our bodies.

seer: A person who is conscious in nine dimensions simultaneously.

seismic tomography: Chemical analysis of rocks, magma, and crystals by measuring the waves generated by Earth movements.

Selfish Biocosm hypothesis: James N. Gardner's theory of replication and evolution.

self-mastery or spiritual masters: State of being totally balanced while grounded in 3D and intentionally fielding other-dimensional forces.

self-reflective: Reading our own energy fields.

seventh dimension (7D): The realm of cosmic sound that is the Galaxy's communication system, and whose Keeper is Andromeda.

shamans: Healers who can travel in other worlds to find information.

silica-based humans: People who speak their truth because their throats are swirling with light-encoded filaments and who are transmuting into silica-based (rather than carbon-based) beings.

singularity: A point of zero size but almost infinite gravity when a star has collapsed, which emerges as a white hole, a new universe.

sirians: Beings from the Sirius star system, who are the Keepers of 6D.

sixth dimension (6D): The realm of geometric forms that replicates in 3D and is held in form by the Sirians.

Sma: A beautiful ancient Egyptian symbol that expresses the wisdom of the heart.

solar flares: Storms on the Sun's surface that eject matter into the solar wind.

sonics: The study of sound to discover the changes in matter that occur by frequencies, such as noting how frequencies can alter the geometry in a medium.

sound: The vibration of air molecules that we measure in hertz.

space: Energy fields permeated by all the dimensions.

special relativity: Einstein's theory that time and space seem to be aspects of a four-dimensional reality where events happen that appear to be relative.

speed of light: According to Albert Einstein, it is 186,000 miles per second; beyond that, energy goes into hyperspace, thus the speed of light is the boundary of light in 3D.

sphere: A solid that is bounded by a surface consisting of all points equidistant from its center.

spherical force fields: Vibrating curved fields that exist by the connection of the intersecting points of triangles, squares, and pentagons.

spherical geometry: The geometric forms that exist within perfect spheres.

spin at the subatomic level: The primal movement that begins any materialization.

spinmasters: Elite lackeys who get paid to distort and twist the truth.

spiritual science: The laws of harmony and correspondences.

standing waves: Wavelengths that can be measured by height and length.

starlore: The repository of cellular memory contained in the stars that reawakens perennially according to stellar cycles.

string theory: A theory that says fundamental ingredients of nature are "strings" or stringlike.

strings: Tiny, one-dimensional filaments vibrating to and fro that are the smallest thing in nature and have no content.

strong nuclear force: The force that binds quarks, which make protons and neutrons.

subtle dimensions, frequencies, or fields: Realms beyond the solid world that are less dense than physicality.

supernova: The explosion of a large star.

superstring theory: String theory that incorporates supersymmetry.

supersymmetry: The symmetry principle that relates the properties of particles with a whole number amount of spin (bosons) to those with half (fermions).

symbiotic: Intimate association of two different entities.

symmetry: A property of a physical system that does not change when the system is transformed in some manner; for example, the appearance of a sphere does not change when it is rotated.

synaesthesia: Sound-induced experiences of color, such as can occur by drumming.

synchronicity: Parallel possibilities in 3D that create events that make it possible to detect the Divine.

taus: High-energy particles that are produced when cosmic rays strike Earth's atmosphere.

tectonic: Forces involved in the deformation of the crust of a moon or planet, such as volcanism.

telepathy: Two or more beings connected in an immediate and intimate way by feelings in their bodies or knowing in their minds.

television: An electronic box that projects images designed by the Elite to destroy the imagination of the public.

telluric energy fields and realms: The world of tectonic forces beneath Earth's surface, specifically the outer core, mantle, lithosphere, and inner crust of Earth.

tenth dimension (10D): The vertical axis that generates all nine dimensions.

tetractys: Pythagorean tetrahedral face divided by ten equidistant dots that depict a Platonic cube; the Ten Words of God.

tetrahedral: Having the form of a tetrahedron, which has four triangular faces and is the primal bond of matter.

Tetrahedron Land: According to Julian Barbour, the 6D limitless, timeless, eternal world of tetrahedrons.

thin disk (also thick disk): A plane in the Galaxy where many stars lie.

third dimension (3D): All life and things on Earth's surface and their relationships.

time capsules: Fixed patterns that encode change, also called history.

time in 3D: The locator for past, present, and future.

time in 9D: The creator of programs or timelines for Earth.

time warp: When time is lost or skips into the past or future.

time waves: Creative projects coming out of the Galactic Center that are received by the 8D Divine Mind, such as sacred calendars.

tinnitus: Unexplainable ringing in the ears and inner head.

topology or knot theory: The mathematics of correspondences and continuity that finds formulas to describe knots, which are places where cords cross an axis that generates things. Regarding landscapes, topology studies the qualities of places.

torus: Doughnut-shaped surface generated by the revolution of a circle around another circle.

Transfiguration: The transmutation of the physical body into pure light, as with Christ.

transmutation: The conversion of base materials into finer elements.

transubstantiation: Changing one substance into another one.

trauma: Emotional blocks locked in our bodies from difficult experiences.

Triangle Land: Julian Barbour's limitless, timeless, eternal world of triangles.

trigonometric: In accordance with trigonometry, which is the study of the properties of triangles, and especially offering information or based on Ptolemy's theorem of chords, which is the basis of diatonic ratios.

tuning forks: Steel devices with a handle that splits into two forks and calibrated by size to make tones of varying frequencies when they are struck.

Tzolk'in: The Keeper of 9D and the creator of the Mayan calendar.

unbroken wholeness: Physicist David Bohm's theory that the dynamic relations of particles depend on the whole system.

unconscious: State of being stuck on one side or the other of a duality so that the center or resolution is unknown.

unmasking the gods: Exposing the true nature of gods by mocking their ridiculous, limiting, and power-hungry tendencies.

vacuum: Space devoid of air.

vertical axis: A line or force that is generated at ninety-degree angles to planes. The Pleiadian vertical axis is the force generated between 1D and 9D that maintains the nine dimensions.

vibrational frequencies: Full range of the electromagnetic spectrum.

Virga Supercluster: A cluster of galaxies that our local cluster orbits around.

virus: Submicroscopic infective agents that come alive when they invade cells.

visible light spectrum (VLS): The range in the Schumann Resonance chart (see figure 1.2) in which things are visible, which is 10^{15} hertz.

vortex: Region within a medium in which the medium has angular velocity.

war: The huge game run by the Global Elite from 4D that is used to hold humankind in perpetual enslavement.

weak nuclear force: The force that causes nuclear decay.

Wheel of Twelve: Barbara Hand Clow's division of 4D space into six polarities, which enables us to balance ourselves in 3D and safely expand our consciousness. In sacred geography, gigantic wheels once divided the landscape into twelve divisions.

whistle-blowers: People who risk themselves to bust the pyramid to free systems.

wounded healer complex: Systemic and permanent healing of trauma complexes accomplished by healing the originating basis.

X-rays: Waves of energy that are vibrating at frequencies between ultraviolet radiation and gamma rays.

Yahweh: The god of the Hebrews who also rules the Christians.

yoga: A system of postures that align our bodies with 6D.

Zeus: The head god of the Greek pantheon.

zodiac: The division of the sky or the land into twelve signs, and some astrological systems have more than twelve divisions.

Endnotes

Introduction

1. These channelings and the reception of the monad occurred in Lakeville, Connecticut. Regarding the possible validity of these transmissions, I was lucky to get several rather astonishing confirmations. In 1994–95, I was the acquisitions editor for Bear & Company, where I handled around 7,000 submittals per year. During the summer and fall in 1995, while my manuscript was being edited, I received four submittals that discussed the same data bank—a cosmology from the Pleiades describing Earth's transformation from 1987 to December 21, 2012, which involved the Sirians, Andromedans, Orion, and the Galactic Center. One of these submittals was a rough but complete manuscript; two others were detailed outlines; and a fourth one was a description offered in a phone conversation. Regrettably, I had to inform these other authors that a similar book was already in editorial stages, namely *The Pleiadian Agenda.*

2. Richard Rudgley, *The Lost Civilizations of the Stone Age,* 100.

Chapter One

1. William J. Broad, "The Core of the Earth May Be a Gigantic Crystal Made of Iron," *New York Times,* April 4, 1995, C1.

2. Ibid. The Ps say the iron core crystal is the primal activator of magnetic waves that come to Earth's surface. Scientifically, the outer core is molten iron, and its churnings are thought to be the cause of Earth's magnetic field. Then the core crystal seems to have a magnetic field itself, since the closely packed hexagonal crystalline structure is a huge alignment. Seismic waves going through the inner core north-south go faster than those going east-west.

3. Carl Johan Calleman, *The Mayan Calendar and the Transformation of Consciousness,* 54–58. The measurable pulse of Earth at 40 Hz is described here as coming from the core (generated by spin). As the electromagnetic waves move

through the outer core, they slow down to 13.5 Hz, then they slow down to 7.5 Hz in Earth's crust. According to science, Earth's surface is like a giant electrical circuit, and there are quasi-standing waves (Schumann Resonance) between Earth's surface and the inner edge of the ionosphere, which is about 35 miles above Earth. These waves are normally around 7.8 Hz at the surface and then diminish to 2 Hz in the outer regions of the ionosphere.

4. Measuring gravity is described by John Noble Wilford, "Test Lets Scientists Clock the Force of Gravity for the First Time," *Miami Herald*, January 8, 2003, 8A.

5. Gravity traveling faster than the speed of light in higher dimensions is explored by Amir D. Aczel in *Entanglement*. Entanglement allows particles to travel at infinite speed in the subatomic realm.

6. Broad, "The Core of the Earth May Be a Gigantic Crystal Made of Iron," C1.

7. Ibid. Regarding the power of the vertical axis, the Ps say that gravity holds the dimensions together on the axis, which made me think about how this would work if there were a pole reversal. The lines of force of Earth's magnetic field show a persistent four-degree tilt. If Earth were a perfect bar magnet, the field lines at the magnetic equator should parallel Earth's surface, but they do not; they show a constant four-degree tilt. Earth's north and south magnetic poles have reversed repeatedly in the past. Scientists propose that during a reversal, Earth's magnetic field is weakened, which allows the core to strengthen its magnetic force. During a reversal, the poles linger near the southern end of South America and around Western Australia. This is because the powerful inner field actually captures the outer one, which forces it to correspond with its own poles. (When the poles are near reversal, as they apparently are now, this potent tension between the inner Earth and the surface generates the vertical axis of consciousness.)

8. Paul Recer, "Telescope Spots Supermassive Black Hole," *Miami Herald*, January 7, 2003, 8A. (Also, see chapter 9.)

9. Regarding the Pleiadian chakra system and the dimensions, our understanding of this relationship has evolved after teaching Satya's description for seven years. The Ps seem to watch us from afar, and to them, we are a chakra system with seven chakras that correspond to the nine dimensions. Hence we feel 1D in our root (coccygeal) chakra resonating with the core, 2D and 3D resonating in our sexual (sacral) chakra, and 8D and 9D in our crown chakra. Regarding the difference between how the Pleiadians see the human chakra system and how humans experience it, it is possible that the Ps are seeing us humans in our light-body modality, and once we evolve further, we humans may begin to experience our chakras according to the Pleiaidan model; in other words, we would experience our root (coccygeal) chakra as an Earth chakra located off-body at the iron core crystal.

Chapter Two

1. The master alchemist Fulcanelli (in *The Dwellings of the Philosophers*) has much to say about mining 2D elementals. With a wonderful sense of elemental life, he says that "metals as well as animals and vegetables, bear in themselves the faculty of multiplying their species" (62). Then he says that when "ordinary

metals are torn out of their ore-bearing earth to satisfy the demands of industry . . . they seem to be the victims of a glaring evil spell" (301).

2. Barbara Hand Clow, *Catastrophobia*, 106–07; Lynn Picknett, *Mary Magdalene*, 71–79.

3. Resolving the question of whether cellular phones are safe or not is complicated by conflicting information about electromagnetic fields (EMFs). The physics and engineering community is mainly in control of the funding for biological research regarding EMFs and cellphones, and its mind-set does not tend to favor looking at the health consequences of EMFs. B. Blake Levitt, an award-winning medical and science journalist, comments that cellphones transmit in the microwave frequencies; they can emit more radiation than the FDA allows for microwave ovens. The phones are used right next to people's brains, yet they are exempt from FCC regulations. Similar to smokers affecting the health of others who breathe their smoke, these devices affect nearby people—and in some cases, such exposures are greater than for the user. They are already banned for children under eighteen in most European countries, and some suggest they should never be used except in emergencies, such as being stranded on the highway. B. Blake Levitt, *Electromagnetic Fields*, 272–75.

4. Picknett, *Mary Magdalene*, 59, 178, 180.

5. Ibid., 192, 225; Clow, *Catastrophobia*, 210–12.

6. The Catholic Church built its churches on the ancient sacred sites according to a plan. For example, in 601 A.D., Pope Gregory I urged Saint Augustine (bishop in England) to seek out pagan temples, purify them, and convert them to Catholic churches. Clow, *Catastrophobia*, 107.

7. The dimensional knowledge of healers and shamans from 5000 B.C. to 500 A.D. was phenomenal, and we can see now that it is coming back again. Gordon Strachan, *Jesus the Master Builder*, 214–82.

8. Regarding the inner Earth and the Church's program to break the people's connection with it, this program was especially intense in Celtic and Anglo-Saxon countries. From 1 A.D. through 1066 A.D., the surface world was the Middle Earth and the inner Earth was below. The inner Earth was thought of as heaven and the abode of the spirits, and if people and clans were in harmony with it, they were healthy and thriving. The Church broke this relationship down to control all the people. Brian Bates, *The Real Middle Earth*, 120–28.

9. Andrew Collins and Chris Ogilvie-Herald, *Tutankhamun: The Exodus Conspiracy*, 185–229.

10. Regarding Transfiguration and Transubstantiation (Holy Communion), I do not mean to express lack of respect for these mysteries; it was grafting them together that resulted in the perversion. Transfiguration is what happens when a person is fully activated multidimensionally and still in his or her body. Holy Communion is actually a very powerful healing tool; before the Church fully controlled people, the Eucharist was taken home to be used for healing purposes.

11. The reason Communion is so predominant in the Church goes back to 100 to 325 A.D. when the early Church was consolidating itself under the early Church fathers (especially Irenaeus of Lyon) through the Council of Nicea, 325 A.D. In various Gospels and Acts that were excluded from the Canon, another view of Jesus' last supper comes through. John's Gospel, unlike Matthew's,

Mark's, and Luke's, *leaves out* an account of the last supper, and a follower of Valentinus fills in what *did* occur—The Round Dance of the Cross. All of the works of Valentinus and his followers were declared heretical, and most of them were destroyed. They only became available to modern eyes in 1945, when the Nag Hammadi scrolls were discovered. It turns out that on the night of the last supper, Jesus invited his disciples to dance and sing with him and invited them to see themselves in him. This is a radically different approach than sharing his body and blood in a sacrificial ritual, and perhaps it was his real intended sharing. Elaine Pagels, *Beyond Belief*, 120–25.

12. The ongoing process of the Internet and metallic EM technologies is definitely challenging. As I often mention in workshops, the higher dimensions resonate with higher frequencies of the EM spectrum, so perhaps the increasing frequencies in our environment are awakening our multidimensional consciousness!

13. Various related theories of the inner Earth and Agartha are discussed by Joscelyn Godwin in *Arktos: The Polar Myth in Science, Symbolism, and Nazi Survival*, 27–104; Trevor Ravenscroft in *The Spear of Destiny*, 235–59; and Jacques Bergier and Louis Pauwels, *The Morning of the Magicians*, 140–200.

Chapter Three

1. For more information about morphogenesis, see Rupert Sheldrake, *The Presence of the Past: Morphic Resonance and the Habits of Nature*.

2. Many students have asked me over the years about the calendar *Dreamspell*, invented by José Argüelles. I am not in disagreement with him; I simply find that people most easily escape from clock time by living by lunar cycles, equinoxes, and solstices.

3. Forecasting the weather by the local conditions at the New Moon is around eighty percent accurate for the two weeks from the New Moon to the Full Moon, and often it even holds for another week, and then the pattern changes during the last quarter. Watch this for a year or two, since it is the easiest way to get concrete evidence for the influence of the New Moon "seed." This cycle is taught each month at my website: www.handclow2012.com.

4. The 18.6-year Metonic Cycle, which is very hard to track, was often one of the purposes of megalithic circles. Because ancient people thought this cycle was so important for thousands of years, I have observed this cycle very closely since the early 1970s. It offers much wisdom about patterns on Earth and in our lives, and it is much more complex than just following monthly lunar cycles. Also, the Metonic cycle is involved with the Pleiades-rising cycle.

Considering the focus on the Metonic Cycle at megalithic sites, Gordon Strachan in *Jesus the Master Builder* offers some very interesting insights from the Roman writer Diodorus Siculus. Diodorus Siculus wrote about the Hyperboreans (extreme Northerners), who visited Greek sacred sites every nineteen years (Metonic Cycle), because that was when stars return to relatively the same places in the skies. Regarding the return of the Hyperborean god Apollo, he plays the cithera (Chiron's musical instrument) and dances continuously the night of the Spring Equinox until the Pleiades rise. It was understood that Apollo would travel to Hyperborea for this dance, and Strachan makes a very good case that

Hyperborea is the British Isles, which links up the megalithic culture with the Pythagorean Greeks. This is a deep teaching about the Moon synchronizing with the Sun by this 18.6-year cycle. Gordon Strachan, *Jesus the Master Builder*, 236–37.

5. Barbara Hand Clow, *The Liquid Light of Sex*, 62–67.

Chapter Four

1. A similar description of Nibiru and the Annunaki is available in Zecharia Sitchin, *The Twelfth Planet*.

2. Regarding Yahweh as the Judeo/Christian God during the last 3000 years, this God first arose during the Age of Aries in the Middle East. I stressed the continuance of Yahweh during the Age of Pisces, simply because Zeus, Dionysius, Ammon, and so forth have not had such a long ride. Certainly, the concept of "Yahweh," used as a Global Elite tool, calls for some thought in light of the state of the world today.

3. The big battle in the early Church between the orthodoxy and the heretics was over whether individual Christians had the right or ability to seek the Light on their own. This critical conflict—which is still carried on by the Elite—has now been elucidated in many of the Nag Hamadi texts. For example, *On the Origins of the World* (author unknown) says that in the Garden of Eden the luminous *epinoia* "appeared to them [Adam and Eve] shining with light, and awakened their consciousness." *Epinoia* was a common term for intuition and insight that can offer anyone revelation. When John in *The Secret Book of John* asks whether everyone receives this luminous *epinoia*, Jesus says, "The power will descend upon every person, for without it, no one can stand." Pagels, *Beyond Belief*, 164–65.

4. Regarding how my definition of 4D compares with Einstein's theory of four-dimensional "space-time," Einstein's first three dimensions in space are width, depth, and height, which can be drawn as simple lines and angles, and the fourth dimension is space-time. My theory describes a geometric model that exists because of the vertical axis (from the core to the Galactic Center) and has nine dimensions that are planal. These dimensions form and integrate the material world with the cosmos, a concept that is similar to superstring theory described in chapter 7. I disagree with Einstein fundamentally because he was not able to unify gravity—the propelling force for the vertical axis—with the other forces in nature. The 6D Calabi-Yau spaces described in chapter 6 went further in unifying gravity with the other forces, and space-time is five-dimensional. String theory calls for nine to eleven dimensions. Since physics and cosmology are going beyond Einstein now, so are we and the Ps.

5. The quantum mechanical revolution which began around 1900 is actually the scientific beginning of the Age of Aquarius, since it will be an age of exploring frequencies and vibrations.

6. My summary of quantum mechanics was guided by Itzhak Bentov, *Stalking the Wild Pendulum;* David Bohm, *Wholeness and the Implicate Order,* 141–217; Paul Davies, *The Mind of God* and *About Time;* Brian Greene, *The Elegant Universe;* João Magueijo, *Faster Than the Speed of Light;* William C. Mitchell, *Bye Bye Big Bang: Hello Reality;* and Michael Talbot, *Mysticism and the New Physics.*

7. Proof that the New World Order is in residence in Washington, D.C., can be found in David Ovason, *The Secret Architecture of Our Nation's Capital.*

Chapter Five

1. Considering indigenous clans and the Pleiades, prehistorian Boris Frolov notes that the Pleiades were called the Seven Sisters by native people in North America, Siberia, and Australia. This points to a common heritage, which goes back at least 40,000 years, when Australia was first peopled. Richard Rudgley comments that the peopling of Australia is now pushed back to 100,000 years ago by a number of archaeologists. Rudgley, *The Lost Civilizations of the Stone Age*, 100.

2. For more information about the cycles of the Sun and the Pleiades, see Hunbatz Men, *Los Calendarios Mayas y Hunab K'U;* and John Major Jenkins, *Maya Cosmogenesis 2012.* Jenkins says that for Chichén Itzá, the Sun-Pleiades zenith alignment (i.e., located directly overhead) has to do with the shifting of world ages, major celestial alignments, and vast epochs of time (78). Thus this spiral from Alcyone to the Sun may be a Pleiadian method for expressing the zenith cycles. Since modern Maya are saying that we are in the midst of a great alignment at the end of the Long Count (Mayan calendar), then it would not be surprising that there may be major cycles between Alcyone and the Sun.

3. In May 1998, a gamma-ray burst occurred that was described as "the most powerful cosmic event since the Big Bang" (*New York Times*, January 28, 1999, 7). Then on August 27, 1998, the most powerful gamma-ray burst ever detected caused the sky to writhe with light and the ionosphere to shrink, which shut down two NASA spacecraft as well as many scientific instruments (*New York Times*, August 27 and October 6, 1998, no page reference). (This incredible event was observed by my son Tom at 5:22 A.M. EDT; he was so enthralled that he didn't think to wake me up!)

4. Regarding the hypernova theory, on December 12, 2001, an orbiting X-ray observatory picked up the chemical footprints of the elements in a gamma-ray burst, which makes it almost certain that these bursts are coming from hypernovas. "Cosmic Bursts Demystified," *Discover Magazine*, January 3, 2003, Vol. 24, No. 1.

5. Gamma rays and consciousness are considered by aerospace engineer Roland Beanum in *Unicus Magazine*, 1995, Vol. 4, No. 2.

6. Regarding the outrageous Pleiadian theory that Earth's biology is to seed the Milky Way on December 21, 2012, it turns out that such ideas are the cutting edge in biology. Science writer James N. Gardner in *Biocosm* advocates the "Selfish Biocosm Theory," which posits that within a life-friendly universe, evolution is "selfish," or focused upon achieving its own replication (175–80). The emergence of life and advanced intelligence is inextricably involved with the birth, evolution, and reproduction of the cosmos. Eventually, a universe, such as the biological system of Earth, will reach a critical threshold or "eschaton," and it will replicate its codes and transmit them to a new "baby universe," which could occur by "Calabi-Yau shape engineering" (167–70, 252–58).

7. Astronomers reported in 2003 of hearing a black hole singing! This black hole in the center of the Perseus Galaxy cluster is playing the lowest note in the universe—sounds like low B flat—and this sound probably explains how galaxies grow and structure themselves. Dennis Overbye, "Music of the Heavens Turns Out to Sound a Lot Like a B Flat," *New York Times*, September 16, 2003, Science Section, D3.

8. Hunbatz Men said the Maya say that human orgasms move the Galaxy (during a teaching for the Mayan Initiatic 1989 tour from Palenque to Chichén Itzá).

9. Wilhelm Reich discovered cosmic superimposition of spin (the basic movement in the universe), which posits that sexual tension (longing for orgasm) is what calls us to cosmic functions. The superimposition of two orgone energy streams reaches beyond biology into bliss, which is the same thing as the Maya saying human orgasms move the Galaxy! Wilhelm Reich, *Cosmic Superimposition*, 15–19.

10. Mathematician Dr. Jeffrey Weeks hypothesizes that space is a twelve-sided hall of mirrors (a dodecahedron!), in which the illusion of infinity is created. If so, we can see most of the universe now via the recent radio map of the beginning of our universe—the Wilson Microwave Anisotropy Probe. This new idea will be resolved rather quickly, now that the Wilson Probe is available to all scientists. Dennis Overbye, "Cosmic Soccer Ball?" *New York Times*, October 9, 2003, A22.

11. Brian Greene, *The Elegant Universe*, 136.

12. Rupert Sheldrake, *The Presence of the Past*.

13. Julian Barbour, *The End of Time*.

14. Ibid., 9–19.

15. Ibid.

16. I contend that the EM waves are 5D and the shapes are the 6D forms; the shapes are the geometric source of the knots; and 7D is a higher-level unitization zone.

17. Julian Barbour's book, *The End of Time*, was reviewed by Oxford philosopher Simon W. Saunders, who notes that Barbour's idea of Platonia "is so good that it can be applied to Einstein's theory of gravity (relativity) as well as to Newton's." Simon W. Saunders, "Clock Watcher," *New York Times*, March 26, 2000, Book Review section, 10. This brilliant work is having a profound influence on contemporary physics.

18. Julian Barbour, *The End of Time*, 40–46, 116–17, 345. The great sacred geometrician Robert Lawlor says, "The formation of any volume structurally requires triangulation, hence the trinity is the creative basis of all focus." Robert Lawlor, *Sacred Geometry*, 35.

19. Julian Barbour, *The End of Time*, 51.

20. Ibid., 43.

21. Ibid., 44–45.

22. Ibid., 30–34.

23. Ibid., 33.

Chapter Six

1. The Ps insist that Sirius, the Pleiades, and our solar system travel in the same locational relationship around the Galactic Center. Astronomically, Sirius and the Pleiades are located in our galactic plane, in what is called the "Young Thin Disk," while the Sun is located in the "Old Thin Disk." Stars in the Young Thin Disk are younger than one billion years, while stars in the Old Thin Disk are between one and ten billion years old; hence our Sun is 4.6 billion years old and

is located in the Old Thin Disk. All these stars are located in the Orion Arm, so this Pleiadian structure could be correct. Ken Croswell, *The Alchemy of the Heavens*, 5, 79, 153–57.

2. Robert Temple, *The Sirius Mystery*, 55–79.

3. Sacred architecture was secret knowledge until the Pythagorean School was founded around 500 B.C. Pythagoras was born around 580 B.C. and died around 500 B.C., and he traveled to Egypt, Persia, and the British Isles to study sacred tradition, from which he founded his school. Pythagoras taught a fourfold understanding of number—the *Quadrivium*. Number as such was arithmetic; number in space, geometry; number in time, musical harmonics; and number in space-time, astronomy/astrology. This is how the correspondences between humankind and the cosmos were viewed, and then sacred architecture was based on all the principles of the Quadrivium to focus the macrocosmic energies into the microcosm, so that human beings could apprehend the Divine in physical form. Gordon Strachan, *Jesus the Master Builder*, 217–18.

4. After a few years of teaching the Activations, I realized that the nine-dimensional model in *The Pleiadian Agenda* is the same as the teachings of the Heliopolitan Mystery Schools (3500 to 1500 B.C.) of ancient Egypt. This school has potent mist in Platonia, and this wisdom existed in the megalithic cultures and early Egypt, which suggests a common origin that is much older. Then in 500 B.C., we find Pythagoras gathering up the threads from the Druids, the Egyptian temples, and the Zoroastrians in Persia. Now we see this potent mist emerging again, as it always does when people are severed from the Divine.

5. I have practiced yoga since the early 1970s, including Hatha, Iyengar, and Kripalu yoga, all of which were wonderful. The most activating yoga for me now is Kali Ray's TriYoga, which I have practiced since 2000. I love this yoga because all the asanas (postures) flow into each other as a dance, and many masters in India have given respect to this great teacher, Kali Ray (who now calls herself Kaliji). Contact: P.O. Box 6367, Malibu, CA, 90264; phone: 310-589-0600, fax: 310-589-0783; www.triyoga.com.

6. Julian Barbour, *The End of Time*, 30.

7. The ferocity of the destruction of sacred power objects in Peru and Bolivia is meticulously described by William Sullivan in *The Secret of the Incas*, 24.

8. Hakim of Giza took me to see the ancient ones in the Cairo Museum, and Hakim lives so much in the past, present, and future that these great beings came alive in his presence.

9. Julian Barbour, *The End of Time*, 23.

10. The basic language of physics today is the language of relativity, which is based on three main tenets: 1) the speed of light is constant and is a cosmic speed limit; 2) our world is described as a four-dimensional realm; and 3) per the famous formula, $E=mc^2$, energy equals mass times the speed of light squared. João Magueijo, *Faster Than the Speed of Light*, 32–38.

11. Regarding difficulty visualizing the configurations, see Clifford A. Pickover, *Surfing Through Hyperspace*.

12. Freddy Silva, *Secrets in the Fields*, 178–79.

13. Regarding sacred geometry in nature, the Fibonacci series is critically important because its sequence of patterns and processes in nature are ubiqui-

tous and very easy to observe. Among many other things, it governs the reflection of light in mirrors; gains and losses of energy radiation; breeding patterns of rabbits; male-female ratio of bees in hives; leaf distribution in plants; branch distribution in trees; seed distribution in daisy and sunflower heads; proportions of animal and human bodies; spiral growth of many shells; growth of the fetus in animals and humans; spirals of the inner ear (speaking of sound creating geometry!); the unfolding bracken; animal horns; and distant nebulae. The series of ratios of the Fibonacci numbers lies at the heart of the growth patterns in nature and is thus the signature of the Creator in creation. Gordon Strachan, *Jesus the Master Builder*, 119–20; Robert Lawlor, *Sacred Geometry*, 48–59.

14. Jeremy Narby, *The Cosmic Serpent*.

15. Ibid., 126. Narby is quoting the scientific journalist Suren Erkman.

16. Ibid., 127. Narby is quoting biologists Galle et al. (1991), Gu (1992), and Ho and Popp (1993).

17. Jean Richer, *Sacred Geography of the Ancient Greeks*.

18. John Michell and Christine Rhone, *Twelve-Tribe Nations and the Science of Enchanting the Landscape*, 78–80. The authors note that the birth of Christ coincided with the beginning of the Age of Pisces, and the birth of an age traditionally brings spiritual renewal. Led by the Essene esoteric scholars, the Jews (tribes of Judah and Benjamin at Jerusalem) awaited the return of the missing ten tribes of Israel, and the Christians, who also drew much of their new traditions from the Essenes, shared a similar hope. The twelve disciples of Jesus were symbolic of the twelve tribes, and in Revelation, John of Patmos described his vision of the twelve-tribe city, with twelve angels by its twelve gates. Also, the authors note that at the beginning of the 2,160-year Piscean Age, Israel became the Holy Land for Christians, as well as the Jews (153). Also, they note that the Age of Aquarius is to be a spiritual renewal. It is certainly interesting that in the "choreography of twelve nations" that was revived through Christian revelation, Egypt with the Giza Plateau as the center is the Holy Land during the Age of Aquarius (140–43).

19. Anthropologists and archaeologists ignored the findings of Richer, Michell, and Rhone. Photographs taken by once-secret American surveillance satellites have revealed to archaeologists sites of ancient settlements that have previously escaped detection, and they have begun to map ancient roads and settlements that crossed the landscape four thousand to five thousand years ago. The roads radiate out from key center locations like spokes on wheels, and they are oriented on a general east-west axis. "Surveillance satellites mapping ancient settlements in Middle East," *Miami Herald*, International Edition, January 30, 2003, 7.

20. John Michell and Christine Rhone, *Twelve-Tribe Nations*, 7–17, 89–96.

21. Barbara Hand Clow, *Catastrophobia*, 80–81.

22. John Michell and Christine Rhone, *Twelve-Tribe Nations*, 89–96.

23. Ibid., 76.

Chapter Seven

1. Ken Croswell, *The Universe at Midnight*, 234–35. According to blueshift calculations of Andromeda's speed minus the speed of the Sun orbiting the Milky Way (which is roughly in the direction of Andromeda), Andromeda's approach

velocity toward the Milky Way is currently six million miles per day. Astronomers will be able to determine how soon our Galaxy will meet Andromeda within the next twenty years. If they collide, this will create a supergalaxy; the dark halos of each probably are already brushing each other.

2. Michael Baigent, Richard Leigh, and Henry Lincoln, *Holy Blood, Holy Grail;* and Strachan, *Jesus the Master Builder.*

3. Ibid.; Margaret Starbird, *The Woman with the Alabaster Jar;* and Lynn Picknett, *Mary Magdalene.*

4. John Beaulieu, BioSonic Enterprises, P.O. Box 487, High Falls, NY 12440. On the Web at www.BioSonicEnterprises.com.

5. Hans Jenny, *Cymatics,* 207–238. Jenny notes that once the amplitude produces patterns, these patterns—harmonic oscillations—are extremely regular with regard to number, proportion, and symmetry (Platonic solids). These vibrational patterns arise in the medium (liquid or sand) from the natural vibrations within it, and they shift by the sound that vibrates the medium. This is the same orderliness that underlies all action in nature.

6. Freddy Silva, *Secrets in the Fields,* 194–99.

7. Brian Greene, *The Elegant Universe,* 145.

8. Ibid., 377–78.

9. Ibid., 378.

10. Ibid., 374–84, 386. String theory is a cogent framework for integrating gravity and QM. Experimentally confirmed concepts, such as spin, qualities of matter particles, gauge symmetry, and messenger particles, all emerge easily in string theory; yet it has no adjustable parameters being used to ensure experimental measurements. These three factors predict that the theory will be verified, even though experimental verification, such as in particle accelerators, has not occurred yet.

11. Ibid., 321, 340. For extremal black holes, string theory has been successfully used to account for the microscopic constituents and the associated entropy (1997). This success has provided important and convincing evidence for string theory, since black holes are close to observable phenomena.

12. Ibid., 332.

13. Ibid., 300–03.

14. Ibid., 283–88.

15. Ibid., 207–09.

16. Ibid., 283–319.

17. Ibid., 310. Edward Witten's theory went from ten dimensions to eleven in 1995 because he realized that the strongly coupled Heterotic-E string gets stretched into a cylindrical shape and a new dimension appears. The Ps say the 10D vertical axis is the force that holds the nine dimensions or branes in place; it is the force that has the energy to manifest the planes of reality. Witten noted that 10D is not a dimension in which Heterotic-E strings can vibrate; instead, it is a dimension locked within the structures of the strings themselves.

18. João Magueijo, *Faster Than the Speed of Light,* 228.

19. Ibid., 229.

20. Jacob Atabet was a mystic who lived in North Beach in San Francisco during the 1960s, who reputedly transmuted his physical body into light—i.e., a mod-

ern Transfiguration. I heard about Atabet when I lived in San Francisco in the 1960s. Michael Murphy, who founded the Esalen Institute, wrote a novel about Jacob Atabet, *Jacob Atabet*, which inspired many people in the New Consciousness movement (see bibliography).

21. João Magueijo, *Faster Than the Speed of Light*, 228–229. Regarding a variable speed of light (VSL) on three levels, Magueijo says that ultra high-energy cosmic rays have been observed going faster than the speed of light (255–56). With that in mind, some physicists (see latter part of this note) think that the light of different colors travels at different speeds. Regarding the use of primary colors in all spiritual traditions—red is low frequency, yellow is medium, and blue is high—I wonder if 1D through 3D are at the red speed, 4D through 6D at yellow, and 7D through 9D are blue (don't forget the bluebirds!). A VSL is highly theoretical at this time, yet light speed (Einstein's "constant-c") is best thought of as the edge or boundary of light in 3D. Light could easily move faster in higher dimensions, which have not been measured yet. For example, Magueijo notes that physicists Kiritsis Alexander and Stephen Alexander studied the motion of light "stuck" to the three-brane (extended objects with three spatial dimensions), and they found its speed varied. They calculated that *the speed of light as seen on the brane was simply related to its distance to the black hole*. As the brane approached the hole, a VSL would be realized (242). Obviously, if you think about it, the very nature of time dilation in black holes suggests a VSL.

22. Muons are produced when cosmic rays strike Earth's atmosphere. They stretch time because when they move close to the speed of light, their time becomes extremely warped. Fixing the frame of time to Earth, a moving muon becomes stretched out (dilated) perhaps by a thousand times. The Geiger counter measures this bizarre phenomenon by clicks. Paul Davies, *About Time*, 55–58. (I don't think we've even begun to imagine the bizarre affects of cosmic rays.)

23. João Magueijo and physicist Stephen Alexander considered the *zero brane*, which is possibly the most fundamental ingredient in M-theory—an object that behaves like a point particle at great distances but has drastically different properties at short ones. Based on recent calculations, a new and unconventional framework takes over called *noncommutative geometry*, a geometric framework in which the conventional notions of space and distance between points melt away. This is relevant here because they discovered that *the speed of light in noncommutative spaces is color-dependent and increases at very high frequencies* (another proof of a VSL). Since there are three primary colors—red, yellow, and blue—you can see why I suspect that red holds the speed of light for 1D–3D, yellow for 4D–6D, and blue for 7D–9D. João Magueijo, *Faster Than the Speed of Light*, 240–47; and Brian Greene, *The Elegant Universe*, 379.

24. Paul Devereux, *Stone Age Soundtracks*.

25. Ibid., 124.

26. Ibid., 110–15.

27. From 1983 until 1993, I frequently watched Hopi and Jemez Pueblo rain dances, and I could see the priests (along with the dancers) using brain waves to alter waves in the air.

28. Paul Devereux, *Stone Age Soundtracks*, 76–89.

29. The Boyne River Valley temples, such as Knowth, Dowth, and Newgrange, were actually a nine-dimensional teaching complex, and when I went there in 1985, I felt this very strongly. From these temples we can deduce that the return of the light at the Winter Solstice is key to this teaching, and this is why I emphasize attunement to equinoxes and solstices at www.handclow2012.com. Once I figured this out, then I discovered that our ability to access nine dimensions simultaneously is greatly heightened from December 18 to December 25. Try it! The *Lacnunga* compiled the Anglo-Saxon healing wisdom of the Middle Earth around 1000 A.D., and it contains the wisdom of people from the megalithic times to the end of Middle Earth. Regarding the Boyne River Valley in Celtic mythology, it was named after the goddess Boann, and the valley is described as a "shining fountain, with five streams flowing out of it." The river itself would have been the energy of the Otherworld, which is ready to sweep a person away at any moment, and this was the ideal way to realize how the spiritual landscape (5D–9D) intersects with the physical landscape (3D). The river perceived as a shining fountain with five streams flowing out of it expresses 5D–9D fanning out of the canopy. The saga goes on to say that "Nine hazels [nine dimensions] grew over the well" (the spring that accesses the Underworld). This brings in all nine dimensions. Brian Bates, *The Real Middle Earth*, 124–25; he is quoting Alwyn Rees and Brinley Rees, *Celtic Heritage*, but he gives no page numbers.

30. Paul Devereux, *Stone Age Soundtracks*, 56.

31. Ibid., 89–92. A more recent version of a similar science of symbols and sound exists in the famous Templar site, Rosslyn Chapel, near Edinburgh, Scotland. It has 213 cubes on the wall that are believed to be musical notations. Eight scientists from around the world have been attempting to understand the relationships between the symbols. One of the theories is that "the notes were recorded using a brass plate covered with sand. When the brass plate was struck with a bow, it vibrated, creating a distinctive pattern of sand lines for that particular note." Claire Gardner, "Japanese Bid to Solve Musical Mystery of the Rosslyn Cubes," *Scotsman,* June 16, 2002, International Edition, 22. (This sure sounds like a medieval cymatics machine to me!)

32. Pierre Mereaux's research on Carnac was translated by Roslyn Strong, in "Carnac, Stones for the Living: A Megalithic Seismograph?" *NEARA Journal,* Winter 2001, Vol. 35, No. 2, 62–79.

33. Ibid., 74–79. I include here some information about Rosslyn Chapel because both Carnac and Rosslyn Chapel seem to have been working with sound for healing. I have seen both, and I have often wondered why anybody would go to so much trouble. Author and historian Stephen Prior, who has been researching the history of Rosslyn Chapel, believes "the cubes could hold the key to a health-giving chant from the Middle Ages." Claire Gardner, *op. cit.* (Rosslyn was built in 1477, at the end of the Middle Ages, and many believe it is a library or code book of ancient science that the Templars built to save knowledge that was being destroyed by the Catholic Church. As you will see in the following note, this information may involve the survival of the human species.)

34. Regarding fecundity and megalithic science, some sites have stones with holes in them, and in various locations, legends say people crawled through them to get healed or pregnant. Some of the earliest sites with these stone monu-

ments—in the Gulf of Morbihan in Brittany, France—are from the Mesolithic period, which precedes the Neolithic. From analysis of burial remains, the people had many maladies, some congenital, such as spinal problems and arthritis, and they were short in stature. Pierre Mereaux believes the healing science of the megaliths was developed so they could survive and reproduce. Roslyn Strong, *op. cit.*, 78. (Roslyn Strong only translated half of Mereaux's book on Carnac. The second half is very detailed information on healing technologies, which are difficult to translate because so little is understood about these ideas. Roslyn Strong, phone conversation, July 2002.)

35. When a healer uses tuning forks to vibrate a client's body with primary tones such as C-F-G, very powerful energy is often released. In my opinion, this kind of release indicates that the trauma locks from the series of catastrophes I examined in *Catastrophobia* (2001) are being released.

Chapter Eight

1. Helioseismic holography is a recently invented technique that enables scientists to monitor sunspots on the far side of the Sun. Helioseismology has discovered that "the Sun is a humming ball of sound waves launched by turbulent convective motions" in its outer layers. Solar sound waves are mostly trapped inside the Sun; they refract away from the hot core and reflect back and forth in different parts of the photosphere. By monitoring this surface that vibrates with sound waves, "helioseismologists can probe the stellar interior in much the same way that geologists use seismic waves from earthquakes to probe the inside of our planet." See: www.Spaceweather.com/glossary/farside.html. (Scientists do not consider what the sound waves of the Sun might create for Earth, yet by the nine-dimensional model, the solar sound waves make it physically possible for humans to tune directly in to the Sun.)

2. Regarding personification of the Light as Yahweh, some of the sources excluded from the Canon suggest that personifying the Light is the main reason people never experience *epinoia,* or direct revelation through the Light. For example, the *Secret Book of John* tells a story to show that many people mistook Yahweh for God, who was a jealous God who did not know the blessed one— Mother-Father God. So when Adam and Eve experienced the Light—*epinoia*—he punished them and cursed Earth. Elaine Pagels, *Beyond Belief,* 166.

3. In the Algonquin Nation, the Manitou is the energy force in nature, which we can feel when we are in harmony with nature. The people of this Nation began a new phase of their culture in North America 11,500 years ago, and America is filled with stone circles, dolmens, and cairns that come from the same science as Carnac (see chapter 7). Since the official archaeological dogma of the Elite in the United States teaches that America was discovered in 1492, the existence of all these sites is denied, and most people are unaware of them. The megalithic stone science was the way people attuned to the Sun because the solar sound waves make vibrations in the stones. Attuning by these systems enables people to directly access 8D; and one of the most important sites is a Sun sanctuary near Upton, Massachusetts, that is aligned with the Pleiades. James Mavor and Byron Dix, *Manitou,* 33–55.

4. The cycle of Orion rising is first of all a *yearly cycle:* Orion seems to hover right over the equator from the perspective of people living in northern latitudes

because our Sun is located in the inner part of the Orion spiral arm. As we look out in the sky opposite the Galactic Center (toward Orion), we see the stars of the Orion constellation way out beyond our solar system. Because these stars are in the galactic plane—as are we—and the tilted Earth orbits the Sun causing the Sun to seem to move back and forth from the Tropic of Cancer to the Tropic of Capricorn, Orion rises and lowers dramatically in the sky during the year. Second, the cycle of Orion rising in the sky is a precessional cycle. Over the centuries stars and constellations rise, due to precession, at different points on the horizon, and the parts of the sky visible from certain locations gradually shift. Viewing Orion from the Giza Plateau, as well as other sites at 30 degrees north latitude, it is currently at its highest point above the horizon in 11,500 years. Gordon Strachan, *Jesus the Master Builder*, 5–7, 145–53; and John and Peter Filbey, *Astronomy for Astrologers*, 142–44.

5. David Icke, . . . *and the truth shall set you free.* Although I endorse David Icke's description of the pyramid, I am not as comfortable with his definition of reptilian energy in humans. Reptiles, such as snakes and turtles, are wonderful 3D animals. The cold-blooded, serpent-like force that seems to rule most people who abuse power is a 4D malevolent force that distorts human behavior when creativity is suppressed. People do not become reptiles in 3D; rather, the malevolent force rules their lives, such as can be seen with the Hanoverian Royals of England and their distant American cousins, the Bushes.

6. For more good books exposing the Global Elite, see William Cooper, *Behold a Pale Horse;* David Icke, *Alice in Wonderland and the World Trade Center Disaster;* John Kaminski, *America's Autopsy Report;* and Jan van Helsing, *Secret Societies and the Power in the 20th Century.*

7. Regarding orthodox belief systems—as in religions, societies such as the Masons, the Knights of Columbus, country clubs, or most charitable systems—these systems were created in the first place to harness a person's normal desire to be good, to belong, and to worship. They are set up as pyramids used to monitor people's day-to-day behavior; they keep people in line.

8. João Magueijo, *Faster Than the Speed of Light*, 240–47, 255–56; and Brian Greene, *The Elegant Universe*, 379.

9. João Magueijo, *Faster Than the Speed of Light*, 256–58.

10. To visualize dimensionality, see Clifford Pickover, *Surfing through Hyperspace*, 119–139.

11. Brian Greene, *The Elegant Universe*, 142–46.

12. The three physicists are Dr. Nima Arkani-Hamed (Harvard), Dr. Savras Dimopoulos (Stanford), and Dr. Gia Dvali (New York University). Dennis Overbye, "Other Dimensions? She's in Pursuit," *New York Times*, September 30, 2003, Science, F1.

13. John Kaminski, *America's Autopsy Report*, 24–30.

14. I learned this manifestation technique by studying DMA, a self-improvement course created by Robert Fritz, in 1983.

15. After using manifestation for many years, I think the medulla oblongata is the most powerful gravity center in our bodies. Using it as a television screen communicates our requests to all nine dimensions; thus the correct dimension for responding to our requests gets the signal. Our third eyes are where we can visualize the most powerfully.

16. An analysis of the qualities of each New Moon is available every month free of charge at www.handclow2012.com; tune in just before the New Moon.

17. An analysis of the qualities of the equinoxes and solstices is posted at www.handclow2012.com just before each seasonal change.

18. By manifesting your desires when the year begins at the Spring Equinox, your normal powers are greatly expanded, which seems to have been known by most if not all sacred cultures on Earth. Since humans can so easily free themselves from Elite control by taking advantage of this, the Church diverted people's creative focus to sacrifice and the cross by creating Good Friday and Easter Sunday.

Chapter Nine

1. Brian Swimme, *The Hidden Heart of the Cosmos*, 85–86.

2. Barbara Hand Clow, *Catastrophobia*, 9–11.

3. James Gardner, *Biocosm*, 251–58.

4. José Argüelles, *The Mayan Factor.*

5. Barbara Hand Clow, *The Pleiadian Agenda*, 48–49.

6. Ibid., 35. Regarding silica-based biology, the Ps say that dandelions, which are solar flowers, cannot seed until they've used up their carbon energy. Then they restructure as silica filaments, which carry the seeds on the wind. For humans to be silica-based as light-encoded filaments, the Ps say we should imagine billions of light-encoded filaments swirling around our throats that become rods of light when we speak our truths. Then our bodies will lift like umbrellas of filaments that will carry us into the Galaxy to seed it with our biology.

7. This transmutation is very intense because radiation is in the core of Galactic Centers. Radiation is the central creative element in stars, which brings light or photons to Earth. In 8D, radiation opens densities; pure truth will dominate regardless of people's beliefs, which are simply personal attempts to understand their lives. The third dimension processes creativity in other dimensions by making things solid; thus humans have been experimenting with radiation now that 8D is impulsing us in 3D. When a civilization is poised to become multidimensional, experiments with radiation usually occur; encountering fission ultimately causes greater honesty.

8. Dr. Edward Harrison suggests that our universe was created by lifeforms possessing superior intelligence from another universe in which the constants of physics were finely tuned and similar to ours. Therefore perhaps our own descendants in the far future might have the knowledge and technology to build baby universes. The idea is that the universe was in fact designed by minds similar to our own, and it can happen again. James Gardner, *Biocosm*, 158–59. Of course, Gardner's book is based on the "Anthropic Principle," which posits that the universe has evolved to the current level so that we, mankind, can figure out how it works. Meanwhile, many scientists are searching the cosmos for other systems that have evolved as far as ours has, and currently that idea dominates astronomy.

A very thorough analysis of what it takes to get this far was carried out by paleontologist Dr. Peter D. Ward and noted astronomer Dr. Donald C. Brownlee, and they published their conclusions in *Rare Earth* in 2000. Considering how long evolution takes, and the extreme unlikelihood there are any other habitable zones in the universe (based on analysis of the nature of galaxies and solar systems), these authors think we are it. This would support the Anthropic Principle and possibly encourage Earthlings to cherish their planet. William S. Broad, "Maybe We *Are* Alone in the Universe," *New York Times,* February 8, 2000, F1.

9. Terrence McKenna, et al., *Trialogues at the Edge of the West,* 33.

10. Dennis Overbye, "Other Dimensions? She's in Pursuit," *New York Times,* September 30, 2003, Science, F1.

11. Brian Swimme notes that the omnicentricity of our supercluster means that we are in the very center of the universe that is centered on its own expansion: "The beginning is centered upon itself at each place of its existence. . . . To be in existence is to be at the center of the complexifying whole." Brian Swimme, *The Hidden Heart of the Cosmos,* 81–86.

12. John Noble Wilford, "Astronomers Glimpse Objects, Open New Mysteries," *Miami Herald,* January 15, 2003, 12A. The most likely scenario is that the ring stars are remnants of smaller galaxies that came too close, and they were captured by our Galaxy's overpowering gravity.

13. Ken Croswell, *The Alchemy of the Heavens,* 234; and Kenneth Chang, "Down on the Galactic Highway, a Head-On Collision Shapes Up," *New York Times,* May 9, 2000, F5.

14. Ken Croswell, *The Alchemy of the Heavens,* 189–90.

15. Ibid., 60, 157.

16. The solar flares in October and November 2003 were astonishing, since they occurred during a so-called dormant phase. The flares began within an hour of the New Moon, October 25, and they intensified through the November 8 Full Moon eclipse. Before these solar explosions, there was a great solar flare in early August 1972, which was rated an X-20, G-4, the highest rating ever—until 2003. Then on October 28, there was a second X-20 flare, but this one was rated as a G-5. Then on November 4 there was a mega-flare rated *X-28,* while the Sun was also developing a big coronal hole. See: www.SpaceWeather.com.

17. The confirmation of the black hole in the center of the Milky Way came in late 2002. Astronomers using the Chandra X-ray telescope made images that "show it is starved and puny compared with black holes in other galaxies." The Milky Way black hole spends most of its time emitting X-rays about equal to the energy of the Sun. Yet, "at least once a day the black hole suddenly flares, erupting with X-ray bursts 10 to 45 times more powerful than all the Sun's energy." No other supermassive black hole has exhibited this behavior, and the black hole may be starved for energy because "nearby star explosions in the past have blown away most of the gas and dust that would feed the black hole." Paul Recer, "Telescope Spots Supermassive Black Hole," *Miami Herald,* January 7, 2003, 8A. Since the Chandra X-ray has only been able to make these images in 2003: 1) we have no way of knowing whether this is new behavior possibly connected with the galactic alignment, and 2) I wonder if it is possible to see this phenomenon partly if not all because of the galactic Winter Solstice. Whatever, we are all discovering that we live in a very violent universe.

18. Ken Croswell, *The Alchemy of the Heavens,* 195–97; and Paul Recer, "Telescope Spots Supermassive Black Hole," *Miami Herald,* January 7, 2003, 8A.

19. Itzhak Bentov, *Stalking the Wild Pendulum,* 134–39.

20. Ibid., 136–40.
21. Ibid., 137.
22. Ibid., 136–40.
23. Kip Thorne, *Black Holes and Time Warps,* 24–26.
24. "Star Zaps Earth with Super X-rays," *New York Times,* August 27, 1998; and Charles R. Eisendrath, "The Light Fantastic," *New York Times,* October 6, 1998 (no page references for either article). Of course, this phenomenon may have been triggered or made visible due to the 1998 alignment of our solar system to the plane of the Galaxy.
25. James Glanz, "Theorists Ponder a Cosmic Boost from Far, Far Away," *New York Times,* February 15, 2000, Science, F5.
26. "The Strange Case of Earth's New Girth," *Discover Magazine,* January 2003, 52.
27. Dennis Overbye, "Other Dimensions? She's in Pursuit," *New York Times,* September 30, 2003, Science, F1.
28. Carl Johan Calleman, *The Mayan Calendar and the Transformation of Consciousness,* 125. As an International Mayan Elder, I am a ceremonial leader, not a Daykeeper or an expert on the Mayan calendar. *Alchemy of Nine Dimensions* uses the Mayan calendar for the timing of planetary evolution and humanity's attainment of nine-dimensional consciousness. For a truly revolutionary book on the Mayan calendar, I recommend *The Mayan Calendar and the Transformation of Consciousness* by Carl Johan Calleman, Ph.D., which was published in 2004. I did not have the time to integrate this book with *Alchemy of Nine Dimensions,* so I'd like to quote Calleman's thoughts about Tzolk'in because they express such profound knowledge about the Mayan calendar.

"The Creator seems to have concluded that the tzolkin [sic] is the optimal pattern of creation, the pattern behind the evolution of all things. This realization of the Maya and the Mexica [indigenous people of Mexico], that the tzolkin is a filtration pattern of light that pervades the universe and seeks expression on many different levels, is one of their greatest contributions to human spirituality.

"Ultimately, the tzolkin is a code that describes a pre-set divine program for the oscillations of the World Tree, a program that was conceived beyond space and time. The tzolkin is much larger and much more profound than any lunar cycle, biorhythm, or solar phase. On a deeper level the tzolkin is timeless. If its changing energies create our experience of time, it should be obvious that time is an illusion and has no existence independently of divine creation. The tzolkin is, more than anything else, the pattern ultimately behind all rhythms and all structuring of energies."

Chapter Ten

1. Regarding Circlemakers communicating directly with researchers, it is either that, or the researchers are very much in tune with the cycles of time. It is legendary that the arts of the Pythagorean Quadrivium—number as arithmetic musical harmony; astrology; astronomy; and geometry—permeate the mist of Earth when the Great Ages change, such as during our current transition into the Aquarian Age. John Michell and Christine Rhone note that numbers existed as unmanifested archetypes before there was anything to quantify. The Creator's

thought was a harmonious code of number, from which developed all the forces and phenomena of nature. John Michell and Christine Rhone, *Twelve-Tribe Nations and the Science of Enchanting the Landscape*, 82. As we are leaving the Piscean Age, Michell and Rhone describe the recent advent of the crop circles as a sign the Quadrivium is imprinting Earth again (137).

2. José Argüelles, *The Mayan Factor.*

3. Regarding ongoing ceremonies at Teotihuacan, Alberto Ruz Buenfil was leading ceremonies with me in 1989 at Uxmal when he told me about the numbers of celebrants at Teotihuacan at the spring equinoxes.

4. Hunbatz Men visited our house in Santa Fe in January 1989 to discuss the upcoming Mayan Initiatic Tour. Since I was teaching on the tour without Gerry, he was wondering what Hunbatz was planning on doing, so he asked. Hunbatz replied, "We Maya will be moving the Sun." Before we could imagine what he meant, a bright white arc of electricity blew out of a plug in the adjoining dining room and seared into the nearby living room into another plug, and all the power went out! Luckily, an electrician came over in a few hours, and after looking at the circuit breakers, he emerged from the garage with a confused expression on his face. He said, "Something has occurred that is totally impossible! The wires going into the breaker for these plugs fused together and melted." Then when my son Tom and I arrived at the airport in Mexico City just before the journey, massive solar flares in early March 1989 had knocked out all the power. I have since experienced many situations in which Mayan shamans (as well as other indigenous shamans) influence the Sun and electrical forces. Hunbatz told me they knew the asteroid—Quetzalcoatl—would come at the culmination of the 1989 ceremonies because of an alignment with the Sun as measured by the Templo de las Muñecas near Mérida and because of secret calendars given to Hunbatz by his uncle.

5. Freddy Silva, *Secrets in the Fields*, 285.

6. Regarding changes in Earth in 1998, from 10,000 years ago until 1998, high-latitude regions have been rebounding from the weight of the glaciers, which caused Earth's mass to shift gradually to the poles. These changes are monitored by measuring how Earth's gravity affects the orbits of satellites. Suddenly in August 1998, the gravity field began getting stronger at the equator and weaker at the poles, and Earth's rotation slowed slightly. Also, assuming what people are discovering reflects changes in the mental plane of Earth, based on the discovery in 1996 that the expansion of the universe is speeding up, cosmologists began speculating in 1998 that cosmic acceleration may be an effect from another universe. James Glanz, "Theorists Ponder a Cosmic Boost from Far, Far Away," *New York Times*, February 15, 2000, Science, F2. "Another universe" can also be thought of as another dimension, such as the 9D Galactic Center.

7. Freddy Silva, *Secrets in the Fields*, photo section, 96, 140, 220.

8. Judith Moore and Barbara Lamb, *Crop Circles Revealed*, 46–49.

9. See: ascension2000.com/convergenceIII/c313.htm.

10. Freddy Silva, *Secrets in the Fields*, 124–33.

11. Freddy Silva was kind to go over this chapter just before it went to the publisher. In an e-mail in November 2003 he said that hoaxing got completely out of hand in 2003, when he believes ninety-seven percent of the crop circles

were hoaxed! I felt the 2003 circles didn't feel right when I saw photos of them. Silva and I both believe there is an elaborate effort to keep the public in ignorance and confusion. I would add that perhaps the Circlemakers found it difficult to work in Earth's atmosphere in 2003 because of the extremely ugly vibrations existing as Bush and Blair ganged up to attack a sovereign nation, Iraq. Also, the military may have gotten quite good at a technique with advanced equipment, which they are using to block our path to enlightenment.

12. Freddy Silva, *Secrets in the Fields,* 127–28.

13. Ibid., 120–24.

14. Ibid., 106.

15. Ibid., 129–30.

16. Ibid., 137. Regarding vacuum states, Silva notes that Dr. Shiuji Inomata, in *Paradigm of New Science: Principia for the Twenty-First Century,* proposes that "the vacuum state is an energy field in which consciousness is integrated with electromagnetic and gravitational forces to create matter."

17. When I did the past-life regressions (1982–85) that are the basis of *Eye of the Centaur,* I experienced a series of lifetimes as an Owl Clan priestess in the Avebury region 25,000 to 5,000 years ago.

18. Hakim lives at the foot of the sphinx in Giza, and a one-hour video was made of our work together called *Nine Initiations on the Nile.* The best book describing the teachings of Abd'El Hakim is *The Land of Osiris* by Stephen Mehler.

19. Of the circles involved with the megalithic system, many if not most are near barrows and stone circles, such as Avebury and Stonehenge, as if the Circlemakers want humanity to rebuild the ancient system again.

20. Regarding axial tilt, *Catastrophobia* posits that Earth's axis tilted to about 23 degrees during the 9500 B.C. cataclysm in the solar system, and that the axis was vertical before that time. Barbara Hand Clow, *Catastrophobia,* Appendix D: "Reflections on Earth's Tilting Axis," 252–59.

21. The therapist who worked on these sessions was Greg Paxson of Chicago. See his introduction to *Eye of the Centaur,* 1–20.

22. Freddy Silva offered additional information on the Sanctuary at Avebury in his November 2003 e-mail. He says that the Sanctuary was originally a charnel house where the bones of deceased shamans were stripped of their flesh in preparation for interment in Avebury or West Kennett long barrow. Being crystalline, the bones hold cellular memory, so the bones of the shamans would be used to consult the shaman's wisdom. Later the Sanctuary became a place for initiates to focus before they walked down the Avenue and into Avebury temple. Perhaps in the Druid regression, I was accessing a long-lost technique used by ancient shamans.

23. Barbara Hand Clow, *Signet of Atlantis,* 171–80.

24. The best source on the Avebury goddess is *The Silbury Treasure,* by Michael Dames.

25. Alfred Mann, *Shadow of a Star,* 82–91.

Chapter 11

1. Barbara Hand Clow, *Signet of Atlantis,* xix; and Freddy Silva, *Secrets in the Fields,* 268.

2. "Third Earth Conference at the Crop Circles and Stonehenge," Salisbury, England, Power Places Tours, July 27 to August 1, 1993.

3. Freddy Silva, *Secrets in the Fields*, 210–11.

4. Ibid., 268–70.

5. Ibid., 188–89.

6. "The Sixth Annual International Conference on Crop Circles, Stonehenge, and UFOs," Salisbury, England, Power Places Tours, July 19 to August 5, 1997.

7. Freddy Silva, *Secrets in the Fields*, 186–87.

Chapter Twelve

1. I often visualize a Temple of Neutrality, like a special building in a city park somewhere (and maybe eventually everywhere!), much as the United Nations might have originally been intended to be. You could just walk into this Temple, be cleansed of all the positive and negative charges you are carrying, and be allowed to be present, in the now, and *neutral*. That's all: no messages, no dogma, just Neutral. Someday I'll write a book about this Temple, but for now, bring this idea into your life, and let it be neutral. And for those of you who dream about driving your car, remember that your car often represents your spirit, wanting to move you to that special place you are going to next in your life.

2. I learned the term "Inner Work" from a gifted, super-observant teacher, Andreas Lederman, Registered Polarity Practitioner, who leads workshops in Switzerland, England, and the United States on this form of process-oriented psychology (POP). It is an approach very similar to what I was doing (unconsciously) as an adolescent, as I lay in my bed in what I call the "Tom Sawyer pose" and would process through whatever it was that was bothering me at that time. Today I like to think of "Inner Work" as useful for both kinds of explorations: first, as to what is "coming up for me today," and second, as a tool for experiencing feelings at a deeper, fuller, more meaningful level. Both approaches ask for the participant to make whatever is "coming up" larger (as Andreas says, in his delicious Swiss-English accent: "Amplify it! Make it larger!"), and then, once that has happened, to allow the awarenesses to connect with yourself (as Andreas says: "Integrate it!"). Both Andreas and I are Aquarians with Moon in Scorpio, which may explain our similar styles in integrating consciousness.

3. Joseph Chilton Pearce, *The Biology of Transcendence*.

Bibliography

Aczel, Amir, *Entanglement: The Greatest Mystery in Physics*, Four Walls Eight Windows, New York, 2002.

Argüelles, José, *The Mayan Factor: Path Beyond Technology*, Bear & Company, Santa Fe, New Mexico, 1987.

Baigent, Michael, Richard Leigh, and Henry Lincoln, *Holy Blood, Holy Grail*, Delacorte Press, New York, 1982.

Barbour, Julian, *The End of Time: The Next Revolution in Physics*, Oxford University Press, New York, 2000.

Bates, Brian, *The Real Middle Earth: Magic and Mystery in the Dark Ages*, Sidgwick & Jackson, London, 2002.

Beaulieu, John, *Bija Mantras* (video), Biosonic Enterprises, P.O. Box 487, High Falls, NY 12440.

Bentov, Itzhak, *Stalking the Wild Pendulum: On the Mechanics of Consciousness*, Destiny Books, Rochester, Vermont, 1988.

Bohm, David, *Wholeness and the Implicate Order*, Routledge and Kegan Paul, Boston, 1981.

Calleman, Carl Johan, *The Mayan Calendar and the Transformation of Consciousness*, Inner Traditions/Bear & Company, Rochester, Vermont, 2004.

Clow, Barbara Hand, *Eye of the Centaur: A Visionary Guide into Past Lives*, Bear & Company, Santa Fe, New Mexico, 1986.

————, *Chiron: Rainbow Bridge Between the Inner and Outer Planets,* Llewellyn, St. Paul, Minnesota, 1987.

————, *Heart of the Christos: Starseeding from the Pleiades,* Bear & Company, Santa Fe, New Mexico, 1989.

————, *The Liquid Light of Sex: Kundalini, Astrology, and the Key Life Transitions,* Bear & Company, Santa Fe, New Mexico, 1991, 1996, 2001.

————, *Signet of Atlantis: War in Heaven Bypass,* Bear & Company, Santa Fe, New Mexico, 1992.

————, *The Pleiadian Agenda: A New Cosmology for the Age of Light,* Bear & Company, Santa Fe, New Mexico, 1995.

————, *Catastrophobia: The Truth Behind Earth Changes in the Coming Age of Light,* Inner Traditions/Bear & Company, Rochester, Vermont, 2001.

Collins, Andrew, and Chris Ogilvie-Herald, *Tutankhamun: The Exodus Conspiracy,* Virgin Books, London, 2002.

Conty, Patrick, *The Genesis and Geometry of the Labyrinth,* Inner Traditions/Bear & Company, Rochester, Vermont, 2002.

Cooper, William, *Behold a Pale Horse,* Light Technology, Sedona, Arizona, 1991.

Croswell, Ken, *The Alchemy of the Heavens: Searching for Meaning in the Milky Way,* Anchor Books, New York, 1995.

————, *The Universe at Midnight: Observations Illuminating the Cosmos,* Free Press, New York, 2001.

Dames, Michael, *The Silbury Treasure: The Great Goddess Rediscovered,* Thames and Hudson, London, 1976.

Davies, Paul, *The Mind of God: The Scientific Basis for a Rational World,* Simon & Schuster, New York, 1992.

————, *About Time: Einstein's Unfinished Revolution,* Simon & Schuster, New York, 1995.

Devereux, Paul, *Stone Age Soundtracks: The Acoustic Archaeology of Ancient Sites,* Vega, London, 2001.

Filbey, John, and Peter Filbey, *Astronomy for Astrologers,* Aquarian Press, Northamptonshire, England, 1984.

Fox, Matthew, *Meditations with Meister Eckhart,* Bear & Company, Santa Fe, New Mexico, 1983.

Fulcanelli, *The Dwellings of the Philosophers,* Archive Press, Boulder, Colorado, 1998.

Gardner, James N., *Biocosm: The New Scientific Theory of Evolution: Intelligent Life Is the Architect of the Universe,* Inner Ocean, Maui, Hawaii, 2003.

Godwin, Joscelyn, *Arktos: The Polar Myth in Science, Symbolism, and Nazi Survival,* Adventures Unlimited, Kempton, Illinois, 1996.

Gold, Thomas, *The Deep Hot Biosphere,* Copernicus, New York, 1999.

Graves, Robert, *Greek Myths,* Penguin, London, 1992.

Greene, Brian, *The Elegant Universe: Superstrings, Hidden Dimensions, and the Quest for the Ultimate Theory,* Vintage, New York, 2000.

Grey, Alex, *Sacred Mirrors: The Visionary Art of Alex Grey,* Inner Traditions, Rochester, Vermont, 1990.

Icke, David, *. . . and the truth shall set you free,* Bridge of Love Publications, Isle of Wight, 1995.

———, *I Am Me, I Am Free: The Robot's Guide to Freedom,* Bridge of Love Press, Cambridge, England, 1996.

———, *Alice in Wonderland and the World Trade Center Disaster,* Bridge of Love Publications, Isle of Wight, 2002.

Jenkins, John Major, *Maya Cosmogenesis 2012,* Bear & Company, Santa Fe, New Mexico, 1998.

Jenny, Hans, *Cymatics: A Study of Wave Phenomena and Vibrations,* MACROmedia, Newmarket, New Hampshire, 2001.

Kaminski, John, *America's Autopsy Report,* Dandelion Books, Tempe, Arizona, 2003.

Kerényi, Carl, *Dionysos: Archetypal Image of Indestructible Life,* Princeton University Press, Princeton, New Jersey, 1976.

Lawlor, Robert, *Sacred Geometry: Philosophy and Practice,* Thames and Hudson, London, 1982.

Levitt, B. Blake, *Electromagnetic Fields: A Consumer's Guide to the Issues and How to Protect Ourselves,* Harcourt Brace, New York, 1995.

Magueijo, João, *Faster Than the Speed of Light: The Story of a Scientific Speculation,* Perseus, Cambridge, Massachusetts, 2003.

Mann, Alfred K., *Shadow of a Star: The Neutrino Story of Supernova 1987A,* W.H. Freeman, New York, 1997.

Matthews, John, *Taliesin: Shamanism and the Bardic Mysteries in Britain and Ireland,* Aquarian, London, 1991.

Mavor, James W., Jr., and Byron E. Dix, *Manitou: The Sacred Landscape of New England's Native Civilization,* Inner Traditions, Rochester, Vermont, 1989.

McKenna, Terence, Ralph Abraham, and Rupert Sheldrake, *Trialogues at the Edge of the West,* Bear & Company, Santa Fe, New Mexico, 1989.

Mehler, Stephen S., *The Land of Osiris,* Adventures Unlimited, Kempton, Illinois, 2002.

Men, Hunbatz, *Los Calendarios Mayas y Hunab K'U,* Ediciones Horizonte, Juarez, Mexico, 1983.

Michell, John, and Christine Rhone, *Twelve-Tribe Nations and the Science of Enchanting the Landscape,* Phanes Press, Grand Rapids, Michigan, 1991.

Mitchell, William C., *Bye Bye Big Bang: Hello Reality,* Cosmic Sense, Carson City, Nevada, 2002.

Moore, Judith, and Barbara Lamb, *Crop Circles Revealed: Language of the Light Symbols,* Light Technology, Flagstaff, Arizona, 2001.

Murphy, Michael, *Jacob Atabet: A Speculative Fiction,* Celestial Arts, Millbrae, California, 1977.

Narby, Jeremy, *The Cosmic Serpent: DNA and the Origins of Knowledge,* Jeremy P. Tarcher/Putnam, New York, 1998.

Ovason, David, *The Secret Architecture of Our Nation's Capital,* HarperCollins, New York, 2000.

Pagels, Elaine, *Beyond Belief: The Secret Gospel of Thomas,* Random House, New York, 2003.

Pauwels, Louis, and Jacques Bergier, *The Morning of the Magicians,* Stein and Day, New York, 1963.

Pearce, Joseph Chilton, *The Biology of Transcendence: A Blueprint of the Human Spirit,* Park Street Press, Rochester, Vermont, 2002.

Picknett, Lynn, *Mary Magdalene: Christianity's Hidden Goddess,* Carrol & Graf, New York, 2003.

Pickover, Clifford A., *Surfing through Hyperspace: Understanding Higher Universes in Six Easy Lessons,* Oxford University Press, New York, 1999.

Ravenscroft, Trevor, *The Spear of Destiny,* Weiser, York Beach, Maine, 1982.

Rees, Alwyn, and Brinley Rees, *Celtic Heritage: Ancient Tradition in Ireland and Wales,* Thames and Hudson, London, 1973.

Reich, Wilhelm, *Cosmic Superimposition,* Wilhelm Reich Foundation, Rangeley, Maine, 1951.

Richer, Jean, *Sacred Geography of the Ancient Greeks: Astrological Symbolism in Art, Architecture, and Landscape,* State University of New York, Albany, 1994.

Rudgley, Richard, *The Lost Civilizations of the Stone Age*, Free Press, New York, 1999.

Schaafsma, Polly, *Rock Art in New Mexico*, Museum of New Mexico Press, Santa Fe, New Mexico, 1992.

Shearer, Tony, *Lord of the Dawn: Quetzalcoatl and the Tree of Life*, Naturegraph Publishers, Happy Camp, California, 1971.

Sheldrake, Rupert, *The Presence of the Past: Morphic Resonance and the Habits of Nature*, Times Books, New York, 1988.

Silva, Freddy, *Secrets in the Fields: The Science and Mysticism of Crop Circles*, Hampton Roads, Charlottesville, Virginia, 2002.

Sitchin, Zecharia, *The Twelfth Planet*, Avon Books, New York, 1978.

Starbird, Margaret, *The Woman with the Alabaster Jar: Mary Magdalene and the Holy Grail*, Bear & Company, Santa Fe, New Mexico, 1993.

Strachan, Gordon, *Jesus the Master Builder: Druid Mysteries and the Dawn of Christianity*, Floris Books, Edinburgh, 1999.

Sullivan, William, *The Secret of the Incas: Myth, Astronomy, and the War Against Time*, Crown, New York, 1996.

Swimme, Brian, *The Hidden Heart of the Cosmos: Humanity and the New Story*, Orbis Books, Maryknoll, New York, 1996.

Talbot, Michael, *Mysticism and the New Physics*, Bantam Books, New York, 1980.

Temple, Robert K. G., *The Sirius Mystery*, St. Martin's Press, New York, 1976.

Thorne, Kip S., *Black Holes and Time Warps: Einstein's Outrageous Legacy*, W.W. Norton, New York, 1994.

Tompkins, Peter, *Secrets of the Great Pyramid*, Harper & Row, New York, 1971.

van Helsing, Jan, *Secret Societies and the Power in the 20th Century*, Ewertverlag, Gran Canaria, Spain, 2002.

Index

About the Authors

Barbara Hand Clow has been studying classical thought and spiritual sources since she was a little girl. Her tutors, starting at age four, were her Cherokee grandfather, Gilbert Hand, and her Celtic (Hebridean) grandmother, Mabel Austin Hand, in Bay City, Michigan, downriver from her home in Saginaw.

Barbara was an honors student at the University of Michigan and Seattle University and received her master's in theology from Matthew Fox's Institute in Creation-Centered Spirituality at Mundelein College/Loyola University in Chicago. Her master's thesis compared Jungian analysis with past-life regression. Shortly after graduation, her first book of the Mind Chronicles series, *Eye of the Centaur*, was published, which was followed by seven other titles, all related to a search for deeper understanding of ourselves as multidimensional beings.

Barbara teamed up with her husband, Gerry Clow, to cofound Bear & Company Publishing with Matthew Fox in 1983. Bear specialized in creation-centered spirituality and alternative health, producing such bestsellers as *Original Blessing*, *The Mayan Factor*, *Medicine Cards*, *Bringers of the Dawn*, and *Vibrational Medicine* during its first decade in business.

Gerry Clow was the president of Bear & Company from 1983 to 2000. His training is as a journalist and art critic, having graduated with a bachelor's degree in art history from Yale in 1970, then working for three years as an arts columnist for the *Boston Globe*. Gerry discovered the power of healing touch in 1994 while working in the King's Chamber at the Great Pyramid at Giza, and since then has studied and practiced spiritual healing, Polarity Therapy, and Craniosacral Therapy.

Ordering Information

We have created a one-hour CD, *Journeys through Nine Dimensions*, with composer Michael Stearns that musically describes the nine dimensions. The CD presents the dimensions in order, starting with the first, and completes with a medley of all the dimensions on the tenth track.

We have also helped produce a one-hour, film-quality video, *Nine Initiations on the Nile*, which beautifully shows Barbara leading a group of spiritual seekers down the Nile in 1994. The video is an introduction both to the power of Barbara's ceremonial teachings and to the power of the ancient Egyptian temples, now awakened for all of us to experience.

If you would like to purchase our CD, video, or other books, or you would like to invite us to teach a workshop, please contact:

Wise Awakening
P.O. Box 31547
Bellingham, WA 98228
Tel: 360-312-9240
Fax: 360-312-9730
www.wiseawakening.com
diana@wiseawakening.com

We also recommend our website, www.handclow2012.com, which includes monthly New Moon forecasts by Barbara (see "AstroFlash") as well as solstice and equinox readings, and our workshop schedule.

Hampton Roads Publishing Company

. . . for the evolving human spirit

HAMPTON ROADS PUBLISHING COMPANY publishes books on a variety of subjects, including metaphysics, spirituality, health, visionary fiction, and other related topics.

For a copy of our latest trade catalog, call toll-free, 800-766-8009, or send your name and address to:

HAMPTON ROADS PUBLISHING COMPANY, INC.
1125 STONEY RIDGE ROAD • CHARLOTTESVILLE, VA 22902
e-mail: hrpc@hrpub.com • www.hrpub.com